THE HOGARTH ESSAYS

THE HOGARTH ESSAYS

Compiled by
LEONARD S. WOOLF
and
MRS. VIRGINIA S. WOOLF

Essay Index Reprint Series

BOOKS FOR LIBRARIES PRESS
FREEPORT, NEW YORK

First Published 1928

Reprinted 1970

STANDARD BOOK NUMBER:

8369-1709-X

LIBRARY OF CONGRESS CATALOG CARD NUMBER:

70-121478

PRINTED IN THE UNITED STATES OF AMERICA

Contents

MR. BENNETT AND MRS. BROWN

BY

VIRGINIA WOOLF ·

MR. BENNETT AND MRS. BROWN*

It seems to me possible, perhaps desirable, that I may be the only person in this room who has committed the folly of writing, trying to write, or failing to write, a novel. And when I asked myself, as your invitation to speak to you about modern fiction made me ask myself, what demon whispered in my ear and urged me to my doom, a little figure rose before me—the figure of a man, or of a woman, who said, "My name is Brown. Catch me if you can."

Most novelists have the same experience. Some Brown, Smith, or Jones comes before them and says in the most seductive and charming way in the world, "Come and catch me if you can." And so, led on by this will-o'-the-wisp, they flounder through volume after volume, spending the best years of their lives in the pursuit, and receiving for the most part very little cash in exchange. Few catch the phantom; most have to be content with a scrap of her dress or a wisp of her hair.

My belief that men and women write novels because they are lured on to create some character which has thus imposed itself upon them has the sanction of Mr. Arnold Bennett. In an article from which I will quote he says: "The foundation of good fiction is character-creating and nothing else. . . . Style counts; plot counts; originality of outlook counts. But none of

*A paper read to the Heretics, Cambridge, England, on May 18, 1924.

these counts anything like so much as the convincing-
ness of the characters. If the characters are real the
novel will have a chance; if they are not, oblivion will
be its portion. . . ." And he goes on to draw the
conclusion that we have no young novelists of first-rate
importance at the present moment, because they are
unable to create characters that are real, true, and convincing.

These are the questions that I want with greater
boldness than discretion to discuss to-night. I want to
make out what we mean when we talk about "character" in fiction; to say something about the question of
reality which Mr. Bennett raises; and to suggest some
reasons why the younger novelists fail to create characters, if, as Mr. Bennett asserts, it is true that fail
they do. This will lead me, I am well aware, to make
some very sweeping and some very vague assertions.
For the question is an extremely difficult one. Think
how little we know about character—think how little
we know about art. But, to make a clearance before I
begin, I will suggest that we range Edwardians and
Georgians into two camps; Mr. Wells, Mr. Bennett,
and Mr. Galsworthy I will call the Edwardians; Mr.
Foster, Mr. Lawrence, Mr. Strachey, Mr. Joyce, and
Mr. Eliot I will call the Georgians. And if I speak in
the first person, with intolerable egotism, I will ask
you to excuse me. I do not want to attribute to the
world at large the opinions of one solitary, ill-informed,
and misguided individual.

My first assertion is one that I think you will grant—
that every one in this room is a judge of character. Indeed it would be impossible to live for a year without
disaster unless one practised character-reading and had

some skill in the art. Our marriages, our friendships depend on it; our business largely depends on it; every day questions arise which can only be solved by its help. And now I will hazard a second assertion, which is more disputable perhaps, to the effect that on or about December, 1910, human character changed.

I am not saying that one went out, as one might into a garden, and there saw that a rose had flowered, or that a hen had laid an egg. The change was not sudden and definite like that. But a change there was, nevertheless; and, since one must be arbitrary, let us date it about the year 1910. The first signs of it are recorded in the books of Samuel Butler, in *The Way of All Flesh* in particular; the plays of Bernard Shaw continue to record it. In life one can see the change, if I may use a homely illustration, in the character of one's cook. The Victorian cook lived like a leviathan in the lower depths, formidable, silent, obscure, inscrutable; the Georgian cook is a creature of sunshine and fresh air; in and out of the drawing-room, now to borrow *The Daily Herald,* now to ask advice about a hat. Do you ask for more solemn instances of the power of the human race to change? Read the *Agamemnon,* and see whether, in process of time, your sympathies are not almost entirely with Clytemnestra. Or consider the married life of the Carlyles, and bewail the waste, the futility, for him and for her, of the horrible domestic tradition which made it seemly for a woman of genius to spend her time chasing beetles, scouring saucepans, instead of writing books. All human relations have shifted—those between masters and servants, husbands and wives, parents and children. And when human relations change there is at the same time a change in religion, conduct, politics, and literature. Let us agree to place one of these changes about the year 1910.

I have said that people have to acquire a good deal of skill in character-reading if they are to live a single year of life without disaster. But it is the art of the young. In middle age and in old age the art is practised mostly for its uses, and friendships and other adventures and experiments in the art of reading character are seldom made. But novelists differ from the rest of the world because they do not cease to be interested in character when they have learnt enough about it for practical purposes. They go a step further; they feel that there is something permanently interesting in character in itself. When all the practical business of life has been discharged, there is something about people which continues to seem to them of overwhelming importance, in spite of the fact that it has no bearing whatever upon their happiness, comfort, or income. The study of character becomes to them an absorbing pursuit; to impart character an obsession. And this I find it very difficult to explain: what novelists mean when they talk about character, what the impulse is that urges them so powerfully every now and then to embody their view in writing.

So, if you will allow me, instead of analyzing and abstracting, I will tell you a simple story which, however pointless, has the merit of being true, of a journey from Richmond to Waterloo, in the hope that I may show you what I mean by character in itself; that you may realize the different aspects it can wear; and the hideous perils that beset you directly you try to describe it in words.

One night some weeks ago, then, I was late for the train and jumped into the first carriage I came to. As I sat down I had the strange and uncomfortable feeling that I was interrupting a conversation between two people who were already sitting there. Not that they were young or happy. Far from it. They were both elderly, the woman over sixty, the man well over forty. They were sitting opposite each other, and the man, who had been leaning over and talking emphatically to judge by his attitude and the flush on his face, sat back and became silent. I had disturbed him, and he was annoyed. The elderly lady, however, whom I will call Mrs. Brown, seemed rather relieved. She was one of those clean, threadbare old ladies whose extreme tidiness—everything buttoned, fastened, tied together, mended and brushed up—suggests more extreme poverty than rags and dirt. There was something pinched about her—a look of suffering, of apprehension, and, in addition, she was extremely small. Her feet, in their clean little boots, scarcely touched the floor. I felt that she had nobody to support her; that she had to make up her mind for herself; that, having been deserted, or left a widow, years ago, she had led an anxious, harried life, bringing up an only son, perhaps, who, as likely as not, was by this time beginning to go to the bad. All this shot through my mind as I sat down, being uncomfortable, like most people, at travelling with fellow passengers unless I have somehow or other accounted for them. Then I looked at the man. He was no relation of Mrs. Brown's I felt sure; he was of a bigger, burlier, less refined type. He was a man of business I imagined, very likely a respectable corn-chandler from the North, dressed in good blue serge with a pocket-knife and a silk handkerchief, and a stout leather bag. Obviously, however, he had an unpleasant business to settle with Mrs. Brown; a secret, perhaps sinister business, which they did not intend to discuss in my presence.

"Yes, the Crofts have had very bad luck with their servants," Mr. Smith (as I will call him) said in a considering way, going back to some earlier topic, with a view to keeping up appearances.

"Ah, poor people," said Mrs. Brown, a trifle condescendingly. "My grandmother had a maid who came when she was fifteen and stayed till she was eighty" (this was said with a kind of hurt and aggressive pride to impress us both perhaps).

"One doesn't often come across that sort of thing nowadays," said Mr. Smith in conciliatory tones.

Then they were silent.

"It's odd they don't start a golf club there—I should have thought one of the young fellows would," said Mr. Smith, for the silence obviously made him uneasy.

Mrs. Brown hardly took the trouble to answer.

"What changes they're making in this part of the world," said Mr. Smith looking out of the window, and looking furtively at me as he did so.

It was plain, from Mrs. Brown's silence, from the uneasy affability with which Mr. Smith spoke, that he had some power over her which he was exerting disagreeably. It might have been her son's downfall, or some painful episode in her past life, or her daughter's. Perhaps she was going to London to sign some document to make over some property. Obviously against her will she was in Mr. Smith's hands. I was beginning to feel a great deal of pity for her, when she said, suddenly and inconsequently,

"Can you tell me if an oak-tree dies when the leaves have been eaten for two years in succession by caterpillars?"

She spoke quite brightly, and rather precisely, in a cultivated, inquisitive voice.

Mr. Smith was startled, but relieved to have a safe topic of conversation given him. He told her a great deal very quickly about plagues of insects. He told her that he had a brother who kept a fruit farm in Kent. He told her what fruit farmers do every year in Kent, and so on, and so on. While he talked a very odd thing happened. Mrs. Brown took out her little white handkerchief and began to dab her eyes. She was crying. But she went on listening quite composedly to what he was saying, and he went on talking, a little louder, a little angrily, as if he had seen her cry often before; as if it were a painful habit. At last it got on his nerves. He stopped abruptly, looked out of the window, then leant towards her as he had been doing when I got in, and said in a bullying, menacing way, as if he would not stand any more nonsense,

"So about that matter we were discussing. It'll be all right? George will be there on Tuesday?"

"We sha'n't be late," said Mrs. Brown, gathering herself together with superb dignity.

Mr. Smith said nothing. He got up, buttoned his coat, reached his bag down, and jumped out of the train before it had stopped at Clapham Junction. He had got what he wanted, but he was ashamed of himself; he was glad to get out of the old lady's sight.

Mrs. Brown and I were left alone together. She sat in her corner opposite, very clean, very small, rather queer, and suffering intensely. The impression she made was overwhelming. It came pouring out like a draught, like a smell of burning. What was it composed of— that overwhelming and peculiar impression? Myriads of irrelevant and incongruous ideas crowd into one's head on such occasions; one sees the person, one sees Mrs. Brown, in the centre of all sorts of different scenes. I thought of her in a seaside house, among queer ornaments: sea-urchins, models of ships in glass cases. Her husband's medals were on the mantelpiece. She popped in and out of the room, perching on the edges of chairs, picking meals out of saucers, indulging in long, silent stares. The caterpillars and the oak-trees seemed to imply all that. And then, into this fan-tastic and secluded life, broke Mr. Smith. I saw him blowing in, so to speak, on a windy day. He banged, he slammed. His dripping umbrella made a pool in the hall. They sat closeted together.

And then Mrs. Brown faced the dreadful revela-tion. She took her heroic decision. Early, before dawn, she packed her bag and carried it herself to the station. She would not let Smith touch it. She was wounded in her pride, unmoored from her anchorage; she came of gentlefolks who kept servants—but details could wait. The important thing was to realize her character, to steep oneself in her atmosphere. I had no time to ex-plain why I felt it somewhat tragic, heroic, yet with a dash of the flighty, and fantastic, before the train stopped, and I watched her disappear, carrying her bag, into the vast blazing station. She looked very small, very tenacious; at once very frail and very heroic. And I have never seen her again, and I shall never know what became of her.

The story ends without any point to it. But I have not told you this anecdote to illustrate either my own ingenuity or the pleasure of travelling from Richmond to Waterloo. What I want you to see in it is this. Here is a character imposing itself upon another person. Here is Mrs. Brown making someone begin almost automatically to write a novel about her. I believe that all novels begin with an old lady in the corner opposite. I believe that all novels, that is to say, deal with character, and that it is to express character—not to preach doctrines, sing songs, or celebrate the glories of the British Empire, that the form of the novel, so clumsy, verbose, and undramatic, so rich, elastic, and alive, has been evolved. To express character, I have said; but you will at once reflect that the very widest interpretation can be put upon those words. For example, old Mrs. Brown's character will strike you very differently according to the age and country in which you happen to be born. It would be easy enough to write three different versions of that incident in the train, an English, a French, and a Russian. The English writer would make the old lady into a "character"; he would bring out her oddities and mannerisms; her buttons and wrinkles; her ribbons and warts. Her personality would dominate the book. A French writer would rub out all that; he would sacrifice the individual Mrs. Brown to give a more general view of human nature; to make a more abstract, proportioned, and harmonious whole. The Russian would pierce through the flesh; would reveal the soul—the soul alone, wandering out into the Waterloo Road, asking of life some tremendous question which would sound on and on in our ears after the book was finished. And then besides age and country there is the writer's temperament to be considered. You see one thing in character, and I another. You say it means this, and I that. And when it comes to writing each makes a further selection on principles of his own. Thus Mrs. Brown can be treated in an infinite variety of ways, according to the age, country, and temperament of the writer.

But now I must recall what Mr. Arnold Bennett says. He says that it is only if the characters are real that the novel has any chance of surviving. Otherwise, die it must. But, I ask myself, what is reality? And who are the judges of reality? A character may be real to Mr. Bennett and quite unreal to me. For instance, in this article he says that Dr. Watson in *Sherlock Holmes* is real to him: to me Dr. Watson is a sack stuffed with straw, a dummy, a figure of fun. And so it is with character after character—in book after book. There is nothing that people differ about more than the reality of characters, especially in contemporary books. But if you take a larger view I think that Mr. Bennett is perfectly right. If, that is, you think of the novels which seem to you great novels—*War and Peace, Vanity Fair, Tristram Shandy, Madame Bovary, Pride and Prejudice, The Mayor of Casterbridge, Villette*— if you think of these books, you do at once think of some character who has seemed to you so real (I do not by that mean so lifelike) that it has the power to make you think not merely of it itself, but of all sorts of things through its eyes—of religion, of love, of war, of peace, of family life, of balls in county towns, of sunsets, moonrises, the immortality of the soul.

There is hardly any subject of human experience that is left out of *War and Peace* it seems to me. And in all these novels all these great novelists have brought us to see whatever they wish us to see through some character. Otherwise, they would not be novelists; but poets, historians, or pamphleteers.

But now let us examine what Mr. Bennett went on to say—he said that there was no great novelist among the Georgian writers because they cannot create characters who are real, true, and convincing. And there I cannot agree. There are reasons, excuses, possibilities which I think put a different colour upon the case. It seems so to me at least, but I am well aware that this is a matter about which I am likely to be prejudiced, sanguine, and near-sighted. I will put my view before you in the hope that you will make it impartial, judicial, and broad-minded. Why, then, is it so hard for novelists at present to create characters which seem real, not only to Mr. Bennett, but to the world at large? Why, when October comes round, do the publishers always fail to supply us with a masterpiece?

Surely one reason is that the men and women who began writing novels in 1910 or thereabouts had this great difficulty to face—that there was no English novelist living from whom they could learn their business. Mr. Conrad is a Pole; which sets him apart, and makes him, however admirable, not very helpful. Mr. Hardy has written no novel since 1895. The most prominent and successful novelists in the year 1910 were, I suppose, Mr. Wells, Mr. Bennett, and Mr. Galsworthy. Now it seems to me that to go to these men and ask them to teach you how to write a novel —how to create characters that are real—is precisely

like going to a bootmaker and asking him to teach you
how to make a watch. Do not let me give you the impression that I do not admire and enjoy their books.
They seem to me of great value, and indeed of great
necessity. There are seasons when it is more important
to have boots than to have watches. To drop metaphor, I think that after the creative activity of the
Victorian age it was quite necessary, not only for literature but for life, that someone should write the
books that Mr. Wells, Mr. Bennett, and Mr. Galsworthy have written. Yet what odd books they are!
Sometimes I wonder if we are right to call them books
at all. For they leave one with so strange a feeling of
incompleteness and dissatisfaction. In order to complete them it seems necessary to do something—to join
a society, or, more desperately, to write a cheque.
That done, the restlessness is laid, the book finished;
it can be put upon the shelf, and need never be read
again. But with the work of other novelists it is different. *Tristram Shandy* or *Pride and Prejudice* is complete in itself; it is self-contained; it leaves one with
no desire to do anything, except indeed to read the
book again, and to understand it better. The difference
perhaps is that both Sterne and Jane Austen were interested in things in themselves; in character in itself;
in the book in itself. Therefore everything was inside
the book, nothing outside. But the Edwardians were
never interested in character in itself; or in the book
in itself. They were interested in something outside.
Their books, then, were incomplete as books, and required that the reader should finish them, actively and
practically, for himself.

Perhaps we can make this clearer if we take the

liberty of imagining a little party in the railway carriage—Mr. Wells, Mr. Galsworthy, Mr. Bennett are
travelling to Waterloo with Mrs. Brown. Mrs. Brown,
I have said, was poorly dressed and very small. She
had an anxious, harassed look. I doubt whether she was
what you call an educated woman. Seizing upon all
these symptoms of the unsatisfactory condition of our
primary schools with a rapidity to which I can do no
justice, Mr. Wells would instantly project upon the
windowpane a vision of a better, breezier, jollier, hap-
pier, more adventurous and gallant world, where these
musty railway carriages and fusty old women do not
exist; where miraculous barges bring tropical fruit to
Camberwell by eight o'clock in the morning; where
there are public nurseries, fountains, and libraries,
dining-rooms, drawing-rooms, and marriages; where
every citizen is generous and candid, manly and magnificent, and rather like Mr. Wells himself. But nobody is in the least like Mrs. Brown. There are no
Mrs. Browns in Utopia. Indeed I do not think that
Mr. Wells, in his passion to make her what she ought
to be, would waste a thought upon her as she is. And
what would Mr. Galsworthy see? Can we doubt that
the walls of Doulton's factory would take his fancy?
There are women in that factory who make twenty-
five dozen earthenware pots every day. There are
mothers in the Mile End Road who depend upon the
farthings which those women earn. But there are em-
ployers in Surrey who are even now smoking rich
cigars while the nightingale sings. Burning with indig-
nation, stuffed with information, arraigning civilization, Mr. Galsworthy would only see in Mrs. Brown
a pot broken on the wheel and thrown into the corner.

Mr. Bennett, alone of the Edwardians, would keep his eyes in the carriage. He, indeed, would observe every detail with immense care. He would notice the advertisements; the pictures of Swanage and Portsmouth; the way in which the cushion bulged between the buttons; how Mrs. Brown wore a brooch which had cost three-and-ten-three at Whitworth's bazaar; and had mended both gloves—indeed the thumb of the left-hand glove had been replaced. And he would observe, at length, how this was the non-stop train from Windsor which calls at Richmond for the convenience of middle-class residents, who can afford to go to the theatre but have not reached the social rank which can afford motor-cars, though it is true, there are occasions (he would tell us what), when they hire them from a company (he would tell us which). And so he would gradually sidle sedately towards Mrs. Brown, and would remark how she had been left a little copyhold, not freehold, property at Datchet, which, however, was mortgaged to Mr. Bungay the solicitor—but why should I presume to invent Mr. Bennett? Does not Mr. Bennett write novels himself? I will open the first book that chance puts in my way—*Hilda Lessways*. Let us see how he makes us feel that Hilda is real, true, and convincing, as a novelist should. She shut the door in a soft, controlled way, which showed the constraint of her relations with her mother. She was fond of reading *Maud;* she was endowed with the power to feel intensely. So far, so good; in his leisurely, sure-footed way Mr. Bennett is trying in these first pages, where every touch is important, to show us the kind of girl she was.

But then he begins to describe, not Hilda Lessways,

but the view from her bedroom window, the excuse being that Mr. Skellorn, the man who collects rents, is coming along that way. Mr. Bennett proceeds:

"The bailiwick of Turnhill lay behind her; and all the murky district of the Five Towns, of which Turnhill is the northern outpost, lay to the south. At the foot of Chatterley Wood the canal wound in large curves on its way towards the undefiled plains of Cheshire and the sea. On the canal-side, exactly opposite to Hilda's window, was a flour-mill, that sometimes made nearly as much smoke as the kilns and the chimneys closing the prospect on either hand. From the flour-mill a bricked path, which separated a considerable row of new cottages from their appurtenant gardens, led straight into Lessways Street, in front of Mrs. Lessways' house. By this path Mr. Skellorn should have arrived, for he inhabited the farthest of the cottages."

One line of insight would have done more than all those lines of description; but let them pass as the necessary drudgery of the novelist. And now—where is Hilda? Alas. Hilda is still looking out of the window. Passionate and dissatisfied as she was, she was a girl with an eye for houses. She often compared this old Mr. Skellorn with the villas she saw from her bedroom window. Therefore the villas must be described. Mr. Bennett proceeds:

"The row was called Freehold Villas: a consciously proud name in a district where much of the land was copyhold and could only change owners subject to the payment of 'fines,' and to the feudal consent of a 'court' presided over by the agent of a lord of the manor. Most of the dwellings were owned by their occupiers, who, each an absolute monarch of the soil, niggled in his sooty garden of an evening amid the flutter of drying shirts and towels. Freehold Villas symbolized the final triumph of Victorian economics, the apotheosis of the prudent and industrious artisan. It corresponded with a Building Society Secretary's dream of paradise. And indeed it was a very real achievement. Nevertheless, Hilda's irrational contempt would not admit this."

Heaven be praised, we cry! At last we are coming to Hilda herself. But not so fast. Hilda may have been this, that, and the other; but Hilda not only looked at houses, and thought of houses; Hilda lived in a house. And what sort of a house did Hilda live in? Mr. Bennett proceeds:

"It was one of the two middle houses of a detached terrace of four houses built by her grandfather Lessways, the tea-pot manufacturer; it was the chief of the four, obviously the habitation of the proprietor of the terrace. One of the corner houses comprised a grocer's shop, and this house had been robbed of its just proportion of garden so that the seigneurial garden-plot might be triflingly larger than the other. The terrace was not a terrace of cottages, but of houses rated at from twenty-six to thirty-six pounds a year; beyond the means of artisans and petty insurance agents and rent-collectors. And further, it was well built, generously built; and its architecture, though debased, showed some faint traces of Georgian amenity. It was admittedly the best row of houses in that newly settled quarter of the town. In coming to it out of Freehold Villas Mr. Skellorn obviously came to something superior, wider, more liberal. Suddenly Hilda heard her mother's voice. . . ."

But we cannot hear her mother's voice, or Hilda's voice; we can only hear Mr. Bennett's voice telling us facts about rents and freeholds and copyholds and fines. What can Mr. Bennett be about? I have formed my own opinion of what Mr. Bennett is about—he is trying to make us imagine for him; he is trying to hypnotize us into the belief that, because he has made a house, there must be a person living there. With all his powers of observation, which are marvellous, with all his sympathy and humanity, which are great, Mr. Bennett has never once looked at Mrs. Brown in her corner. There she sits in the corner of the carriage—that carriage which is travelling, not from Richmond to Waterloo, but from one age of English literature to the next, for Mrs. Brown is eternal, Mrs. Brown is human nature, Mrs. Brown changes only on the surface, it is the novelists who get in and out—there she sits and not one of the Edwardian writers had so much as looked at her. They have looked very powerfully, searchingly, and sympathetically out of the window; at factories, at Utopias, even at the decoration and upholstery of the carriage; but never at her, never at life, never at human nature. And so they have developed a technique of novel-writing which suits their purpose; they have made tools and established conventions which do their business. But those tools are not our tools, and that business is not our business. For us those conventions are ruin, those tools are death.

You may well complain of the vagueness of my

language. What is a convention, a tool, you may ask, and what do you mean by saying that Mr. Bennett's and Mr. Wells's and Mr. Galsworthy's conventions are the wrong conventions for the Georgians? The question is difficult: I will attempt a short cut. A convention in writing is not much different from a convention in manners. Both in life and in literature it is necessary to have some means of bridging the gulf between the hostess and her unknown guest on the one hand, the writer and his unknown reader on the other. The hostess bethinks her of the weather, for generations of hostesses have established the fact that this is a subject of universal interest in which we all believe. She begins by saying that we are having a wretched May, and, having thus got into touch with her unknown guest, proceeds to matters of greater interest. So it is in literature. The writer must get into touch with his reader by putting before him something which he recognizes, which therefore stimulates his imagination, and makes him willing to coöperate in the far more difficult business of intimacy. And it is of the highest importance that this common meeting-place should be reached easily, almost instinctively, in the dark, with one's eyes shut. Here is Mr. Bennett making use of this common ground in the passage which I have quoted. The problem before him was to make us believe in the reality of Hilda Lessways. So he began, being an Edwardian, by describing accurately and minutely the sort of house Hilda lived in, and the sort of house she saw from the window. House property was the common ground from which the Edwardians found it easy to proceed to intimacy. Indirect as it seems to us, the convention worked admirably, and thousands of Hilda Lessways were launched upon the world by this means. For that age and generation, the convention was a good one.

But now, if you will allow me to pull my own anecdote to pieces, you will see how keenly I felt the lack of a convention, and how serious a matter it is when the tools of one generation are useless for the next. The incident had made a great impression on me. But how was I to transmit it to you? All I could do was to report as accurately as I could what was said, to describe in detail what was worn, to say, despairingly, that all sorts of scenes rushed into my mind, to proceed to tumble them out pell-mell, and to describe this vivid, this overmastering impression by likening it to a draught or a smell of burning. To tell you the truth, I was also strongly tempted to manufacture a three-volume novel about the old lady's son, and his adventures crossing the Atlantic, and her daughter, and how she kept a milliner's shop in Westminster, the past life of Smith himself, and his house at Sheffield, though such stories seem to me the most dreary, irrelevant, and humbugging affairs in the world.

But if I had done that I should have escaped the appalling effort of saying what I meant. And to have got at what I meant I should have had to go back and back and back; to experiment with one thing and another; to try this sentence and that, referring each word to my vision, matching it as exactly as possible, and knowing that somehow I had to find a common ground between us, a convention which would not seem to you too odd, unreal, and far-fetched to believe in. I admit that I shirked that arduous undertaking. I let my Mrs. Brown slip through my fingers.

I have told you nothing whatever about her. But that is partly the great Edwardians' fault. I asked them— they are my elders and betters—How shall I begin to describe this woman's character? And they said, "Begin by saying that her father kept a shop in Harrogate. Ascertain the rent. Ascertain the wages of shop assistants in the year 1878. Discover what her mother died of. Describe cancer. Describe calico. Describe——" But I cried, "Stop! Stop!" And I regret to say that I threw that ugly, that clumsy, that incongruous tool out of the window, for I knew that if I began describing the cancer and the calico, my Mrs. Brown, that vision to which I cling though I know no way of imparting it to you, would have been dulled and tarnished and vanished for ever.

That is what I meant by saying that the Edwardian tools are the wrong ones for us to use. They have laid an enormous stress upon the fabric of things. They have given us a house in the hope that we may be able to deduce the human beings who live there. To give them their due, they have made that house much better worth living in. But if you hold that novels are in the first place about people, and only in the second about the houses they live in, that is the wrong way to set about it. Therefore, you see, the Georgian writer had to begin by throwing away the method that was in use at the moment. He was left alone there facing Mrs. Brown without any method of conveying her to the reader. But that is inaccurate. A writer is never alone. There is always the public with him—if not on the same seat, at least in the compartment next door. Now the public is a strange travelling companion. In England it is a very suggestive and docile creature,

which, once you get it to attend, will believe implicitly
what it is told for a certain number of years. If you
say to the public with sufficient conviction, "All women
have tails, and all men humps," it will actually learn
to see women with tails and men with humps, and
will think it very revolutionary and probably improper
if you say "Nonsense. Monkeys have tails and camels
humps. But men and women have brains, and they have
hearts; they think and they feel,"—that will seem to
it a bad joke, and an improper one into the bargain.

But to return. Here is the British public sitting by
the writer's side and saying in its vast and unanimous
way, "Old women have houses. They have fathers.
They have incomes. They have servants. They have
hot water bottles. That is how we know that they are
old women. Mr. Wells and Mr. Bennett and Mr.
Galsworthy have always taught us that this is the way
to recognize them. But now with your Mrs. Brown—
how are we to believe in her? We do not even know
whether her villa was called Albert or Balmoral; what
she paid for her gloves; or whether her mother died of
cancer or of consumption. How can she be alive? No;
she is a mere figment of your imagination."

And old women of course ought to be made of
freehold villas and copyhold estates, not of imagination.

The Georgian novelist, therefore, was in an awkward predicament. There was Mrs. Brown protesting
that she was different, quite different, from what people
made out, and luring the novelist to her rescue by the
most fascinating if fleeting glimpse of her charms;
there were the Edwardians handing out tools appropriate to house building and house breaking; and there

was the British public asseverating that they must see
the hot water bottle first. Meanwhile the train was
rushing to that station where we must all get out.

Such, I think, was the predicament in which the
young Georgians found themselves about the year
1910. Many of them—I am thinking of Mr. Forster
and Mr. Lawrence in particular—spoilt their early
work because, instead of throwing away those tools,
they tried to use them. They tried to compromise.
They tried to combine their own direct sense of the
oddity and significance of some character with Mr.
Galsworthy's knowledge of the Factory Acts, and Mr.
Bennett's knowledge of the Five Towns. They tried
it, but they had too keen, too overpowering a sense of
Mrs. Brown and her peculiarities to go on trying it
much longer. Something had to be done. At whatever
cost of life, limb, and damage to valuable property
Mrs. Brown must be rescued, expressed, and set in her
high relations to the world before the train stopped
and she disappeared for ever. And so the smashing
and the crashing began. Thus it is that we hear all
round us, in poems and novels and biographies, even in
newspaper articles and essays, the sound of breaking
and falling, crashing and destruction. It is the prevail-
ing sound of the Georgian age—rather a melancholy
one if you think what melodious days there have been
in the past, if you think of Shakespeare and Milton and
Keats or even of Jane Austen and Thackeray and
Dickens; if you think of the language, and the heights
to which it can soar when free, and see the same eagle
captive, bald, and croaking.

In view of these facts—with these sounds in my ears
and these fancies in my brain—I am not going to deny

that Mr. Bennett has some reason when he complains
that our Georgian writers are unable to make us believe
that our characters are real. I am forced to agree that
they do not pour out three immortal masterpieces with
Victorian regularity every autumn. But instead of being
gloomy, I am sanguine. For this state of things is, I
think, inevitable whenever from hoar old age or callow
youth the convention ceases to be a means of communication between writer and reader, and becomes
instead an obstacle and an impediment. At the present moment we are suffering, not from decay, but from
having no code of manners which writers and readers
accept as a prelude to the more exciting intercourse of
friendship. The literary convention of the time is so
artificial—you have to talk about the weather and nothing but the weather throughout the entire visit—that,
naturally, the feeble are tempted to outrage, and the
strong are led to destroy the very foundations and
rules of literary society. Signs of this are everywhere
apparent. Grammar is violated; syntax disintegrated;
as a boy staying with an aunt for the week-end rolls in
the geranium bed out of sheer desperation as the solem-
nities of the Sabbath wear on. The more adult writers
do not, of course, indulge in such wanton exhibitions of
spleen. Their sincerity is desperate, and their courage
tremendous; it is only that they do not know which
to use, a fork or their fingers. Thus, if you read Mr.
Joyce and Mr. Eliot you will be struck by the indecency
of the one, and the obscurity of the other. Mr. Joyce's
indecency in *Ulysses* seems to me the conscious and calculated indecency of a desperate man who feels that
in order to breathe he must break the windows. At
moments, when the window is broken, he is magni-

ficent. But what a waste of energy! And, after all,
how dull indecency is, when it is not the overflowing
of a super-abundant energy or savagery, but the determined and public-spirited act of a man who needs fresh
air! Again, with the obscurity of Mr. Eliot. I think
that Mr. Eliot has written some of the loveliest single
lines in modern poetry. But how intolerant he is of the
old usages and politenesses of society—respect for the
weak, consideration for the dull! As I sun myself upon
the intense and ravishing beauty of one of his lines,
and reflect that I must make a dizzy and dangerous
leap to the next, and so on from line to line, like an
acrobat flying precariously from bar to bar, I cry out,
I confess, for the old decorums, and envy the indolence
of my ancestors who, instead of spinning madly
through mid-air, dreamt quietly in the shade with a
book. Again, in Mr. Strachey's books, *Eminent Victorians* and *Queen Victoria,* the effort and strain of
writing against the grain and current of the times
is visible too. It is much less visible, of course, for
not only is he dealing with facts, which are stubborn
things, but he has fabricated, chiefly from eighteenth-
century material, a very discreet code of manners of
his own, which allows him to sit at table with the highest in the land and to say a great many things under
cover of that exquisite apparel which, had they gone
naked, would have been chased by the men-servants
from the room. Still, if you compare *Eminent Victorians* with some of Lord Macaulay's essays, though
you will feel that Lord Macaulay is always wrong, and
Mr. Strachey always right, you will also feel a body,
a sweep, a richness in Lord Macaulay's essays which
show that his age was behind him; all his strength

went straight into his work; none was used for purposes of concealment or of conversion. But Mr. Strachey has had to open our eyes before he made us see; he has had to search out and sew together a very artful manner of speech; and the effort, beautifully though it is concealed, has robbed his work of some of the force that should have gone into it, and limited his scope.

For these reasons, then, we must reconcile ourselves to a season of failures and fragments. We must reflect that where so much strength is spent on finding a way of telling the truth the truth itself is bound to reach us in rather an exhausted and chaotic condition. Ulysses, Queen Victoria, Mr. Prufrock—to give Mrs. Brown some of the names she has made famous lately—is a little pale and dishevelled by the time her rescuers reach her. And it is the sound of their axes that we hear—a vigorous and stimulating sound in my ears—unless of course you wish to sleep, when, in the bounty of his concern, Providence has provided a host of writers anxious and able to satisfy your needs.

Thus I have tried, at tedious length, I fear, to answer some of the questions which I began by asking. I have given an account of some of the difficulties which in my view beset the Georgian writer in all his forms. I have sought to excuse him. May I end by venturing to remind you of the duties and responsibilities that are yours as partners in this business of writing books, as companions in the railway carriage, as fellow travellers with Mrs. Brown? For she is just as visible to you who remain silent as to us who tell stories about her. In the course of your daily life this past week you have had far stranger and more interesting experiences than the one I have tried to describe. You have overheard scraps of talk that filled you with amazement. You have gone to bed at night bewildered by the complexity of your feelings. In one day thousands of ideas have coursed through your brains; thousands of emotions have met, collided, and disappeared in astonishing disorder. Nevertheless, you allow the writers to palm off upon you a version of all this, an image of Mrs. Brown, which has no likeness to that surprising apparition whatsoever. In your modesty you seem to consider that writers are of different blood and bone from yourselves; that they know more of Mrs. Brown than you do. Never was there a more fatal mistake. It is this division between reader and writer, this humility on your part, these professional airs and graces on ours, that corrupt and emasculate the books which should be the healthy offspring of a close and equal alliance between us. Hence spring those sleek, smooth novels, those portentous and ridiculous biographies, that milk-and-watery criticism, those poems melodiously celebrating the innocence of roses and sheep which pass so plausibly for literature at the present time.

Your part is to insist that writers shall come down off their plinths and pedestals, and describe beautifully if possible, truthfully at any rate, our Mrs. Brown. You should insist that she is an old lady of unlimited capacity and infinite variety; capable of appearing in any place; wearing any dress; saying anything and doing heaven knows what. But the things she says and the things she does and her eyes and her nose and her speech and her silence have an overwhelming fascination, for she is, of course, the spirit we live by, life itself.

But do not expect just at present a complete and satisfactory presentment of her. Tolerate the spasmodic, the obscure, the fragmentary, the failure. Your help is invoked in a good cause. For I will make one final and surpassingly rash prediction—we are trembling on the verge of one of the great ages of English literature. But it can only be reached if we are determined never, never to desert Mrs. Brown.

THE HOGARTH ESSAYS

THE PROSPECTS OF LITERATURE

BY

LOGAN PEARSALL SMITH

Break their teeth, O God, in their mouth: break out the great teeth of the young lions, O Lord.

Ps. 58: 6.

THE PROSPECTS OF LITERATURE

MRS. VIRGINIA WOOLF, in one of her delightful essays, states her belief that "we are trembling," as she puts it, "on the verge of one of the great ages of English literature." I should very much like to agree with Mrs. Woolf: it would be pleasant to feel that one was at the dawn of a great epoch; nor indeed is it difficult to discover at the present time much that seems full of encouragement and promise. Our younger writers are undoubtedly daring and sincere, and they seem most anxious to tell the truth about what they think and feel in all sorts of circumstances. They have broken down many of the old conventions, and have banished most of the taboos which used to be so hampering to freedom. There is also to-day a large public which is eager to welcome experiments; nor do I believe that there has ever been a time in our literary history when talent was more sure to meet with immediate recognition. All this, as I say, seems full of promise; but is it enough to justify Mrs. Woolf's belief that a golden day of letters is about to dawn upon us? By a great age of literature she means—she must mean—something more than a plentiful output of books of contemporary interest; her phrase suggests the production of enduring masterpieces—of works which will be read and re-read by succeeding generations, and regarded as permanent additions to the literature of our race. Ages which abound in masterpieces of this kind are the result of a number of complex circumstances; they have occurred, after all, very rarely in the history of literature, and, according to my reading of that history, they have been due above all to the happy coincidence of two conditions, neither of which can be said to characterize our time. In the great periods of Greece and Rome, at the Classical revivals in Italy and France and England, as at the Romantic revivals in those countries—and these were the greatest epochs of literary creation—men shared in common certain convictions which they took more or less for granted; and it was the coherence of their beliefs and ideals, the grandiose completeness, rather than the ultimate truth, of their scheme of things, which gave them that imaginative dominion over experience which produces greatness. They had, in fact, a solution which sufficed them for life's problems, a formula, an agreed convention; it was this that enabled them to handle their material with the ease of masters; and even our predecessors of the Victorian era worked together on a basis of accepted ideas, which we, of the twentieth century, with our miscellaneous, shattered view of the world, are very far from possessing.

But even this by itself is not enough. Literature is not a branch of philosophy or of social science; it is an art, and the arts only blossom freely—and how rarely they blossom with any freedom!—under certain technical conditions, and when their material, their medium happens to be in a state favourable to their right development. Great thoughts seem only able to produce great literature when they happen to coincide with a special condition of the means of expression—

with what I may call a certain plastic state of language. This plastic state is due either to the unhackneyed freshness of an unexploited idiom, full of unconscious poetry, and with the dew of the morning, so to speak, upon it,—and an unexhausted form of speech like this, as with the Greeks, the Romans, and the Elizabethan English, has formed the medium of the supremest literature; or it may be due, as at the Romantic period, to what is called linguistic renovation, to the vigour borrowed from popular speech, and to the revival of an old vocabulary which had fallen out of use. So important is this need of an unhackneyed, expressive diction to give to thought an enduring form, or at least so important does it seem to me (but I am perhaps a faddist on the subject), that I should hardly consider it a paradox to regard what we call the great imaginative periods of literature as being, in fact, linguistic phenomena—incidents, not so much in the history of man's mind, as in that of his language.

Of the preoccupation with language, the verbal preciosity and experiment which absorbed so much attention in the age of Ronsard in France, and in that of Shakespeare in England, or of that search for a renewed vocabulary which inaugurated the Romantic revivals in these countries,—of any of this kind of linguistic ferment, which is the surest sign of a revival of letters, I can see, however, little or no evidence today. Almost all our younger writers appear to be perfectly content with the common and current vocabulary; save for a few almost grotesque aberrations, the diction and style of each of them is indistinguishable, to me at least, from the diction and style of any of the others.

The very conditions, moreover, which I have already mentioned as being apparently so full of encouragement—the widespread interest in literature, the large reading public, the prompt recognition of merit,—all these things are hardly as favourable as they might seem to the development of literary talent. Enduring excellence in any art is not at all a necessary result—it would seem indeed to be more like an accidental by-product—of artistic activity; and a general interest in the art, and enthusiasm for it, often tends, by making it fashionable, to hamper and impede, rather than to foster it. And is not this what is happening to-day? A large number of people who would do well to concern themselves with other things are now led by fashion to take an intelligent, or semi-intelligent, interest in new books; they form enthusiastic cliques, so eager to welcome and make notorious any novelty, that the clever young writer is able to attain recognition much too easily. Success is, indeed, as a famous writer has said, a necessary poison; but they are fortunate, he wisely adds, to whom it comes late in life and in small doses.

The effects of this easy success—and of the many dangers in the path of the would-be artist, premature success is probably the most dangerous,—the results of this quickly won popularity are not difficult to observe all about us. As soon as any glimmering of talent, any freshness of originality, makes its appearance, it is immediately noted and exploited. Editors of the weekly and even of the daily papers seize upon it; they have acquired, one may almost say of them, the habits of cannibals or ogres; they suck the brains of young writers, and then replace them by a new levy of

adolescent talent. Their victims find it easy at the out-
start to make money; even the fashion-papers pay them
large sums for their little essays; they acquire expensive
habits; they are introduced by benevolent patrons into
what is called good society; and losing before long, as
journalists are apt to lose, the power of reading and
of nourishing their minds by disinterested study, they
soon exhaust their little stock of originality: they have
nothing more to say; their contributions are no longer
wanted; a new set of beginners supplants them, to be
soon exhausted and supplanted in their turn.

I do not mean to suggest that journalism, the habit
of rapid composition for the press, is always inimical
to talent. Often, indeed, to men of matured minds it
is a fortunate incentive, which compels them, as it
compelled Hazlitt for instance, to give the world their
accumulated treasures of reading and meditation, to
pour out the richness of their minds upon paper. But to
the young, the inexperienced, the immature, how can
this marketing of unripe fruit be anything but in-
jurious?

Publishers also compete nowadays with editors in
killing the goose whose golden eggs they live on. As
soon as a young author makes a success his publisher
urges him to repeat it at once; other publishers are
eager to win his patronage, and he is not infrequently
offered a fixed income on the condition that he shall
regularly provide one or two volumes a year. It is
difficult for the impecunious young to refuse these
offers; but they stimulate, they indeed necessitate, that
kind of hasty and abundant composition which must
be harmful to any young writer, unless indeed he is
endowed with the supremest talent. A great genius, it

is true, born in a great age of literary creation, and
finding ready at hand a plastic medium in which to
embody his imaginations, is sometimes able to produce
abundant masterpieces, one after the other, and to
write down without care pages which are destined to
endure for ever. These fortunate epochs, however,
occur but rarely, and the great unscrupulous artists
who, like Shakespeare or Molière, can cater for the
market without harm, and blamelessly worship the
golden calf on the highest peaks of Parnassus, are so
divinely gifted and so exceptional, that they are quite
outside all the ordinary rules.

It would be invidious to mention names, but in following the careers of the more recent writers whose
first books have charmed me, I almost invariably find
that their earliest publications, or at least their earliest successes, are their best achievements; their promise
ripens to no fulfilment; each subsequent work tends to
be a feeble replica and fainter echo of the first. In
recent years, and especially since the war, similar conditions have prevailed in France and in America; in
these countries, as in England, the number of miscar-
riages of talent, the rate of infant mortality among
gifts of promise, seems to be ever increasing. And,
indeed, with all the advertisement and premature pub-
licity of our time, where can we hope to find that
leisurely ripening of talent in the shade of obscurity,
that slow development by experiment and failure, by
which it can best be mellowed and matured? If what
a fine critic has told us be true, that "no great work
has ever been produced except after a long interval
of still and musing meditation," it is difficult to see how
a successful and money-making author can find under

modern conditions the leisure for such spells of con-
templative musing. And those above all who have the
misfortune to be the authors of best-sellers—what of
those unhappy moths, as they scorch and flare and
shrivel in the limelight?

No; the old, hard conditions were surely better. It
was much better to stone the prophets than to crown
them, as we now crown them, with immediate roses.
They are stifled by the roses, but the stones in the old
days of stoning only drove them out into the desert
to meditate on their mission and perfect their gifts, so
that they might return at last to take their revenge on
the world which had scorned them.

Is all lost then? If we live in an age which demands
and abundantly rewards improvisation, but in which
the improviser is extremely unlikely to produce enduring work; if all the circumstances of our time seem co-
ordinated and organized to smother talent; if Mrs.
Woolf's surmised dawn is the late twilight that it
seems to me, is there nothing to be done but to lay
aside our pens and wait till the winter of our inanition
be over? Must we console ourselves with the reflection that such winters are beneficent seasons of repose
for the human spirit, and that Beauty, after being
buried for a while, will shine at its rediscovery—a
hundred or two hundred years hence perhaps—with a
new brightness? Or is there a way of keeping the lamp
still alight, and handing it on to others through the
dark; a path out of the wilderness, which can be followed under unfavourable as well as favourable circumstances; a means of achieving excellence which is
more or less independent of the age one lives in?

In that lazy perusal of old books in which I spend so great a part of my existence, I sometimes come on a sentence, a phrase, an image which seems to arouse a faint echo somewhere within me. "That's for you; make a note of it; copy it out!" my Good Angel whispers; but too often I pay no attention to that wise admonition. Then afterwards, often days afterwards, some dim reverberation of that forgotten sentence begins to haunt me; I begin to feel that some mysterious good had been embodied in it; that it had revealed perhaps the secret of a charming way of life, or had solved some perplexing problem, or had aptly expressed, it may be, some meaning of my own, giving importance to my private thought, and making it more true and lucid. In any case, back through all the books I have been reading, I must search for that lost phrase until again I find it.

Je trouve au coin d'un bois le mot qui m'avoit fui—

This line of Boileau's is the latest of these recaptures; and now that I have read it again in the epistles of that old bewigged poet, it creates for me an enchanting picture of a special kind of lettered existence, of a life of toil and leisure, devoted to the development of talent —the life of Horace at his Sabine farm, of Boileau in his garden at Auteuil, of Pope at Twickenham, of Gray in his college rooms at Cambridge. Writers of this studious kind are more concerned with the conquests than the gifts of art, with what can be achieved by scrupulous correction, by the curious felicity of phrasing, by constant revision, and the assiduous labour of the file. They do not improvise, they are carried away by no sudden fits of inspiration; their industry is rather like that of the laborious bee, to which Horace, the master of them all, compared his toil; and their hives are enriched by the diligently gathered spoil of innumerable flowers. Or, to change the image, we may compare their method to the delicate chiselling of gems; nor is this old comparison an unfitting one, since their verses often possess a gem-like quality which enables them to resist the wrong of time.

Although these laborious writers can seldom vie in achievement with the inspired poets, the great writers without scruples of the creative ages, they have for us at least one great advantage; we can imitate them and learn from them, for they have much to teach us. We must honour the genius, and rejoice that he has existed, but we must take good care not to try to follow in his footsteps. The example of the man of genius is, as Flaubert was fond of pointing out, the worst kind of example for the man of talent; and talent and the development of talent amid unfavourable conditions is my subject in this paper. I have spoken of poets; but for writers of careful prose, like Flaubert for instance, or Walter Pater, the methods of cultivating a gift and creating a style are not in any way different.

Should the age then provide no great impulse, and beget no genius, talent may still find its opportunity for development; and by the inspiration of technique and the study of the best models it may produce work of enduring value. If the thought of the time we live in gives us no general scheme of ideas and no agreed convictions, we may still be able to discover in our own thought and our own temperament, if we search for it, some point of view which will enable us to dominate our own experience; some meaning which, for ourselves at least, is central and significant. Should the language of the day be set in fixed formulas and moulds, and the vocabulary have lost its freshness, it is still possible to discard those formulas and break those moulds, to make one's own vocabulary and create one's own individual and expressive style.

To write as if we were geniuses, and to imitate the easy carelessness of those great men in an age which does not produce them, must almost certainly lead to artistic failure. But to cultivate a talent is always possible; and how many beautiful and enduring works of literature are the fruits of talent brought by labour and care to its utmost perfection! Delightful it must be, no doubt, to live in a great epoch and be hypnotized by it, and become its mouthpiece, to have mighty words, words one cannot help, rush to one's lips in the ecstasy of inspiration; but to shut oneself away from hostile circumstance in some pleasant solitude, and devote the leisure of one's mornings to the labour of the file; to search for the word one wants, and then to walk abroad and find it perhaps at the corner of a wood,— is not this also a delightful way of living, and may it not be that those who spend their days in this delicate and learned labour taste what are after all the more conscious, the more exquisite, the more aristocratic joys of the career of letters?

But to lead this life, to taste these joys, certain qualities of temper are needed, and the ability is also needed to make certain renunciations. The labor of creating one's own style can only be undertaken by one to whom that labour is in itself delightful; his pains must be his pleasures also, he must love the medium he works in, delight in playing with words and phrases, as the painter delights in playing with his palette and paints and brushes. He must be willing, if necessary, to be poor, for his fastidious pen will not support him, and if he must earn his living he must earn it by other means than those of literature. He must not repine at obscurity, for poverty and obscurity are likely to be for many years his companions; nor should he envy too much the early successes of his more popular contemporaries, or of those who are younger than himself.

This is indeed an old-fashioned way of life which I find myself recommending; and it is only, I think, by means of a desire, a purpose, an ideal aim which appears to be equally out of fashion to-day, that it has ever been possible to adopt, or at least to maintain, it.

The youth of to-day seem to me, as I have said, intensely interested in life, and I like them for it; but, if I observe them rightly, it is life more as a means to experience, than as an opportunity for achievement, which absorbs and excites them. To undergo one experience after another, to tell the truth about each, and thus to win the attention of their contemporaries, —something of this kind strikes me as being in the main their animating motive. That life can be above all an opportunity for carrying out a preconceived plan, for striving onwards towards a distant goal; that it should only be crowned at last, if at all, by that enduring fame which is the final reward of a rounded career,—this is an antique ideal which seems to be so forgotten now, and even the words which express it sound curiously out of date in our more modern vocabulary.

It is natural enough that, to a generation disillusioned by the war, the notions embodied in high-sounding terms like Fame and Glory should seem somewhat pompous and absurd. Perhaps they are so, perhaps all such aims are folly; perhaps those who are devoid of such ambitions are superior, as they certainly are more amiable and easy-going, human beings. Only —and this is the point I want to emphasize—we must not expect them to leave much enduring work behind them. Unless an artist regards achievement in his art, and the lasting fame it brings, as infinitely worth while, esteems it as far above immediate success and the applause of his contemporaries; unless he be sustained and spurred on, and, if you like, deluded, by a faith, a fanaticism, a folly of this kind, he is not in the least likely to maintain his purpose, striving ever onwards towards that excellence which, we are told, "dwells among rocks hardly accessible, and a man must almost wear his heart out before he can reach her." Fame may be the last infirmity of noble mind, but the noblest minds whom Time has crowned with enduring laurel have seldom been untouched by this brave fever. With what a passion the ancient Greeks loved fame, and how abundantly was that love rewarded! The κλέα ἀνδρῶν, the fame of great deeds which might reach heaven, was the high incentive of the Homeric heroes; the thought of it inspired Pindar's odes; and Plato expressed the feeling of this most glorious and vain-glorious people, when he made the wise Diotima exalt the love in mortals of immortal fame, saying that she was persuaded "that all men do all things—and the better they are the more they do them—in the hope of the glorious fame of immortal virtue, for they desire the immortal." With this fine passion the Greeks infected the Romans, handing it on to the nobler among them as a spark of divinest fire. It flashed out again at the Renaissance from the ashes of antiquity; and the French, with their love of *la gloire,* have carried on this, as they have other classical traditions. When the most famous of French critics comes to depict a character devoid of ambition and the love of fame, he notes the absence of this high and animating motive, this desire to excel, as a grave default, a kind of emasculation, and a sign of poverty of spirit. It is easy enough, Sainte-Beuve says, to miss fame by not believing in it; and this, in my analysis of their plight, seems to me likely to be the fate of our younger generation. With the love of fame, the desire to appeal to a more permanent audience than that of one's immediate contemporaries, the other unfavourable conditions of the time, however discouraging, would present no insuperable difficulties; the temptations of money and immediate success could be resisted; but if writers have no belief in lasting renown, and no desire for it, if they produce their works only for the day's consumption, how can they expect to win enduring reputations? it being useless, as Schopenhauer pointed out, for pastry-cooks to appeal to posterity.

Fame indeed is seldom with us so conscious, or at least so openly avowed, an object of ambition as it is in France, and we possess no exact equivalent for the French term *la gloire.* But the ideal of which fame is the old and consecrated symbol, the desire to leave behind one something which the world will be unwilling to let die, and thus to live on in the thoughts of succeeding ages, has been, though they may not have so often confessed it, a most potent incentive to our greatest English writers.

What I am writing sounds no doubt rather priggish;

and I am perfectly aware that it is in a way ridiculous
for ephemeral little mortals like ourselves to be so
anxious about their puny performances and their insignificant reputations. All such thoughts are chilled at
once when we reflect on the almost certain indifference
of posterity, or extend our cogitations as far as the
next glacial epoch. But the desire for enduring renown,
though rooted in the egotism of our vain human nature,
reaches upward towards more permanent things, and
bears fairer fruit upon its branches. Fame, as Hazlitt,
the least priggish of our critics, declared in his
panegyric of that passion, is not popularity, the shout
of the multitude; it is the spirit of man surviving in the
minds and thoughts of other men; and the love of it
is, he says, only another name for the love of excellence; or it is "the ambition to attain the highest excellence, sanctioned by the highest authority—that of
time." "Fame," another critic writes (and I cannot
deny myself the pleasure of copying out this eloquent
passage) :

Fame, as a noble mind conceives and desires it, is not embodied
in a monument, a biography, or the repetition of a strange name by
strangers; it consists in the immortality of a man's work, his
spirit, his efficacy, in the perpetual rejuvenation of his soul in the
world. When Horace—no model of magnanimity—wrote his *exegi
monumentum,* he was not thinking that the pleasure he would continue to give would remind people of his trivial personality, which
indeed he never particularly celebrated, and which had much
better lie buried with his bones. He was thinking, of course, of that
pleasure itself; thinking that the delight, half lyric, half sarcastic,
which those delicate cameos had given him to carve would be
perennially renewed in all who retraced them. Nay, perhaps we
may not go too far in saying that even that impersonal satisfaction was not the deepest he felt; the deepest, very likely, flowed
from the immortality, not of his monument, but of the subject and
passion it commemorated; that tenderness, I mean, and that dis-

illusion with mortal life which rendered his verse immortal. He had expressed, and in expressing appropriated, some recurring human moods, some mocking renunciations, and he knew that his spirit was immortal, being linked and identified with that portion of the truth.*

Such, then, is the incentive which those who do not believe in it run the risk of missing. Is a purpose of this kind lightly to be disregarded? Among all the things that men live for, is the eternity of their thought, or such eternity as earth can give, their least worthy object of desire? Was not Renan right when he said that glory after all is the thing which has the best chance of not being altogether vanity? And even if fame be nothing but a shadow and an illusion, and those who pursue it shadows also, yet surely of all illusions it is the most illustrious, being the image and symbol of the highest excellence. To love fame is no merely egotistic passion; and indeed were it otherwise, were a man's attempt to make his name immortal nothing but a mad and private venture, ought we not to prize it even so for the insolence of so vainglorious a design? Should anyone be touched to-day by this old infatuation, and find himself among the lovers of enduring fame, he may reflect that nowhere else, at least, could he be in better company. And, anyhow, is not life more interesting, is it not more of an adventure, and (if we care to use the old-fashioned word) may we not call it nobler, if we have some impossible aim to live for, some ideal purpose, however unavailing, to animate our dust?

---

*George Santayana: *Reason in Society*, pp. 144-145.

THE HOGARTH ESSAYS

ANONYMITY
AN ENQUIRY

BY

E. M. FORSTER

To L. H. C. S.

ANONYMITY: AN ENQUIRY

Do you like to know who a book's by?

The question is more profound and even more literary than may appear. A poem for example: do we gain more or less pleasure from it when we know the name of the poet? The *Ballad of Sir Patrick Spens*, for example. No one knows who wrote *Sir Patrick Spens*. It comes to us out of the northern void like a breath of ice. Set beside it another ballad whose author is known—*The Rime of the Ancient Mariner*. That, too, contains a tragic voyage and the breath of ice, but it is signed Samuel Taylor Coleridge, and we know a certain amount about this Coleridge. Coleridge signed other poems and knew other poets; he ran away from Cambridge; he enlisted as a Dragoon under the name of Trooper Comberback, but fell so constantly from his horse that it had to be withdrawn from beneath him permanently; he was employed instead upon matters relating to sanitation; he married Southey's sister, and gave lectures; he became stout, pious, and dishonest, took opium and died. With such information in our heads, we speak of the *Ancient Mariner* as "a poem by Coleridge," but of *Sir Patrick Spens* as "a poem." What difference, if any, does this difference between them make upon our minds? And in the case of novels and plays—does ignorance or knowledge of their authorship signify? And newspaper articles—do they

impress more when they are signed or unsigned? Thus
—rather vaguely—let us begin our quest.

Books are composed of words, and words have two
functions to perform: they give information or they
create an atmosphere. Often they do both, for the two
functions are not incompatible, but our enquiry shall
keep them distinct. Let us turn for our next example
to Public Notices. There is a word that is sometimes
hung up at the edge of a tramline: the word "Stop."
Written on a metal label by the side of the line, it
means that a tram should stop here presently. It is an
example of pure information. It creates no atmosphere
—at least, not in my mind. I stand close to the label
and wait and wait for the tram. If the tram comes, the
information is correct; if it doesn't come, the information is incorrect; but in either case it remains information, and the notice is an excellent instance of one
of the uses of the words.

Compare it with another public notice which is sometimes exhibited in the darker cities of England:
"Beware of pickpockets, male and female." Here,
again, there is information. A pickpocket may come
along presently, just like a tram, and we take our
measures accordingly. But there is something else besides. Atmosphere is created. Who can see those words
without a slight sinking feeling at the heart? All the
people around look so honest and nice, but they are
not, some of them are pickpockets, male or female.
They hustle old gentlemen, the old gentleman glances
down, his watch is gone. They steal up behind an old
lady and cut out the back breadth of her beautiful
sealskin jacket with sharp and noiseless pairs of scis-
sors. Observe that happy little child running to buy

sweets. Why does he suddenly burst into tears? A pick-pocket, male or female, has jerked his halfpenny out of his hand. All this, and perhaps much more, occurs to us when we read the notice in question. We suspect our fellows of dishonesty, we observe them suspecting us. We have been reminded of several disquieting truths, of the general insecurity of life, human frailty, the violence of the poor, and the fatuous trustfulness of the rich, who always expect to be popular without having done anything to deserve it. It is a sort of *memento mori,* set up in the midst of Vanity Fair. By taking the form of a warning it has made us afraid, although nothing is gained by fear; all we need to do is to protect our precious purses, and fear will not help us to do this. Besides conveying information it has created an atmosphere, and to that extent is literature. "Beware of pockpockets, male and female," is not good literature, and it is unconscious. But the words are performing two functions, whereas the word "Stop" only performed one, and this is an important difference, and the first step in our journey.

Next step. Let us now collect together all the printed matter of the world into a single heap; poetry books, exercise books, plays, newspapers, advertisements, street notices, everything. Let us arrange the contents of the heap into a line, with the works that convey pure information at one end, and the works that create pure atmosphere at the other end, and the works that do both in their intermediate positions, the whole line being graded so that we pass from one attitude to another. We shall find that at the end of pure information stands the tramway notice "Stop," and that at the extreme other end is lyric poetry. Lyric poetry is absolutely no use. It is the exact antithesis of a street notice, for it conveys no information of any kind. What's the use of "A slumber did my spirit seal" or "Whether on Ida's snowy brow" or "So we'll go no more a roving" or "Far in a western brookland"? They do not tell us where the tram will stop or even whether it exists. And, passing from lyric poetry to ballad, we are still deprived of information. It is true that the *Ancient Mariner* describes an antarctic expedition, but in such a muddled way that it is no real help to the explorer, the accounts of the polar currents and winds being hopelessly inaccurate. It is true that the *Ballad of Sir Patrick Spens* refers to the bringing home of the Maid of Norway in the year 1285, but the reference is so vague and confused that the historians turn from it in despair. Lyric poetry is absolutely no use, and poetry generally is almost no use.

But when, proceeding down the line, we leave poetry behind and arrive at the drama, and particularly at those plays that purport to contain normal human beings, we find a change. Uselessness still predominates, but we begin to get information as well. *Julius Cæsar* contains some reliable information about Rome. And when we pass from the drama to the novel, the change is still more marked. Information abounds. What a lot we learn from *Tom Jones* about the west countryside! And from *Northanger Abbey* about the same country-side fifty years later. In psychology too the novelist teaches us much. How carefully has Henry James explored certain selected recesses of the human mind! What an analysis of a country rectory in *The Way of All Flesh!* The instincts of Emily Brontë—they illuminate passion. And Proust—how amazingly does Proust describe not only French Society, not only the working of his characters, but the personal equipment of the reader, so that one keeps stopping with a gasp to say "Oh! how did he find that out about me? I didn't even know it myself until he informed me, but it is so!" The novel, whatever else it may be, is partly a notice board. And that is why many men who do not care for poetry or even for the drama enjoy novels and are well qualified to criticize them.

Beyond the novel we came to works whose avowed aim is information, works of learning, history, sociology, philosophy, psychology, science, etc. Uselessness is now subsidiary, though it still may persist as it does in the *Decline and Fall* or the *Stones of Venice*. And next come those works that give, or profess to give, us information about contemporary events: the newspapers. (Newspapers are so important and so peculiar that I shall return to them later, but mention them here in their place in the procession of printed matter.) And then come advertisements, time tables, the price list inside a taxi, and public notices: the notice warning us against pickpockets, which incidentally produced an atmosphere, though its aim was information, and the pure information contained in the announcement "Stop." It is a long journey from lyric poetry to a placard beside a tram line, but it is a journey in which there are no breaks. Words are all of one family, and do not become different because some are printed in a book and others on a metal disc. It is their functions that differentiate them. They have two functions, and the combination of those functions is infinite. If there is on earth a house with many mansions, it is the house of words.

Looking at this line of printed matter, let us again ask ourselves: Do I want to know who wrote that? Ought it to be signed or not? The question is becoming more interesting. Clearly, in so far as words convey information, they ought to be signed. Information is supposed to be true. That is its only reason for existing, and the man who gives it ought to sign his name, so that he may be called to account if he has told a lie. When I have waited for several hours beneath the notice "Stop," I have the right to suggest that it be taken down, and I cannot do this unless I know who put it up. Make your statement, sign your name. That's common sense. But as we approach the other function of words—the creation of atmosphere—the question of signature surely loses its importance. It does not matter who wrote "A slumber did my spirit steal" because the poem itself does not matter. Ascribe it to Ella Wheeler Wilcox and the tram will run as usual. It does not matter much who wrote *Julius Cæsar* and *Tom Jones*. They contain descriptions of ancient Rome and eighteenth-century England, and to that extent we wish them signed, for we can judge from the author's name whether the description is likely to be reliable; but beyond that, the guarantee of Shakespeare or Fielding might just as well be Charles Garvice's. So we come to the conclusion, firstly, that what is information ought to be signed; and, secondly, that what is not information need not be signed.

The question can now be carried a step further.

What is this element in words that is not information? I have called it "atmosphere," but it requires stricter definition than that. It resides not in any particular word, but in the order in which words are

arranged—that is to say, in style. It is the power that
words have to raise our emotions or quicken our blood.
It is also something else, and to define that other thing
would be to explain the secret of the universe. This
"something else" in words is undefinable. It is their
power to create not only atmosphere, but a world,
which, while it lasts, seems more real and solid than this
daily existence of pickpockets and trams. Before we
begin to read the *Ancient Mariner* we know that the
Polar Seas are not inhabited by spirits, and that if a
man shoots an albatross he is not a criminal but a
sportsman, and that if he stuffs the albatross afterwards he becomes a naturalist also. All this is common
knowledge. But when we are reading the *Ancient
Mariner,* or remembering it intensely, common knowledge disappears and uncommon knowledge takes its
place. We have entered a universe that only answers
to its own laws, supports itself, internally coheres, and
has a new standard of truth. Information is true if
it is accurate. A poem is true if it hangs together.
Information points to something else. A poem points
to nothing but itself. Information is relative. A poem
is absolute. The world created by words exists neither
in space nor time though it has semblances of both,
it is eternal and indestructible, and yet its action
is no stronger than a flower: it is adamant, yet it is
also what one of its practitioners thought it to be,
namely, the shadow of a shadow. We can best define it
by negations. It is not this world, its laws are not the
laws of science or logic, its conclusions not those of
common sense. And it causes us to suspend our ordinary
judgments.

Now comes the crucial point. While we are reading

the *Ancient Mariner* we forget our astronomy and geography and daily ethics. Do we not also forget the author? Does not Samuel Taylor Coleridge, lecturer, opium eater, and dragoon, disappear with the rest of the world of information? We remember him before we begin the poem and after we finish it, but during the poem nothing exists but the poem. Consequently while we read the *Ancient Mariner* a change takes place in it. It becomes anonymous, like the *Ballad of Sir Patrick Spens*. And here is the point I would support: that all literature tends towards a condition of anonymity, and that, so far as words are creative, a signature merely distracts us from their true significance. I do not say literature "ought" not to be signed, because literature is alive, and consequently "ought" is the wrong word to use. It wants not to be signed. That puts my point. It is always tugging in that direction and saying in effect: "I, not my author, exist really." So do the trees, flowers and human beings say "I really exist, not God," and continue to say so despite the admonitions to the contrary addressed to them by clergymen and scientists. To forget its Creator is one of the functions of a Creation. To remember him is to forget the days of one's youth. Literature does not want to remember. It is alive—not in a vague complementary sense—but alive tenaciously, and it is always covering up the tracks that connect it with the laboratory.

It may here be objected that literature expresses personality, that it is the result of the author's individual outlook, that we are right in asking for his name. It is his property—he ought to have the credit.

An important objection; also a modern one, for in

the past neither writers nor readers attached the high importance to personality that they do to-day. It did not trouble Homer or the various people who were Homer. It did not trouble the writers in the Greek Anthology, who would write and re-write the same poem in almost identical language, their notion being that the poem, not the poet, is the important thing, and that by continuous rehandling the perfect expression natural to the poem may be attained. It did not trouble the mediæval balladists, who, like the Cathedral builders, left their work unsigned. It troubled neither the composers nor the translators of the Bible. The Book of Genesis to-day contains at least three different elements—Jahvist, Elohist, and Priestly—which were combined into a single account by a committee who lived under King Josiah at Jerusalem and translated into English by another committee who lived under King James I at London. And yet the Book of Genesis is literature. These earlier writers and readers knew that the words a man writes express him, but they did not make a cult of expression as we do to-day. Surely they were right, and modern critics go too far in their insistence on personality.

They go too far because they do not reflect what personality is. Just as words have two functions—information and creation—so each human mind has two personalities, one on the surface, one deeper down. The upper personality has a name. It is called S. T. Coleridge, or William Shakespeare, or Mrs. Humphry Ward. It is conscious and alert, it does things like dining out, answering letters, etc., and it differs vividly and amusingly from other personalities. The lower personality is a very queer affair. In many ways it is a perfect fool, but without it there is no literature, because, unless a man dips a bucket down into it occasionally he cannot produce first-class work. There is something general about it. Although it is inside S. T. Coleridge, it cannot be labelled with his name. It has something in common with all other deeper personalities, and the mystic will assert that the common quality is God, and that here, in the obscure recesses of our being, we near the gates of the Divine. It is in any case the force that makes for anonymity. As it came from the depths, so it soars to the heights, out of local questionings; as it is general to all men, so the works it inspires have something general about them, namely beauty. The poet wrote the poem no doubt, but he forgot himself while he wrote it, and we forget him while we read. What is so wonderful about great literature is that it transforms the man who reads it towards the condition of the man who wrote, and brings to birth in us also the creative impulse. Lost in the beauty where he was lost, we find more than we ever threw away, we reach what seems to be our spiritual home, and remember that it was not the speaker who was in the beginning but the Word.

If we glance at one or two writers who are not first class this point will be illustrated. Charles Lamb and R. L. Stevenson will serve. Here are two gifted, sensitive, fanciful, tolerant, humorous fellows, but they always write with their surface-personalities and never let down buckets into their underworld. Lamb did not try: bbbbuckets, he would have said, are bbeyond me, and he is the pleasanter writer in consequence. Stevenson was always trying oh ever so hard, but the bucket either stuck or else came up again full of the R. L. S.

who let it down full of the mannerisms, the self-consciousness, the sentimentality, the quaintness which he was hoping to avoid. He and Lamb append their names in full to every sentence they write. They pursue us page after page, always to the exclusion of higher joy. They are letter writers, not creative artists, and it is no coincidence that each of them did write charming letters. A letter comes off the surface: it deals with the events of the day or with plans: it is naturally signed. Literature tries to be unsigned. And the proof is that, whereas we are always exclaiming "How like Lamb!" or "How typical of Stevenson!" we never say "How like Shakespeare!" or "How typical of Dante!" We are conscious only of the world they have created, and we are in a sense co-partners in it. Coleridge, in his smaller domain, makes us co-partners too. We forget for ten minutes his name and our own, and I contend that this temporary forgetfulness, this momentary and mutual anonymity, is sure evidence of good stuff. The demand that literature should express personality is far too insistent in these days, and I look back with longing to the earlier modes of criticism where a poem was not an expression but a discovery, and was sometimes supposed to have been shown to the poet by God.

Explique moi d'où vient ce souffle par to bouche façonné en mots.

Car quand tu parles, comme un arbre qui de toute sa feuille S'émeut dans le silence du Midi, la paix en nous peu à peu succède à la pensée.

Par le moyen de ce chant sans musique et de cette parole sans voix, nous sommes accordés à la mélodie de ce monde.

Tu n'explique rien, ô poète, mais toutes choses par toi nous deviennent explicables.

Je ne parle pas selon ce que je veux, mais je conçois dans le sommeil,
Et je ne saurais expliquer, d'où je retire ce souffle, c'est le souffle qui m'est retiré.
Dilatant ce vide que j'ai en moi, j'ouvre la bouche,
Et ayant aspiré l'air, dans ce legs de lui même par lequel l'homme à chaque seconde *expire* l'image de sa mort,
Je restitue une parole intelligible,
Et l'ayant dite, je sais ce que j'ai dit.*

The personality of a writer does become important after we have read his book and begin to study it. When the glamour of creation ceases, when the leaves of the divine tree are silent, when the intelligible word is restored to the universe, when the co-partnership is over, then a book changes its nature, and we can ask ourselves questions about it such as "What is the author's name?"; "Where did he live?"; "Was he married?"; and "Which was his favourite flower?" Then we are no longer reading the book, we are studying it and making it subserve our desire for information. "Study" has a very solemn sound. "I am studying Dante" sounds much more than "I am reading Dante." It is really much less. Study is only a serious form of gossip. It teaches us everything about the book except the central thing, and between that and us it raises a circular barrier which only the wings of the spirit can cross. The study of science, history, etc., is necessary and proper, for they are subjects that belong to the domain of information, but a creative subject like literature—to study that is excessively dangerous, and should never be attempted by the immature. Modern education promotes the unmitigated study of literature and concentrates our attention on the relation between

*Claudel: *La Ville* (second version).

a writer's life—his surface life—and his work. That is one reason why it is such a curse. There are no questions to be asked about literature while we read it because *"la paix succède à la pensée."* An examination paper could not be set on the *Ancient Mariner* as it speaks to the heart of the reader, and it was to speak to the heart that it was written, and otherwise it would not have been written. Questions only occur when we cease to realize what it was about and become inquisitive and methodical.

A word in conclusion on the newspapers—for they raise an interesting contributory issue. We have already defined a newspaper as something which conveys, or is supposed to convey, information about passing events. It is true, not to itself like a poem, but to the facts it purports to relate—like the tram notice. When the morning paper arrives it lies upon the breakfast table simply steaming with truth in regard to something else. Truth, truth, and nothing but truth. Unsated by the banquet, we sally forth in the afternoon to buy an evening paper, which is published at mid-day as the name implies, and feast anew. At the end of the week we buy a weekly, or a Sunday, paper, which as the name implies has been written on the Saturday, and at the end of the month we buy a monthly. Thus do we keep in touch with the world of events as practical men should.

And who is keeping us in touch? Who gives us this information upon which our judgments depend, and which must ultimately influence our characters? Curious to relate, we seldom know. Newspapers are for the most part anonymous. Statements are made and no signature appended. Suppose we read in a paper that the

Emperor of Guatemala is dead. Our first feeling is
one of mild consternation; out of snobbery we regret
what has happened, although the Emperor didn't play
much part in our lives, and if ladies we say to one
another "I feel so sorry for the poor Empress." But
presently we learn that the Emperor cannot have died,
because Guatemala is a Republic, and the Empress cannot be a widow, because she does not exist. If the statement was signed, and we know the name of the goose
who made it, we shall discount anything he tells us in
the future. If—which is more probable—it is unsigned
or signed "Our Special Correspondent"—we remain
defenceless against future misstatements. The Guatemala lad may be turned on to write about the Fall of
the Franc and mislead us over that.

It seems paradoxical that an article should impress
us more if it is unsigned than if it is signed. But it
does, owing to the weakness of our psychology. Anonymous statements have, as we have seen, a universal
air about them. Absolute truth, the collected wisdom
of the universe, seems to be speaking, not the feeble
voice of a man. The modern newspaper has taken advantage of this. It is a pernicious caricature of literature. It has usurped that divine tendency towards
anonymity. It has claimed for information what only
belongs to creation. And it will claim it as long as we
allow it to claim it, and to exploit the defects of our
psychology. "The High Mission of the Press." Poor
Press! as if it were in a position to have a mission! It
is we who have a mission to it. To cure a man through
the newspapers or through propaganda of any sort is
impossible: you merely alter the symptoms of his
disease. We shall only be cured by purging our minds

of confusion. The papers trick us not so much by their lies as by their exploitation of our weakness. They are always confusing the two functions of words and insinuating that "The Emperor of Guatemala is dead" and "A slumber did my spirit seal" belong to the same category. They are always usurping the privileges that only uselessness may claim, and they will do this as long as we allow them to do it.

This ends our enquiry. The question "Ought things to be signed?" seemed, if not an easy question, at all events an isolated one, but we could not answer it without considering what words are, and disentangling the two functions they perform. We decided pretty easily that information ought to be signed: common sense leads to this conclusion, and newspapers which are largely unsigned have gained by that device their undesirable influence over civilization. Creation—that we found a more difficult matter. "Literature wants not to be signed" I suggested. Creation comes from the depths—the mystic will say from God. The signature, the name, belongs to the surface-personality, and pertains to the world of information, it is a ticket, not the spirit of life. While the author wrote he forgot his name; while we read him we forget both his name and our own. When we have finished reading we begin to ask questions, and to study the book and the author, we drag them into the realm of information. Now we learn a thousand things, but we have lost the pearl of great price, and in the chatter of question and answer, in the torrents of gossip and examination papers we forget the purpose for which creation was performed. I am not asking for reverence. Reverence is fatal to literature. My plea is for something more vital: imagination. Imagination is as the immortal God which should assume flesh for the redemption of mortal passion (Shelley). Imagination is our only guide into the world created by words. Whether those words are signed or unsigned becomes, as soon as the imagination redeems us, a matter of no importance, because we have approximated to the state in which they were written, and there are no names down there, no personality as we understand personality, no marrying or giving in marriage. What there is down there—ah, that is another enquiry, and may the clergymen and the scientists pursue it more successfully in the future than they have in the past.

THE HOGARTH ESSAYS

IN RETREAT

BY

HERBERT READ

To The Green Howards

. . . No, it is impossible; it is impossible to convey the life-sensation of any given epoch of one's existence—that which makes its truth, its meaning, its subtle and penetrating essence. It is impossible. We live, as we dream—alone. . . .

JOSEPH CONRAD

IN RETREAT

A JOURNAL OF THE RETREAT OF THE FIFTH ARMY FROM ST. QUENTIN, MARCH, 1918.

INTRODUCTION

IT IS now seven years since the incidents here related took place, and six years since I wrote this account. I had preserved, rather by accident than by design, a bundle of messages and field-maps connected with the Retreat, and it occurred to me, in the spring of 1919, that here was circumstantial evidence of a kind which, despite the immensity of the war, was likely to be preserved. My memory of the events associated with these relics was yet vivid enough to give them a real connection, and this I set myself to do. One thing I wished to avoid, and that was any personal interpretation of the events—any expatiation, that is to say, whether of the imagination or of the intellect. I wanted the events to speak for themselves unaided by any art.

I tried to publish this short narrative as soon as I had written it; and in this effort I received encouragement and advice from one whose name should have been sufficient to remove many obstacles. But the state of the public mind, or at least, of that mind as localized in the minds of publishers and editors, refused anything so bleak. The war was still a sentimental illusion: it was a subject for pathos, for platitude, even for rationalization. It was not yet time for the simple facts.

I then resolved to put the narrative away for five years and see what change came over the public mind, or my mind too, in that interval.

Personally I find myself receding from the stern oath of realism I took when in the midst of war; receding, too, from whatever bitterness I then felt against the charlatans who proffered their vicarious interpretations of our experience. I still feel some bitterness that so little that is effectual should have been recorded of the reality; and most bitter, perhaps, at certain states of forgetfulness in the minds of non-combatants. But I have nothing to say

—no desire to say anything—on that aspect of the turn of events. I have grown to think that whatever is effected by the written word must be effected on the plane of imagination and thought.

But these cannot subsist without logical roots in experience. And meanwhile there is historic truth—a necessary science; and this transcript of experience is designed to that end. It does not pretend to be more than a very small fragment of the history of the war; but *in full* that history will never be written.

H. R.

I

WE RECEIVED the warning order just before dinner,
and for a while talked excitedly round the mess fire,
some scoffing at the idea of an imminent battle, others
gravely saying that this time at any rate the warning
was justified. Two deserters, with tales of massing
guns and the night-movement of innumerable troops,
had reached our lines the previous day. Of course, deserters usually had some such tale designed to tempt
a captor's leniency, but this time it was likely to be the
truth. What else could the enemy's long silence mean?
To that question we had no answer. We went early to
bed, expecting an early awakening. The harnessed
horses stood in lowered shafts.

There was scarcely a wall standing in Fluquières:
everywhere demolition and bombardment had reduced
the village to irregular cairns of brick and plaster.
Winding among these cairns were the cleared road-
ways. Men and horses rested in patched sheds and an
occasional cellar. S. and I were in a small repaired
stable, each with a bed-frame in a manger. I had livened
the cleanly whitewashed walls of the place with illustrations from a coloured magazine. That evening all
save our trench-kit had been sent to the transport-
wagons, and we were lying on the bare netting with
only our trench coats thrown over us.

For some time I was too excited to sleep, and none
too warm. But weariness did at length triumph, and

when, a short while afterwards, I was roughly awakened, I had become unconscious enough to forget the continuity of things.

II

Yes: suddenly I was awake. A match was being applied to the candle stuck on the bed-frame above my head. With his excited face illumined by the near candle-light, an orderly bent over me and shook my shoulders. I heard confused shoutings, and the rumble of gunfire. I had hardly need to read the message-form held out to me: "Man Battle Stations"—the code words I knew only too well, and all that they implied. I was shivering violently with the cold, but in the shaking candle-light I scribbled messages repeating the code to the company commanders, the transport officer, and to others. S. was moving on the other side of the wall that divided the mangers.

"We're in for it, my lad," he yelled, above the increasing din.

Just then there was the sudden shrieking rush of a descending shell and its riotous detonation very near. Our candles jumped out, and we were in darkness, with bricks and earth falling like a hail on the roof. My servant came in, and hastily helped me to gather my equipment together. He handled the two or three books I always carried with me, asking me if I would take one in my pocket. I took Thoreau's *Walden*, because I had not yet read it, and anticipated two or three weary days of passive defence. For even if now we realized the actuality of the enemy's attack, so confident were we of our defensive system that we contemplated nothing more than a short successful resistance. When in the front line we had ceaselessly reconnoitred all approaches, and so fine were the sweeping fields of fire that stretched away towards St. Quentin, so skilfully placed were our machine-guns, that always we pitied the folly of the enemy should he assail a defence so deadly. We reckoned with one factor unseen.

I fixed my revolver and ammunition securely, and set out to the orderly room, some five hundred yards away. It was now about five o'clock and still dark. I picked my way along a path which led across the great heaps of rubble. Shells were falling in the village. I still shivered with cold. My electric torch was nearly exhausted, so that I kept falling as I went. When I reached the orderly room, which was in a restored cottage, I found everything in a great hubbub, orderlies coming and going, the sergeant-major shouting orders. Inside, the doctor was bandaging a wounded man.

S., who had been assembling the headquarter staff, came to say that something terrible had happened to the Lewis team (at that time a Lewis-gun team was attached to each battalion headquarters): would I come round with my torch.

They had been sleeping, some six men, beneath tarpaulin sheets, stretched across a half-demolished outhouse. A shell had fallen in the middle of them. In the weak glare of my torch, we saw a mangled mass of red brick-dust and of red glistening blood. Here and there we distinguished a tousled head of hair. One man, pinned beneath beams and brickwork, was still groaning. We quickly began to extricate him, but he died whilst we worked.

I then joined the colonel, and with one or two

orderlies and the sergeant-major we followed the companies along the back lane that led from Fluquières to Roupy, a distance of about a mile and a half. The morning was cold and a heavy dew lay on the ground. As we walked the light of dawn began to reveal a thick wet mist.

III

At 6.50 I sent a message to the brigade, informing them that the battalion was in position. We had been shelled all along the way, and when we neared Roupy, the crossroads seemed to be under a continuous barrage. Nevertheless, we got into position with very few casualties. Safe in the bowels of the headquarter dugout, we thought the worst was over, and began casually to eat the tongue sandwiches and drink the tea provided by the mess-corporal.

The dugout was new and spacious, and odorous of the fresh chalky earth. It was about thirty feet deep, and partitioned into three sections, of which the middle one was occupied by the headquarter officers. Because it was new it was unfurnished, and we had to squat on the bare floor, grouped round a few candles.

For me that cavern is a telephonic nightmare. The instrument, a "D III converted," was placed on the floor in a corner of the dugout. Two signallers sat with their legs straddling round it. At first the companies, then the neighbouring battalions, and, finally, the brigade, kept me there crouching on the floor, yelling till I was hoarse into the execrable instrument. When I was not speaking, the signallers were receiving or sending Morse messages.

Above the ground, the situation was disquieting.

The thick mist of the early dawn persisted: a man ten yards away could not be distinguished. The gunfire, tremendous in its intensity, continued hour after hour to pound into the invisible foreground. The earth vibrated almost hysterically. An occasional shell crashed near us, but after the first three hours (at 7.30) the enemy's fire seemed to be concentrated on our front-line defences. No messages, telephonic or written, came to relieve our anxiety.

The gradual accumulation of our anxiety should be realized. Every minute seemed to add to its intensity. By ten o'clock or so, our hearts were like taut drum skins beaten reverberantly by every little incident.

Then the skin smashed. Bodily action flickered like flame. The sense of duration was consumed away.

Shortly after eleven o'clock, a gun team galloped madly down the main road. Then two stragglers belonging to the Machine-Gun Corps were brought to headquarters. They informed us that the front line had been penetrated. Later, an officer from the front-line battalion, with five or six men, came to us out of the mist. Most of the party were wounded, and as the officer's leg was being bandaged in the dugout, he told us his tale. He was haggard and incoherent, but the sequence was awfully clear to us. The enemy had attacked in great strength at 7.30. They had apparently reached the observation line unobserved, and overpowered the few men there before a warning could be given or an escape made. Advancing under cover of a creeping barrage, they had approached the main line of defence. No fire met them there, or only fire directed vaguely into the fog. The fight at the main line had been short and bloody. Our men,

dazed and quivering after three hours' hellish bombardment (I could see them cowering on the cold mist-wet
earth), had been brave to the limits of heroism; but
pitifully powerless. The ghastly job had been completed by 8.30. About nine o'clock fresh enemy battalions passed through their fellows and advanced
towards the front-line redoubt (L'Épine de Dallon).
Our artillery fire must have been useless by then, still
falling on the old enemy front line. At any rate, the
enemy quickly surrounded the redoubt, and then penetrated it. This officer himself had been captured, and
later had made his escape in the mist. He thought it
possible that the headquarters of his battalion were
still holding out.

We were still questioning our informant when an
excited voice yelled down the dugout shaft: "Boches
on the top of the dugout." Our hearts thumped. There
was no reason why the enemy shouldn't be on us. They
might have been anywhere in that damned mist. We
drew our revolvers and rushed to the shaft. We did
not mean to be caught like rats in a hole.

I remember my emotion distinctly: a quiet despair.
I *knew* I went up those stairs either to be shot or
bayoneted, as I emerged, or, perhaps, to be made pris-
oner and so plunge into a strange unknown existence.

Half-way up the stairs, and a voice cried down:
"It's all right: they're our fellows." Some artillerymen in overcoats, straggling across the open, had
looked sinister in the mist.

We turned to the dugout, the released tension leaving us exhausted.

Patrols from our front companies had been feeling outward all morning, at first without result. At

12.30, B. (commanding the left front company) reported: "Machine-gun and rifle-fire on left and right can be heard. Shelling very hard. Can see nothing. Patrols are being sent out." At 1 p. m. he reported: "Boches are in quarry just in front of me. We are firing Lewis guns and rifles at him. He seems to be firing from our right flank too, with machine-guns."

These and other messages all came by runner. The telephonic communications to the companies had broken down before noon, though I think we remained in touch with the brigade until late in the afternoon.

About midday the mist began to clear a little. At one o'clock the enemy, having massed in the valley five hundred yards immediately in front of us, attacked in mass strength. The fusillade that met them must have been terrific. They came on in good order, extending and manœuvring with precision. At 1.20, B. reported: "No. 5 Platoon report enemy on wire in front. Artillery assistance is asked for. We are firing rifle grenades into them." And again at 1.30: "Boches attacking in strength with sections in front. Front troops are in valley in front. They are also heading to my left flank." Between 1.30 and 1.40 the attack reached its greatest intensity. By 1.45 it had withered completely before the hail of our fire.

At 1.45, B. reported: "Boches running back like hell near Savy. They seem to be running from artillery as much as anything." (Savy was one and a half miles to our left front: it was on the slope that rose away from the valley in front of us where the enemy had massed his forces before his attack.)

For a moment we became elated. There was cause enough. The mist had lifted, and a pale sun shone.

We had defeated a strong attack. We received a message from the Inniskillings on our right to say they still held their positions intact. And wider afield the coördination of the enemy's advance seemed to have broken down.

We made haste to distribute our reserve ammunition, to clear the dressing-station, and generally to make ourselves ready for the next happenings.

In reply to my inquiries B. sent this message, timed 2.15 p.m.: "It is very difficult to tell numbers of enemy. I can see the ground north to Savy, and saw them scattered. The line advancing had about 30 men to every 100 yards. We do not require S.A.A. yet. Can you instruct Rose * to fire up Soup Valley, please? We will want Very lights for the night. Will a supply be forthcoming? Can see no movement now. Boche is putting up white lights all along valley."

IV

The lull was not of long duration. Either we had been deceived by the movements near Savy, or the enemy had made a miraculously swift recovery. At 2.45 I received another message from B.: "Enemy movement at F. 12 at 4.0. They appear to be carrying in wounded. Enemy also advancing across valley on left on F. 5, in small parties. Estimated total strength seen, 50 men. Boche aëroplanes are flying about 300 feet above our lines, and have been for a short while past. There is still some machine-gun fire in front. Is a redoubt holding out?"

The aëroplanes were evidently making a prelim-

---

*Code name for a company.

inary reconnaissance and I guessed the movement to be significant of a new attack.

On the mists clearing, the aëroplanes were able to sight position, and soon the artillery on both sides became active. Our own artillery, alas, fired short, smashing our already weakening defences. The Germans brought up their light field guns with great skill and rapidity. Several batteries were observed coming over the ridge at L'Épine de Dallon—only a few hours ago the headquarters of the battalion we were supporting. We now realized our position in earnest, and I sent a detailed account of the situation to the brigade.

Towards four o'clock, the enemy shelling increased in intensity. The second attack was now imminent. B. sent the following message timed 4.30 p.m.: "Boche is attacking on right about 400 strong, and is massing in the valley right in front of Roupy. We want some more S.A.A. During the Boche retreat the riflemen and Lewis guns did good work, killing many. Shelling very heavy."

The heavy shelling continued, and under cover of its intensity the enemy again massed in the valley in front of us. The men held on grimly. Thus B., timed 5.10 p.m.: "Line holding still with some casualties. Reports not in. Line heavily shelled. S.A.A. received correct. Situation still the same. Touch is being kept with battalion on our right, and patrols go constantly. (Our chloride of lime is missing and cannot be found.) Machine-guns very active." And again at 5.40 p.m.: "The Boche is 50 yards or less from our line, and is also passing down the valley for another attack."

Then suddenly those massed men leapt from cover, and came on in their grey, regular formations. At headquarters we were only aware of the angry surge of rifle and machine-gun fire, deadening even the detonations of shells. All this time I was spending tiring, exasperating hours at the telephone, striving to get in communication with brigade and artillery headquarters. Again and again the wire was broken, and again and again the linesmen went out into the mist to mend it. Then it got disconnected irreparably. We were isolated in that chaos.

About 6.30, B. sent the following momentous message: "Boche got inside our wire on right and left. No. 5 Platoon are all either wiped out or prisoners. No. 7 Platoon took up position on left of keep, but Boches were in it when I left. They also were in trench on right of road left by C. Company, and we killed several on road near camouflage. I am now in redoubt with 25 men."

The climax had come. We had still one card to play —the counter-attack company. On receipt of B.'s message, the colonel decided to order C. to attack in accordance with the preconceived plan.

We only heard of this counter-attack from the mouths of a few survivors. It was one of the most heroic episodes in the retreat. The company gathered together in the shell-battered trench that they had occupied all day, and then took the open. No artillery covered their advance. It was hopeless, insane, suicidal. They had perhaps one hundred and fifty yards to cover. They advanced at a jog-trot, lumbering on the uneven ground. One by one they fell before the fusillade that met them. C. had reached the enemy with about a dozen men. These leapt in among the Boches,

and a hand-to-hand struggle ensued for a few minutes.
C. was last seen cursing, pinned to the trench wall by
a little mob of Germans, in one hand his empty smoking revolver.

V

It was now dusk, and with dusk came peace and
silence. And at dusk this was our position:—The front
rim of the redoubt was in the enemy's possession. The
counter-attack company had disappeared. The com-
pany-keeps still held out with a few men in each. The
inner ring of the redoubt was held by one company,
and the remnants of three. B. had survived with one
of his officers. But several officers in the three front
companies had been either killed, wounded, or captured. There were probably two hundred men still
surviving in the battalion.

In the darkness the colonel and I walked up to the
line. As we went along the road, the stillness was
abruptly broken by the sounds of three or four shots,
screams, and curses. We flung ourselves on the roadside, our revolvers ready. We shouted: "Who goes
there?" English voices answered, and the sergeant-
major went to investigate. Two German privates had
walked into a sentry on the road, *coming from behind
us.* No one could understand what they said, and they
were sent back to brigade headquarters. And I don't
remember that any one of us was perturbed by the
incident, eerie though it was.

Just after one o'clock in the day, we received long-
awaited instructions from the brigade: The battalion
in reserve was to deliver a counter-attack. The line of

deployment was given, and the direction of attack. The battalion was to leave its position at 12.45, and the guns were to start a creeping barrage at 1.33 a.m.

The whole thing was a ghastly failure. The night was black, and the battalion attacking was unfamiliar with the ground it had to cover. We waited hours for a sign of their approach. About two o'clock a stray officer came to us, having lost his company. Eventually, about four o'clock, one company did appear. It went forward in the darkness, but got dispersed and uncontrollable in the effort to deploy into attack formation. Dawn found us as dusk had found us, with the sole difference that some two hundred men of the counter-attack battalion had found refuge in our redoubt, and in the keeps in front.

I think by then we were past hope or despair. We regarded all events with an indifference of weariness, knowing that with the dawn would come another attack. We distributed ammunition, reorganized our Lewis guns, and waited dully, without apprehension.

Again the morning was thickly misty. Our own artillery fire was desultory and useless. Under cover of the mist, the enemy massed in battle formation, and the third attack commenced about 7 a.m. We only heard a babel in the mist. Now our artillery was firing short among our men in the redoubt. About ten o'clock the enemy penetrated our left flank, presumably in the gap between us and the battalion on our left, which was still in position. Machine-gun fire began to harass us from that direction, somewhere in the ruins of the village. We never heard from the battalion on our right, and a runner I sent there did not return. I think they must have withdrawn about ten o'clock.

This new attack petered out. I fancy it was only half-hearted on the part of the enemy—probably only a demonstration to see if we intended to make a determined resistance, or to fight only a rearguard action. Finding the resistance determined enough, they evidently retired to prepare the real thing.

This fourth attack was delivered about midday. The mist still persisted thinly. One could perhaps see objects fifty yards away. I don't know what resistance the platoon-keeps offered. They were in a hopeless position, and would easily have been swamped in a mass attack.

Shortly after midday, the enemy came in direct contact with the inner ring of the redoubt.

We fired like maniacs. Every round of ammunition had been distributed. The Lewis guns jammed; rifle bolts grew stiff and unworkable with the expansion of heat.

In the lull before noon, the colonel and I had left the dugout, in which we were beginning to feel like rats in a trap, and had found an old gun-pit about two hundred and fifty yards farther back, and here we established our headquarters. An extraordinary thing happened. The gun-pit was dug out of the bank on the roadside. About two o'clock one of our guns, evidently assuming that Roupy had been evacuated, began to pound the road between Roupy and Fluquières. One of these shells landed clean on the road edge of our pit. We were all hurled to the ground by the explosion, but, on recovering ourselves, found only one casualty; the colonel had received a nasty gash in the forearm. We then went two hundred to three hundred yards across the open, away from the road, and found a smaller

overgrown pit. The colonel refused to regard his
wound as serious; but he soon began to feel dizzy, and
was compelled to go back to the dressing-station. I
was then left in charge of the battalion.

It was now about 2.30. The attack still persisted in
a guerilla fashion. But the enemy was massing troops
in the trenches already taken. At 4 p.m. the intensity
of the attack deepened suddenly. A new intention had
come into the enemy's mind: he was directing his attack on the flanks of our position in an effort to close
round us like pincers. On the left he made use of cover
offered by the ruined village, and eventually brought
machine-guns to bear against us from our left rear.
On the right he made use of the trenches evacuated by
the Inniskillings.

In the height of this attack, while my heart was
heavy with anxiety, I received a message from the
brigade. Surely reinforcements were coming to our
aid? Or was I at length given permission to withdraw?
Neither: it was a rhetorical appeal to hold on to the
last man. I rather bitterly resolved to obey the command.

Another hour passed. The enemy pressed on relent-
lessly with a determined, insidious energy, reckless of
cost. Our position was now appallingly precarious. I
therefore resolved to act independently, and do as
perhaps I should have done hours earlier. I ordered B.
to organize a withdrawal. This message despatched, I
lay on my belly in the grass and watched through my
field-glasses every minute trickling of the enemy's
progress. Gradually they made way round the rim of
the redoubt, bombing along the traverses. And now we
only held it as lips might touch the rim of a saucer.

I could see the heads of my men, very dense and in a
little space. And on either side, incredibly active,
gathered the gray helmets of the Boches. It was like
a long bowstring along the horizon, and our diminished
forces the arrow to be shot into the void. A great many
hostile machine-guns had now been brought up, and the
plain was sprayed with hissing bullets. They impinged
and spluttered about the little pit in which I crouched.

I waited anxiously for B. to take the open. I saw
men crawl out of the trenches, and lie flat on the
parados, still firing at the enemy. Then, after a little
while, the arrow was launched. I saw a piteous band
of men rise from the ground, and run rapidly towards
me. A great shout went up from the Germans: a cry
of mingled triumph and horror. "Halt Eenglisch!"
they cried, and for a moment were too amazed to fire;
as though aghast at the folly of men who could plunge
into such a storm of death. But the first silent gasp of
horror expanded, then broke the crackling storm. I
don't remember in the whole war an intenser taste of
hell. My men came along spreading rapidly to a line of
some two hundred yards' length, but bunched here and
there. On the left, by the main road, the enemy rushed
out to cut them off. Bayonets clashed there. Along the
line men were falling swiftly as the bullets hit them.
Each second they fell, now one crumpling up, now two
or three at once. I saw men stop to pick up their
wounded mates, and as they carried them along, themselves get hit and fall with their inert burdens. Now
they were near me, so I rushed out of my pit and ran
with them to the line of trenches some three hundred
yards behind.

It seemed to take a long time to race across those

few hundred yards. My heart beat nervously, and I
felt infinitely weary. The bullets hissed about me, and
I thought: then this is the moment of death. But I had
no emotions. I remembered having read how in battle
men are hit, and never feel the hurt till later, and I
wondered if I had yet been hit. Then I reached the
line. I stood petrified, enormously aghast. *The trench
had not been dug, and no reinforcements occupied it.*
It was as we had passed it on the morning of the 21st,
the sods dug off the surface, leaving an immaculately
patterned "mock" trench. A hundred yards on the
right a machine-gun corps had taken up a position, and
was already covering our retreat. I looked about me
wildly, running along the line and signalling to the
men to drop as they reached the slender parapet of
sods. But the whole basis of my previous tactics had
been destroyed. I should never have ordered my men
to cross that plain of death, but for the expectation
that we were falling back to reinforce a new line. We
found an empty mockery, and I was in despair. But I
must steady the line. On the actual plain the men
obeyed my signals, and crouched in the shallow trench.
But even as they crouched, the bullets struck them. On
the road, the straight white road leading to the western safety, there was something like a stampede. S. and
the sergeant-major went and held it with pointed
revolvers. But it was all useless—hopeless. On the
right, I saw the enemy creeping round. They would
soon enfilade us, and then our shallow defence would
be a death-trap. I accordingly gave the signal to withdraw, bidding the two Lewis guns to cover us as long
as possible. Once more we rose and scattered in retreat.
It would be about seven hundred yards to the next

trenches—the village line round Fluquières, and this
we covered fairly well, sections occasionally halting to
give covering fire. The enemy had not yet ventured
from the redoubt, and our distance apart was now
great enough to make his fire of little effect. And I
think as we moved up the slope towards the village
we must have been in "dead" ground, so far as the
enemy advancing on the right was concerned.

We reached Fluquières, which lay on the top of the
slope, and found there some deep trenches on each side
of the road at the entrance of the village. Further to
the left, I found certain London troops commanded
by a major. One of my Lewis guns still remained intact, and this I placed to fire down the straight road
to Roupy. The enemy had now left the redoubt and
were advancing in line formation.

We were at Fluquières about an hour. The enemy
evidently did not intend to rest content with his cap-
ture of the redoubt. It was just beginning to get dusk.
Earlier we had noticed sporadic contact lights go up.
But now they shot into the sky from all along the
plain. Low-flying aëroplanes hovered over the advancing line, and their wireless messages soon put the
German guns on to us. Big black high-explosive shells
began to fall on our position, making our tired flesh
shudder. I now began to be amazed at the advancing
contact lights. They did not merely stretch in a line
*in front of us: they encircled us like a horse-shoe, the
points of which seemed* (and actually were) *miles behind us.* On the right the enemy was enfilading us with
machine-gun fire.

I searched for the major commanding the troops on
my left, but could not find him. By this time I was

determined to act, and therefore gave the order to withdraw. The men filed through the village, gathering fresh ammunition from a dump at the cross-roads. From the village the road went up a slope leading to Aubigny. The enemy's fire soon followed us, and we proceeded along the ditches on each side of the road.

Three-quarters of the way up the slope I observed a trench running at right angles to the road on each side of it. I ordered the London men to go to the left, my own to the right, there to reorganize into companies. The twilight was now fairly deep, and I thought that with evening the enemy's advance would stay. The major I had seen in Fluquières now appeared again, and cursed me for giving the order to retire. I was too tired to argue, and even then a gust of machine-gun fire swept above our heads. They were going to attack again. We could hear them moving in the semi-darkness. Something else we could hear too—the throb of a motor-cycle behind us. It was a despatch rider, and when he drew level to us, he stopped his machine and came towards me with a message. I opened it. It ordered all troops east of the Aubigny defences to retire through Ham.

I was glad. I believe I thought then that it was the end of our share in the battle. I went to the men, and assembled them in companies, and in close artillery formation we retired across country due west. We came to the Aubigny defences, manned by fresh troops, about a mile farther on, and then we gathered on the road again and marched wearily along. I remember coming to a water-tank, where we all drank our fill— our mouths were swollen with thirst. When we reached Ham, an officer met us and ordered us to proceed to

Muille Villette, about two miles farther on, and there billet for the night. Ham, as we walked through its cobbled streets, seemed very hollow and deserted. The last time we had seen it, it had been a busy market-town, full of civilians. Now only a few sinister looters went about the empty houses with candles. We saw one fellow come out of a door with a lady's reticule and other things over his arm. We should have been justi-fied in shooting him, but we were far too tired. We just noticed him stupidly.

The road seemed long, and our pace was slow, but at last we reached the village of Muille Villette. We found it full of artillerymen and a few infantry. Every available shelter seemed to be occupied, but at length we got the men into a school. Our transport had been warned of our station for the night, and turned up with bully-beef and biscuits. These we served out.

I had four officers left with me. We could not find a billet for ourselves, but finally begged for shelter in a barn occupied by artillerymen. They looked on us un-sympathetically, not knowing our experiences. On a stove one of them was cooking a stew of potatoes and meat, and its savour made us lusting beasts. But the artillerymen ate the slop unconcernedly, while we lay down too utterly weary to sleep, languidly chewing bully-beef.

VI

It was after midnight when we came to Muille Villette; I suppose about 2 a.m. we fell into an uneasy sleep. At 4 a.m. we were awakened by the stirrings and shoutings of the artillerymen. I drew my long boots on my aching feet, and went out into the cold dark-

ness. I found an officer of some kind. The enemy were
reported to have attacked and penetrated the Aubigny
defences, and to be now advancing on Ham. All the
troops stationed in Muille Villette had received orders
to withdraw.

We assembled the men, stupid with sleep. I knew
that brigade headquarters were stationed at Golan-
court, a mile and a half along the road. I resolved to
proceed there and ask for orders. We marched away
while the dawn was breaking.

I found the brigade established in a deserted house.
T., the brigade-major, was seated on a bed lacing his
boots. No orders for the brigade had yet been received,
so T. advised me to find billets for the men, where
they could rest and get food. The companies then
sought billets independently, and, what was more
blessed than anything, we managed to get them hot
tea. I went and had breakfast with the brigade staff.
The tea revived me, and I remember how voracious I
felt, and that I tried to hide this fact. The brigadier
came into the room and seemed very pleased to see
me: apparently he was very satisfied with our conduct,
and especially with the frequent reports I had sent
back. Till then I had only felt weariness and baffle-
ment—even shame. But now I began to see that we
were implicated in something immense—something
beyond personal feelings and efforts.

The brigadier told me as much as he knew of the
general situation. It was not much. The communications
had apparently broken down. But it was enough to
make me realize that more than a local attack was in
progress: the whole of the Fifth Army was involved:
but there were no limits to what *might* be happening.

I also learnt that Dury—where the divisional head-quarters had been stationed—a village some five or six miles south-*west* of Roupy, had been captured about two o'clock on the afternoon of the 22nd, several hours before we had evacuated the redoubt. Only a miracle of chance had saved us from being cut off.

The brigade seemed to have difficulty in getting into touch with the division, or, at any rate, in obtaining orders from them. But at 10 a.m. I was told to march to Freniches and await orders there. We assembled in the village street and marched on again. The road was busy with retreating artillery and a few infantry-men. From behind us came the sounds of firing: the enemy were attacking Ham. We trudged on, passing villages whose inhabitants were only just taking steps to flee. They piled beds, chairs, and innumerable bol-sters on little carts, some hand-pulled, some yoked to bony horses. They tied cows behind. There were old men, many old women, a few young women, but no young men. They and their like proceeded with us along the western road.

We had gone perhaps five miles when an orderly on horseback overtook us with orders. We were to report to the —th Division at Freniches.

This we eventually did, and a fat staff colonel studied a map, and then told me to take my battalion to Esmery-Hallon, a village four miles due north, and there take up a defensive position. This was more than I expected. I explained that my men had been fighting continuously for forty-eight hours, and were beaten and spiritless. But I received no comfort: the situation demanded that every available man should be used to the bitter end. I hardly dared to face my men: but I think they were too tired to mind where they went. We turned off at a right angle, and slowly marched on. The road led through a beautiful patch of country, steeped in a calm, liquid sunshine. We tilted our bodies forward, and forced our weary muscles to act.

About two miles south of Esmery-Hallon, an officer (a lieutenant) appeared on a motor-cycle. He was in command of a scrap lot—transport men, cobblers, returned leave men, etc. He seemed to have the impression that the enemy were upon us, and wanted me to deploy and take up a position facing east. I explained that we were much too tired to do any such thing. He expostulated. Did I realize this, that, and the other? I explained that I had cause to realize such things better than he did. He raved. I told him finally that I didn't care a damn, but that I had orders to defend Esmery-Hallon, and thither I must go. He went off in a rage, seeming incredibly silly and fussy to us all.

Esmery-Hallon is a small village perched on a detached conical hill, overlooking the plain on all sides. The defence was simply arranged. Two companies of engineers were entrenched in front of the village. I sent a lookout on to the top of the church tower, and extended my men astraddle the hill on each side of the village, north and south. The men on the south found a ditch, which made an admirable trench. The men on the north extended over the ploughed land, and dug shallow pits for shelter. We had no machine-guns or Lewis guns, but every man had a rifle and a decent amount of ammunition. I established my headquarters on the north side by a quarry, where I had a wide view of the plain.

The day was very still, and the distant rattle of machine-gun fire carried to us. A few enemy shells fell ineffectively about the landscape. I got in touch with a major of the Inniskillings in command of one hundred and fifty men on my right, and we coördinated defences on that wing. My left wing was in the air, so to speak—not a soul visible for miles.

When our dispositions were finally made, I returned to the quarry edge. My servant T. had already been away to search the village, and now came laden with samples of red wine and cider which he had found in a cellar. So I sent him back to the village with other men, telling them to search for food also. They soon returned with bottles of red wine and a large tin of army biscuits. Evidently there was any amount of wine, but I was afraid to distribute it among the men for fear lest on fasting stomachs it should make them drunk. So S. and I each took a wine glass, and starting at different points, we began to go a round of the men. Each man lay curled up in his shallow pit, resting. To each we gave a glass of wine and a few biscuits. They took it thankfully. There was a lull in the distant fighting: I don't remember any noise of fire during that hour. The sun was warm and seemed to cast a golden peace on the scene. A feeling of unity with the men about me suddenly suffused my mind.

VII

It was nearly two o'clock when we got settled. About this time I interrupted a message which gave me the useful information that the enemy had been seen in Ham at 10 a.m. I gussed that the silence meant they were now consolidating along the Somme Canal. Later in the afternoon a cavalry patrol trotted up to our position. Officer, men, and horses all looked very debonair and well fed. The officer was very condescending towards me, but made a message of the information I gave him, thought it would not be worth while venturing farther on to the plain, so rode away back, harness jingling, the sun shining on well-polished occoutrements.

About five o'clock, I judged that we were to be left alone for the night, and made my plans accordingly. I sent the following message to B., who was in charge of the men on the right of the village: "We hold on to our present position unless otherwise ordered. When it is getting dark close your men in a little to form about 7 or 8 pickets. From these pickets send standing patrols out about 150 yards, or to any good observation point within warning distance. Any show of resistance should drive off any enemy patrols. But as far as I can make out the Boche is still east of the canal. Should you be attacked by overwhelming numbers, withdraw fighting in a due westerly direction under your own arrangements. I should do the same in case of need. I suggest you come up to have a look at our position before dark."

But just after dark, I received orders to relieve the Royal Engineers in front of the village. I regretted this order, but had to obey it. We now found ourselves in freshly dug trenches on the flat of the plain, our view to the left and right obstructed by woods.

Included in the orders mentioned was a message to the effect that advance parties of the French would probably arrive that night, and the positions would be

shown to them. This message filled us with wild hope;
we became almost jaunty.

But the night was very cold and heavily wet with
dew. We improved the trenches, and stamped about,
flapping our arms in an effort to keep warm. I sat
with L., bravest and brightest of my runners, on a
waterproof sheet beneath a tree in the centre of our
position. We waited for the dawn: it was weird,
phantasmagorial. Again the fateful mist. As it cleared
a little, the woods near us hung faintly in the whiteness.

At 8 a.m. we began to observe troops retreating in
front of us. They came in little groups down the road,
or straggled singly over the landscape. The mist gradually lifted. We heard machine-gun fire fairly near,
somewhere on the right. The stragglers informed us
that the enemy had crossed the canal in the early dawn,
and was advancing in considerable force. We waited
patiently. At 9 a.m. the enemy came into touch with
our fellows on the left, and here we rebutted him successfully. At 9.30 the troops on our right were reported
to be withdrawing. About ten o'clock there happened
one of those sudden episodes which would be almost
comic with their ludicrous *bouleversement* were they
not so tragic in their results. Seemingly straight from
the misty sky itself, but in reality from our own guns,
descended round after round of shrapnel bursting ter-
rifically just above our heads, and spraying leaden
showers upon us. Simultaneously, from the woods on
our right, there burst a fierce volley of machine-gun
fire, hissing and spluttering among us. We just turned
and fled into the shelter of the village buildings. I
shouted to my men to make for the position by the
quarry. We scuttled through gardens and over walls.

By the time we reached the quarry we had recovered our sang-froid. We extended and faced the enemy, who were advancing skilfully over the plain on our left. We on our part were a scrap lot composed of various units. We hastily reorganized into sections. Retreat was inevitable. Then followed a magnificent effort of discipline. A major took charge of the situation, and we began to retire with covering fire, section by section, in perfect alternation.

We were now on a wide expanse of plain, sloping gently westward. We stretched over this—a thin line of men, perhaps a thousand yards long. We were approaching the Nesle-Noyon Canal. When within a few hundred yards of the canal, we closed inwards to cross a bridge (Ramecourt). At the other end of the bridge stood a staff officer, separating the men like sheep as they crossed, first a few to the left, then a few to the right. Here I got separated from the majority of my men, finding myself with only fifteen. We were told to proceed along the bank of the canal until we found an unoccupied space, and there dig in.

As we crossed the bridge, we saw for the first time the sky-blue helmets of French troops peeping above a parapet. I think our eyes glistened with expectation of relief.

We went perhaps half a mile along the bank of the canal, and there I halted my attenuated company. The sun was now blazing hotly above our heads. We dropped to the ground, utterly exhausted. Presently some of the men began spontaneously to dig. R., the only officer left with me, also took a pick and joined the men. I began to feel ashamed just then, for I would willingly have died. I took a spade (there was

a dump of such things just by us) and began to shovel
the earth loosened by R. I seemed to be lifting utterly
impossible burdens. My flesh seemed to move un-
easily through iron bonds; my leaden lids drooped
smartingly upon my eyes.

We dug about three feet deep, and then ceased,
incapable of more. At the foot of the bank there was
a small pool of water. The enemy was not now in sight,
so we plunged our hot faces and hands into its weedy
freshness, and took off our boots and socks, and bathed
our aching feet.

In the evening, about 5 p.m., a few skirmishing
patrols appeared on the horizon. But our artillery was
now active and fairly accurate, and machine-guns
swept the plain. The patrols retired, without having
advanced any distance. A large German aëroplane,
with a red belly, floated persistently above our line. We
fired hundreds of shots at it, but without effect. T., my
servant, nearly blew my head off in his efforts.

We had gathered a lot of sun-scorched hemlock
and bedded the bottom of our trenches, and when night
came on we posted sentries and huddled down to the
bedding. The night was clear, and I gazed unblink-
ingly at the fierce stars above me, my aching flesh
forbidding sleep. Later, I must have dozed in a wake-
ful stupor.

VIII

The next daybreak, that of the 25th, was less misty.
Bread and bully-beef had come up during the night,
and we fed to get warmth into our bodies. But the sun
was soon up, and we began to feel almost cheerful
once again. There was no immediate sign of the enemy,

and I walked along to the bridge we had crossed the previous day to glean some information of our intentions; but the only plan seemed to be the obvious one of holding on to our positions. I noticed some engineers were there, ready to blow up the bridge if need be.

About 8 a.m. we saw little groups of enemy cavalry appear on the horizon. Through my glasses I could see them consulting maps, pointing, trotting fussily about. Our artillery was planting some kind of scattered barrage on the plain, and an occasional near shot made the horsemen scamper. We watched them rather amusedly till ten o'clock and then we saw signs of infantrymen. They came from the direction of Esmery-Hallon, and at first seemed in fairly dense formation. But they extended as they cut the sky line, and we soon perceived them advancing in open order. As they got nearer, they began to organize short rushes, a section at a time.

We were now well stocked with ammunition—there were piles of it laid about—and as soon as the advancing troops were within anything like range, we began to "pot" them. In fact, the whole thing became like a rifle-gallery entertainment at a fair. But still they came on. Now we could see them quite plainly—could see their legs working like dancing bears, and their great square packs bobbing up and down as they ran. Occasionally one dropped.

Immediately in front of our trench, about eight hundred yards away, there was a little copse of perhaps fifty trees. This they reached about eleven o'clock and halted there. If only our flanks held out, I guessed they would never get farther, for between the copse and our

rifles and Lewis guns there was not a shred of cover;
and we were well entrenched, with a wide canal in front
of us.

Of course, the artillery was busy all the while: not
methodically, but thickly enough to give the day the
appearance of a conventional battle. But then the unexpected (really we had no cause longer to regard it as
unexpected), the fatal thing happened. A battery of
ours shortened its range, and got our position exactly
"tapped." The shells fell thick and fast, right into our
backs. We were, remember, dug in on the top of a
bank, perhaps fifteen feet high. All along this bank
the shells plunged. Immediately on our right, not fifty
yards away, a shell landed cleanly into a trench, and
when the smoke cleared there remained nothing, absolutely nothing distinguishable, where a moment ago
had been five or six men. We grovelled like frightened,
cowed animals. Still the shells fell: and there was no
means of stopping them. I glanced distractedly round;
men on the right were running under cover of the bank
away to the right. Other men on the left were retreating to the left. I resolved to get out of it. Immediately
behind us, fifty yards away, was a large crescent-shaped
mound, very steep, like a railway embankment, and
perhaps sixty feet high. It occurred to me that from
there we should command, and command as effectively
as ever, the plain in front of us. I made my intention
known, and at a given signal we leapt down the bank,
and across the intervening fifty yards. We were evidently in sight, for a hail of machine-gun bullets made
dusty splutters all round us as we ran. But we reached
the mound without a casualty, and climbed safely on

to it. There I found a few men already in occupation, commanded by a colonel, under whose orders I then placed myself.

The enemy's artillery fire now increased in volume. I saw a cow hit in a field behind us, and fall funnily with four rigid legs poking up at the sky.

At 3.30 we saw the French retiring on the right, about a thousand yards away. They were not running, but did not seem to be performing any methodic withdrawal. We then fell into one of those awful states of doubt and indecision. What was happening? What should we do? There was angry, ominous rifle-fire on our immediate left. About 4 p.m. there was a burst of machine-gun fire on our immediate right. I noticed that the stray bullets were coming over our heads. This meant that the enemy were advancing from the right.

I then saw English troops withdrawing about six hundred yards away on the right—evidently the troops that had been defending the bridge. I did not hear any explosion, and so far as I know the bridge remained intact.

At 4.15 I saw the colonel suddenly leave with his men his position on my immediate left. Although I was within sight—within calling distance—he did not give me an order. I was now alone on the mound with my fifteen men.

I did not wait long. I resolved to act on my own initiative once more. We had now moved off the maps I possessed and might as well be in an unknown wilderness. I resolved to proceed due west, taking the sun as a guide. We moved down the back slope of the mound. At the foot we found a stream or off-flow from the canal, about ten feet wide and apparently very deep.

As we hesitated, looking for a convenient crossing, a machine-gun a few hundred yards away opened fire on us. There were a good few trees about which must have obstructed the firer's view: the cut twigs, newly budded, fell into the water. We hesitated no longer: we plunged into the stream. The men had to toss their rifles across, many of which landed short and were lost. The sight of these frightened men plunging into the water effected one of those curious stirrings of the unconscious mind that call up some vivid scene of childhood: I saw distinctly the water-rats plunging at dusk into the mill-dam at Thornton-le-Dale, where I had lived as a boy of ten.

The water sucked at my clothes as I met it, and filled my field-boots. They seemed weighted with lead now as I walked, and oozed for hours afterwards.

We came out facing a wide plain, climbing gently westward. Machine-gun and rifle-fire still played about us. We could see a church steeple on the horizon due west, and I told the men to scatter and make for that steeple. Shrapnel was bursting in the sky, too high to be effective. We ran a little way, but soon got too tired. A., a faithful orderly, had stayed with me, and soon we walked over the fields as friends might walk in England. We came across French machine-gunners, who looked at us curiously, asked for news of the situation, but did not seem very perturbed.

We eventually came to the village on the horizon (probably Solente). An officer of the engineers stood by the side of his horse at the cross-roads, smoking a cigarette. He asked me why I was retreating. The question seemed silly: "We shall have to fight every inch of the way back again," he said. "These Frenchmen will never hold them." I went on, too tired to answer.

Here I saw for the first time a new post stuck on the roadside. It had on it an arrow and "Stragglers Post" in bold letters. So I was a straggler. I felt very bitter and full of despair.

I followed the road indicated by the arrow. It was dotted with small parties of men, all dejected and weary. We trudged along till we came to the village of Carrepuits. Military police met us at the entrance, and told us to report to the Traffic Control in a house a few hundred yards away. It was now getting dusk. I went into the cottage indicated, and here found an officer, very harassed and bored. Men were collected, and separated into the divisions they belonged to, and then given orders to report to such and such a place. I found a party of about fifty men of my division, and was instructed to take them and report to a divisional headquarters situated in a certain street in Roye.

I've forgotten that walk: it was only about two miles, but our utter dejection induced a kind of unconsciousness in us. It would be between ten and eleven o'clock when we got to Roye. I reported to a staff officer, who sent me off to the town major to get billets. The town major I found distracted, unable to say where I should find a billet. Apparently the town was packed with stragglers. We peered into two great gloomy marquees, floored densely with recumbent men. Meanwhile two other officers joined me with their men, and together we went off to search on our own. We found a magnificent house, quite empty, and here we lodged the men. Some kind of rations had been found. They soon had blazing wood fires going, and seemed happy in a way.

The town major had indicated a hut, where we officers might get rest, and perhaps some food. We went round, tired and aching though we were; we lifted the latch and found ourselves in a glowing room. A stove roared in one corner—and my teeth were chattering with cold, my clothes still being sodden—and a lamp hung from the roof. A large pan of coffee simmered on the stove, and the table was laden with bread, tinned foods, butter; food, food, food. I hadn't had a bite since early morning, and then not much.

I forget, if I ever knew, who or what the two occupants were, but they were not stragglers. Roye had been their station for some time. One of them was fat, very fat, with a tight, glossy skin. I don't remember the other. We explained that we would like a billet for the night—anything would do so long as it was warmth. They were sorry: they had no room. Could they spare us some rations? They were sorry: this was all they had got till to-morrow noon. We stood very dejected, sick at our reception. "Come away!" I said. "Before I go away," cried one of my companions, with a bitter voice, "I would just like to tell these blighters what I think of them." Then followed a desperate man's invective. . . . We walked away, back to the men's billet. I looked in at my fellows; most of them were naked, drying their clothes at the fire. Some slept on the floor.

We went upstairs into an empty room. Two of us agreed to make a fire, while the other, the one who had given vent to his feelings, volunteered to go off in search of food. We split up wood we found in the house, and lit a fire. I took off my clothes to dry them, and sat on a bench in my shirt. If I had been asked then what I most desired, besides sleep, I think I would have said: French bread, butter, honey, and hot milky coffee.

The forager soon turned up. God only knows where he got that food from: we did not ask him. But it was French bread, butter, honey, and hot milky coffee in a champagne bottle! We cried out with wonder: I believe we wept. We shared the precious stuff out, eating and drinking with inexpressible zest.

As we supped we related our experiences. I forget their names; I don't think I ever knew them. Were they of the Border Regiment? I'm not sure; but they were Northerners. They had been trapped in a sunken road, with a Boche machine-gun at either end, and Boches calling on them to surrender. I don't think either of them was more than twenty years old: they were fresh and boyish, and had been faced with this dilemma. They put it to the vote: there, with death literally staring them in the face, they solemnly called on the men to show hands as to whether they would surrender or make a run for it. They had voted unanimously for the run. Half of them perished in the attempt. But here, a few hours afterwards, were the survivors, chatting over a blazing wood fire, passing a bottle of coffee round, very unperturbed, not in any way self-conscious. We stacked the fire high and stretched ourselves on the floor in front of it, and slept for a few hours.

IX

We were up at six the next morning, the 26th of March, and reporting to the A.P.M., who was reorganizing stragglers. We congregated in the Town

Square, and I was amazed at the numbers there. The streets were thickly congested with infantrymen from several divisions, with French armoured cars, cavalry, and staff officers. We fell in by divisions, and presently marched off, a column a mile or two in length. Cavalry protected our flanks and rear from surprise.

At Villers-les-Roye I found B., the man who had been separated from me at Ramecourt Bridge. We were glad to be united again, and from there proceeded together. B. had had orders to go to a place called La Neuville, where the first-line transport awaited us. We were now passing through the battlefields of 1916, and everywhere was desolate and ruined. We marched on as far as Hangest-en-Santerre, where we met our battalion cookers loaded with a welcome meal. Just as we had devoured this, and were starting on our way again, we were met by a staff colonel, who, after inquiring who we were, ordered us to turn back and proceed to Folies, where our brigade was reorganizing.

We could but mutely obey, but with dull despair and an aching bitterness. We had never thought since leaving Roye but that we were finally out of the mêlée. To turn back meant, we knew, that we might still be very much in it. We crossed country to Folies, about two miles away, in a blazing sun. There we found the details of the brigade, consisting mostly of returned leave men, already holding a line of trenches. We were told to reinforce them.

Here the second-in-command rejoined the battalion and assumed command. My endurance was broken, and I was ordered down to the transport lines. I pointed out that the men were as weary as I, and had no right to be ordered into action again. It was useless: no man could be spared. But there was not much more for them to bear. Good hot food came up to them again at dusk. The night was warm and restful.

On the morning of the 27th, the enemy had possession of Bouchoir, a village about one mile to the southeast. He commenced to advance during the morning, and a skirmishing fight went on during that day and the next; and during this time the battalion was withdrawn from the line without suffering any serious casualties.

X

But I had gone back with the transport officer on the 26th. I mounted the transport-sergeant's horse, and in a dazed sort of way galloped westward in the dusk. I arrived half-dead at La Neuville, and slept there for twelve hours or more. The next day we went to Braches, and thence on foot to Rouvrel. About here, the country was yet unscathed by war, and very beautiful. On a bank by the roadside, I took *Walden* out of my pocket, where it had been forgotten since the morning of the 21st, and there began to read it. At Rouvrel the rest of the battalion rejoined us the next day. On the 29th I set off on horseback with the transport to trek down the valley of the Somme.

When evening came and the hills of Moreuil were faint in the twilight, we were still travelling along the western road. No guns nor any clamour of war could be heard: a great silence filled the cup of misty hills. My weary horse drooped her head as she ambled along, and I, too, was sorrowful. To our north-east lay the squat towers of Amiens, a city in whose defence we had endured hardships until flesh had been defeated, and the brave heart broken. My mind held a vague wonder for her fate—a wonder devoid of hope. I could not believe in the avail of any effort. Then I listened to the rumbling cart, and the quiet voices of the men about me. The first stars were out when we reached Guignemicourt, and there we billeted for the night. In this manner we marched by easy stages down the valley of the Somme, halting finally at Salenelle, a village near Valery, and there we rested four days.

APPENDIX

A. The scheme, common to the Fifth Army, was a defence by distribution in depth. The original front line was reduced to a line of observation posts, from 100 to 500 yards apart, each consisting of a section of men. These men were not intended to resist: they were to observe and give warning to the main line of defence about 200 to 500 yards behind them. This main line was well dug and well wired. But the battalion fronts were extremely long—as long as 2000 yards—and three companies, perhaps each 100 to 120 strong, became very attenuated along this distance, especially when you had deducted the men on the observation posts. But the line was exceedingly well sited, and, under ordinary circumstances, the machine and Lewis guns, helped by what rifle-fire there was, would have been adequate to cope with any attacking force.

B. Behind the main line of resistance came the battalion redoubt. This was a circular defensive system, perhaps 800 yards in diameter, manned by the company in battalion reserve, battalion headquarters, and a Machine-Gun Corps unit. The construction of these redoubts was not yet completed, especially in the matter of wiring, and I remember how the colonel used to go round raging about the folly of the man who left his back door undefended.

There was one of these redoubts to each battalion, so that between each redoubt there was a gap of some 1000 yards. These gaps were covered by machine-guns, and elaborate barrages were worked out by the artillery to cover the approaches to them.

C. At varying distances behind the front-line system came a second line of redoubts occupied by the brigade in support. These were carefully sited and more or less echeloned with the redoubts 1000 to 3000 yards in front. It was one of these redoubts that we occupied at Roupy, and a detailed description of the defence is given in paragraph *F*.

D. Behind this system of redoubts, resting in near villages and camps, came the brigade in reserve. They could be utilized to reinforce or counter-attack any part of the division's frontage.

E. A line of continuous trenches was in preparation behind the redoubt system, but on our frontage, on the 21st of March, this had only been outlined by removing the sods, and by the construction of one or two machine-gun emplacements. We had only a vague idea of what troops were in Army Reserve, and subsequent experience proved these to be negligible.

F. The defences we occupied on the morning of the 21st were distributed as follows: the headquarters were in Stanley Redoubt: round this core was the wired ring of the redoubt, occupied on its eastern side by one company. Towards the enemy in front of the redoubt a short line was occupied by another company detailed to counter-attack should the line in front be broken. This front line was a crescent-shaped irregular line about 1000 yards long, occupied by two companies. The headquarters of each of these companies was about 200 yards behind the front line in a small keep, wired and defended by a small company-reserve. Communication trenches connected the front-line companies with the counter-attack company, and the counter-attack company with the redoubt. The front-line companies were not well connected with the corresponding companies of the battalion on their flanks. There were gaps which could only be covered by visiting patrols.

The system was, according to British standard, fairly well wired, and the redoubt was well stored with S.A.A. and reserve water and rations.

THE HOGARTH ESSAYS

CATCHWORDS AND CLAPTRAP

BY

ROSE MACAULAY

CATCHWORDS AND CLAPTRAP

THESE discursive and random comments are the indulgence of a private taste, which finds in language as used one of the most amusing subjects for meditation and speculation. This fantastical currency, minted by the requirements of human thought and feeling, circulated by the urgent desire we have to convey these somehow to our fellows, so precisely, so delicately wrought and cast into exact and minute forms, so skilfully adapted to the commerce which is its purpose, and, having been so shaped, shaping in its turn thought itself, stamping it ever freshly with intricate designs— except that nothing in this curious world can well be selected and labelled as odd, it might seem odd that such a currency should have been coined by our simian race.

But what is not by any means odd is that, having contrived for each feeling, each thought, each fact, its appropriate symbol, beautifully neat and fit, so that we may enjoy ready commerce of ideas, we should proceed, in the perversity of our human nature, to confuse the coins together, using one where another should serve. We prefer, as often as not, to express what we mean in phraseology which means precisely something else. It is, possibly, a revolt against the dominance of established usage, a triumphant assertion that man is lord of language, not language of man, a surging up of the eggish pride which said: "When *I* use a word,

it means just what I choose it to mean." It is yet one
more expression of the free spirit of man striving perpetually against a universe which seeks to enthral him
—a triumphant gesture of anarchy. Yet, because prolonged anarchy is impossible to man's law-bound nature, as to that of the universe which bore him, each
attempt at it defeats itself, each new sense given to a
word or phrase becomes stereotyped, becomes rapidly,
not an individual, but a herd sense, the users giving
countenance and encouragement one to the other. What
the coins originally stood for we forget; we fling them
loosely about, sometimes with misapprehension or deliberate misapplication, sometimes merely with a vague
feeling that here are words, let them somehow convey
our meaning. The psychology behind the various mis-
uses is an interesting study.

Many words, many phrases, seem to acquire nimbuses of association, which do rough service for exact
meaning. Such a word is *nameless,* which comes to
some minds haloed with terror. "Avenging," cries
Shelley, carried away by his distaste for fathers, "such
a nameless wrong, as turns black parricide to piety."
He did not mean that the wrong to which he referred
had no name; it was, in fact, named incest; he merely
meant that the word came into his head with a sinister
aura of horror about it that made it seem apt to the
case, as it had seemed apt to the writer of the Book of
Wisdom to say: "Worshipping of idols not to be
named is the beginning, the cause, and the end of all
evil." All those who write of nameless horrors, nameless vices, nameless orgies, know, when they reflect,
that none of these things need actually be nameless to
those with clear heads and good dictionaries; what

they mean is *horrid,* only they prefer a vaguer, less definite, and therefore more terrible adjective. Such another word is *nominal,* which comes so readily to the help of the business man. "A nominal sum," he will say. Does he mean that, though he calls it a sum, there will in point of fact be no sum to be paid? He does not. Rather, in fact, the contrary. What he does mean is "very small." Why, then, does he not say so? There seems no reason but that "nominal" is the inexact rather than the exact word, and therefore sounds smaller, just as "nameless" sounds more dreadful. So with all those words on which pedagogic comment has grown hackneyed—*decimated,* or *annihilated,* for "greatly reduced in numbers," *phenomenal* for "extraordinary," and all the like mathematical or philosophic expressions so often inaccurately applied; and, of course, the stock misuse of *literally* where "metaphorically" is meant, which is not so much inexact as directly opposed to the meaning it strives to convey, and is an excellent example of man's deliberate revolt against the rigidity of language. So, in the same way, is a curious use of the word *precedent* which I came on lately in an evening paper: "The event is regarded as a precedent, and is not likely ever to be repeated." The journalist probably meant "a unique occurrence," and again has provided a good instance of linguistic oppositionism.

But the inaccurate use of single words can be left to the care of etymologists and lexicographers, who are ever busy in the matter. What has been less investigated is the vague and rhetorical use of phrases and ideas which carry with them certain associations in the mind of the user, and which will, he trusts, carry across similar associations to the hearer or reader. The psychologically interesting thing is the belief that these associations, these meanings in the user's mind, will be more effectively transmitted by a vague phrase than by a precise and accurate on. . Sometimes, of course, the inaccuracy arises from a desire to convey not a correct but an incorrect fact, even when the truth is known to be known to the person addressed, so that there is no question of deceit; as when a Frenchman recently exclaimed to an Englishman: "The franc in English money is only worth a sou." One cannot believe that this was the outcome of a belief that the exchange stood at 480 francs to the pound on a day when it actually stood at 170, nor, scarcely, that he hoped to make the Englishman believe it. His statement more likely arose from a feeling that a sou is a small coin, and that he was saying, "The franc is worth scarcely anything at all." Why, then, instead of saying this, did he select a particular and incorrect sum of money? Why did he not say three sous, which would have been approximately correct? The answer in this case is simple: he desired to exaggerate. And here we have what may be called a primary human need, which should be placed by psychologists with the desire for nourishment, for safety, for sense-gratifications, and for appreciation, as one of the elemental lusts of man. Infants exaggerate: they are, indeed, the world's greatest exaggerators. Before they can speak they seek to magnify their woes with louder cries than the situation in which they find themselves placed, lamentable though this usually is, warrants. They give to their grief a rhetorical expression which does not accurately represent it. Feeling a slight discomfort, they exclaim, in the only phraseology as yet known to them, "I am in

torment, in anguish, in hell. Amend my situation forth-
with, or I perish." A little later, when they can speak,
they will apply the largest measures that they know to
trifling distances or heights. "Miles wide," they will
say of streams, or "miles high" of the elephant. They
are using mile as the Frenchman used sou, merely as
an extreme measure. They love the imagination of immensity; they revel in extremes. "How small," they
inquire, with zest, "would be a quite new Esquimaux
baby?" "Why?" responds the indifferent nurse. If the
child understood this elliptical counter-question (which
he does not) and answered it truly, he would say:
"Because I desire to hear of a human creature very,
very tiny indeed." So he loves to be told of giants and
of dwarfs, to behold elephants, to inquire "How high
is the largest mountain in the world?" He is a natural
extremist.

Nevertheless, the child's pure and rational sense of
logic, outgrown all too soon, keeps him from some of
the deliberate excesses of adult life, prevents him even
from understanding them. They are to him a stumbling-
block. "I sha'n't be gone more than a minute," says the
elder. The child, waiting, perceiving that far more
than sixty seconds has elapsed, puts down the adult,
probably not for the first time, as a liar. He does not
yet know that the word "minute" is a common coin,
loosely thrown about, to symbolize "a short time."
Though, as to that, the vague idea we have as to the
actual length of sixty seconds sometimes induces a
contrary procedure. An extraordinary number of
novelists puzzled my literal childhood by making their
people, engaged in conversation, pause a minute, sometimes even "a full minute," before replying to some

remark—a thing seldom done in any ordinary
duologue, and one which would quite break the conversational current. One suspects that the writer often
means about ten seconds, which is actually quite a good
pause, but, for some reason, sounds short. So he says
minute, which he regards as an elastic term of time—
far more so than hour, day, week, or month.

To return to the desire for exaggeration. This seems
to be an immensely important factor in the development of human language, conversation, and literature.
It accounts, of course, for the spreading of many
strange tales, travellers' and others, for a large proportion of the inaccurate use of words, for a large
number of misstatements and loose phraseology, and
for a great deal of the daily press. "Exciting developments," "amazing scenes,"—how rarely do these
journalistic myths actually either excite or amaze. The
favourite word *sensational* one can pass, for every occurrence in the sphere of sense is, of course, that;
further, to hear of it doubtless causes some sensation,
however mild. But one suspects the intention of being
the same as in the other cases—*i.e.,* to give an impression that something more exciting, important, or what
not, has occurred than is actually the case: in short, to
magnify. "A *marvellous* honest fellow," we used to
say a few hundred years back, meaning, merely, very
honest: and, a century or two later, "a *monstrous,* or
an *amazingly,* agreeable man." More lately, "an
awfully nice person," and to-day "a *frightfully,* or *extraordinarily,* good sort." Increasingly down the ages
we have shirked the simple "very" as inadequate to its
appointed task, and reserved it for mild cases. In
order to convey a high degree of the quality on which

we are commenting, we feel the need to imply some imaginary feeling of wonder, amaze, awe, or fear, which such an extremity of quality might be supposed to conjure in our breasts.

This tendency to magnify seems most prevalent and most acute when emotion is most strongly roused. It is at these times that the precise and accurate statement of fact seems most inadequate to the situation's ardent demands, and we cannot endure to leave truth in her nakedness to speak for herself. When the situation is epidemic rather than individual, a phraseology of magnification comes into wide use, and is broadcast through the press or other machinery available. This is noticeable during all wars, revolutions, and other general human troubles. A recent example of such a period in this country was the General Strike of May, 1926, and, in a less degree, the ensuing months of the Coal Strike. During the General Strike, eloquence was to some extent fettered by certain restrictions on the press, which had small room for expansive comment, except the Labour press, which was at the time, and indeed often is, a highly interesting and instructive psychological study. The vocabulary of this press is a very profitable field of research for those interested in what may be called the language of emotion, as opposed to that of cold and precise statement. Very similar language may be heard from the Labour benches in the House of Commons during many debates; pedantic accuracy of speech is, indeed, scarcely to be looked for in any part of either House of Parliament, or in the governing assembly of any country; it would probably be unbecoming in a politician, who should rather cultivate the arts of rhetoric. But to the already sufficient imaginativeness of the politician and the journalist, the Labour members and the Labour journalists seem to add an element of sound and fury signifying nothing, which is highly interesting to observe and analyze. It derives partly, no doubt, from lack of precise scholastic training, of which one of the surest results is a nearer approach to exact speech, a closer fitting together of word and fact, and partly from the strong emotion very naturally engendered by misfortune, by the perpetual oppression of circumstance, by association with, or meditation upon, those who have all the time to be swimming hard in order to keep above water, and even so often sink. The fact that millions of persons lead miserably hard and poor lives, without any of the amenities of a luxurious civilization, while more fortunate beings spend on pleasures in a month what would keep a poor family for a year, and lavishly squander on personal luxury without apparent consciousness of any debt owed to the less lucky —the hot bitterness of this world-wide and world-old fact has perhaps so enflamed and melted the hearts and brains of many of the spokesmen of the poor that they literally cannot, do not know how to, speak in an accurate sense. They speak as men in a blind passion of pity and rage: furthermore, as men who have had no training in logic or in language, but must needs use the first weapon that comes to hand, be it apt or not. It is a pity, for they thereby often spoil a perfectly good case—and indeed their case, taking it by and large, and apart from detail, is the best case in the world—that of the have-nots against those who have and to spare. But nearly always they spoil it in statement by slip-shod cant and invective. In the darkened confusion of their minds they cry "murder" when there is no question of any taking of life, meaning (one supposes) that here is something they think cruel and hard, that murder is cruel and hard, and that therefore this thing must be murder. It is an elementary fallacy, which a first course in logic would make impossible.

And this leads to the question of words and their haloes. In such minds, excited, untrained, and confused, words seem to be rather symbols of some vague body of associations than the precise outward shapes of definite and clear-cut meanings; phrases rush into the mind haloed with pathos, tragedy, vice, or what not. Such a phrase, apparently, is *women and children*. In *A Passage to India,* Mr. E. M. Forster relates the way in which the members of the Anglo-Indian club worked themselves up into a frenzy of excitement and anger by repeating—"the women and children." And, indeed, these words, either severally or combined, do appear to have some curious hypnotic effect. They are called in, these unfortunate women and children (who always seem to be in evil case, threatened by danger, hardship, or sudden death), to do constant duty in emergencies. "Women and Babies Clubbed by Police," ran a heading in a Labour paper during the recent strike. Such police recall less the placid policemen we see about than the brutal constabulary in Ouida's novels, who, as they go about their business, casually brain passing puppies with their batons. "The women and children will be the first to suffer," wrote the kindly persons who published in the press an appeal for help for miners' families. They cannot have believed what they said: they cannot, I think, have intended such a libel on the miner as seriously to mean that he would let his family want before himself. I am sure, in fact, that they meant nothing so unjust or so untrue; they merely sought to strengthen (though they actually weakened) their appeal by the use of a little unconscious claptrap.

"Brass-faced baby-killers," remarked Miss Ellen Wilkinson, M.P., alluding to the Government—I forget the precise occasion of the phrase, and in what manner the Government had at the moment been massacring the innocents, but "baby-killer" was a phrase in great favour during the strike, as during the last European war. It has, indeed, at times been perilously near becoming merely a vague expression of distaste. For *baby* is another of these haloed words, bearing with it infinite associations of pathos and persecuted innocency. "Tighten the binders" was a pathetic slogan of the strike. "A holocaust has only been prevented by the sacrificial heroism of the mothers," said a newspaper; and *mother,* of course, is another charmed word.

Why all this stress upon the sufferings of infants, in reality the section of the population most carefully provided for during any emergency? The answer is simple: a baby is a symbol of helpless innocence, and its name makes a good slogan. If a man making a speech to a simple audience should, gravelled for lack of matter, desire to gain time, all he need do is to say, "I appeal to you in the name of your little children," or, "What about the kiddies?" and he will have the less critical part of his audience cheering long enough to enable him to collect his thoughts and start afresh. So it was during the last European war, and, I dare say, during all the wars that have been. "Go and fight for the women and children" recruiting speeches would exclaim, and alluded with bitter invective to those of our foes who had deliberately selected British babies (or *babes,* which sounds still more moving) as the targets of their bombs. In point of fact, the number of British infants slain by enemy bombs during the war was extremely small, but one might have gathered from the press that they formed the majority of slain non-combatants. In our attacks on conduct we mislike, we wave the corpses of women and children about us like banners as we charge.

The reason for this use of *babies* is, obviously, their tender age, inferior physical and mental condition, and small size. Presumably the similar use of *women,* where it exists, is also based on their comparatively frail physique. But I do not profess to understand the full aura of associations, either comic or moving, which surround the name *woman;* it is said, indeed, and no doubt truly, that no woman can understand them. It is certain that this apparently simple and straightforward word has a considerable element of catchword about it, and has become surrounded by a good deal of claptrap.

So, for that matter, has the word *man.* I have frequently observed the name denoting the male half of humanity to be curiously used, as if it carried with it some kind of association outside its strict meaning. "I said to myself," the wife of a public man recently announced to the world, alluding to her husband, "I said to myself, he is a *man.*" She obviously was not merely announcing species and sex, but intended the word to carry to her audience qualities, presumably admirable, associated in her mind with the male adult creature.

This, indeed, is a not uncommon piece of symbolism, and produces such remarks as "Quit you like men." "And, what is more, you'll be a man, my son," and so forth. ("What would he have turned into if he *hadn't* been able to do all those things in the poem?" as children inquire.) Anyhow, we may take it (and very creditable it is to us that it should be so, after all these centuries) that the word *man*, like the word *human*, carries an aura of, on the whole, favourable associations, just as (and it is a bad mark to the other animal species that it is so) the names of most of our fellow-creatures on this globe, such as dog, hound, cur, swine, ape, cat, rat, cow, ass, peacock, and the rest (two notable exceptions are duck and lamb—both, it may be added, very good eating and requiring peas) carry such poor associations that they have always had a considerable vogue as uncomplimentary epithets for human beings.

Another haloed catchword, and this time the halo is of the purest gold, is the word *cricket* (denoting the game, not the insect), so that to *play cricket*, in the mouths of some persons, seems to mean to behave in a pure and noble manner. I have understood better how this synonym, which has always puzzled me, arose since I overheard this summer some remarks made to one another by the Australian and British cricket teams and broadcasted by the B.B.C. Allowing for a certain confusion of thought and language due to the fact that most of the speakers were probably more at home with bats and balls than with ideas, and that all had just lunched, it did emerge clearly that some of these devotees of the game believed, or said they believed, in some improving moral effect produced by it. One of them said: "Cricket is an antidote to Bolshevism and degeneracy." The speaker did not explain, nor did others present inquire, in what precise manner this game affects the political opinions of its players, nor how many wickets it takes to turn a Bolshevist cricketer into a Fascist. As to degeneracy, it is not clear whether physical or moral degeneracy was meant. If physical, one imagines that a harder and more active game might be even more effective. If mental, would not a game that left degenerates less time on their hands for their own devices be better? One might, surely, go quite far in the process of deterioration while one's side was in. But still, whether or not the supporters of this moral-improvement theory are able to explain it satisfactorily to others, it is apparent that it is held, and it has very likely led to the curious transference of the word *cricket* to the sphere of moral behaviour. The other possible explanation, the analogy of good play and good conduct, seems less tenable, for why, among all the games which can be well played, should cricket be selected? Anyhow, one observes that the persons who believe the game to be morally improving are usually the same as those who use the phrase, which looks as if theory and phrase were allied.

As to *Bolshevism,* alluded to thus unfavourably by cricketers after lunch, it is a good example of a catchword bearing the more sinister type of halo. As used by some people, it seems to have lost any accurate connotation, and to imply less a Russian political system than a state of mind. It is, one gathers, a state of mind usually regarded as undesirable by those who use the word, though, if analyzed even by these, it seems sometimes to resolve itself into a very natural desire for better conditions of work and wages. Oddly, too, it is often used to denote a supposed anarchic desire to rebel against law, order, and authority which seems a queer transversal of meaning, when we consider that Bolshevism *de facto* is probably the severest, most rigorous, and authoritative form of governmental oppression under which man has yet lived, and the furthest removed from either anarchy or liberty. Those who use the name in this sense are probably referring back to the time before Bolshevism was the established order, and when, therefore, it had for a period to take a revolutionary line. So liable are words to somersaults, that none seems stable in its firmament, and before long we may have "pacifist" flung about to brand one who is supposed to desire war. There seems no limit to these verbal acrobatics.

Which is to say that, once you step outside precise dictionary values and depend on a nimbus of associations to carry your meaning across, you are on dangerous ground. For nimbuses are vague and tricky things, changing colour all the time, seen differently by different eyes, and the sense you try to convey by a catchword may suffer a change between your mind and your hearer's. Say "Bolshevist," meaning "one who desires to upset the existing order," or "one who desires to acquire more wealth and wages," to someone who sees Bolshevists as people who firmly uphold an established order and have concentrated wealth into a few governing hands, and you will miss your mark. It is safer, when you invoke the name of a foreign political party, to use it strictly for that foreign political party and for nothing else; just as it is safer, when you say "cricket," to mean merely a game played with bat,

ball, and wickets. It is also safer, when we say "capitalist," not to trust to it, as some do, to carry implica-
tions of greed, wickedness, and large incomes, for to
what may be called dictionary minds it means merely
a person who has invested such wealth as he has in
some productive undertaking (such as a street taxi, a
barrel-organ, a shop, or a dancing bear), instead of
keeping it loose and ready to spend. The dictionary
mind, in its literal unimaginativeness, cannot understand why capitalism is a bad system, or why capitalists
are necessarily wealthy and probably wicked. In half
the contexts in which "capitalist" (sometimes called
in anger ca*pit*alist, as if a cat were spitting) is used
as a term of opprobrium, what is meant is "a man
richer than he should be," and it is wiser to say this,
even though it takes a little longer. I am told, by the
way, that this question of taking longer, of space, is
an important determining factor in newspaper phraseology, and particularly in the wording or headlines. It
often substitutes for "married" the old-fashioned
"wed," and, doubtless, often, too, substitutes the
wrong word for the right. But, in the main, such substitutions have some psychological basis, which is what
makes them an interesting study.

To get back to verbal haloes, these have always
been particularly prevalent in the minds of poets and
other writers. There is a type of poetic mind which
relies instinctively on association, on the repetition of
certain words and phrases, to achieve the effect desired, of beauty, desolation, terror, or what not. The
verse of the late nineteenth and quite early twentieth
centuries, for example, abounds in such words as
purple, pale, dim, strange-coloured, opaline, crystalline,

chrysoprase, shimmering, glimmering, shadowy, grey, blind, swooning, orchard, honey-coloured moon, repeated again and again like an incantation, as Homer repeated οἰνόπα ποντον, of a sea not actually very like wine (the Greeks nearly all loved tags), as Miss Edith Sitwell applies, even when least deserved, such epithets as "creaking," and as the eighteenth-century poets called on nymphs, verdant lawns, enchanting groves, embower'd towers, and the like features of a neat and parklike landscape, to convey the aroma of poetry. Such catchwords have always been used rather vaguely and voluptuously, so that the "purple" and "shadowy" of the late Victorians both symbolized more a spiritual atmosphere than, respectively, a definite colour and a definite arrangement of light and shade. The intention of such repetitions is rather to hypnotize than to be precisely apt. "A chain of roses threaded on a wire and pressed one against the other" (to quote M. Jean Cocteau on the style of Barrès)— this was the kind of effect aimed at by many of the late Victorian poets. To-day it is less often roses that are so threaded than harder, pricklier, less sweetly-scented objects. The poets of to-day do not escape this pitfall of catchwords, but the catchwords are different, as they are in every age. And, on the whole, they are fewer than at many periods of verse-making. A closer exactitude and realism informs much of the verse of to-day; we have, of course, those elegant, fantastic, and romantic anti-realists, the Sitwells and their imitators, but many poets seem to be inspired with a desire to impart precise and detailed information as to the form and colour of the objects they have observed. Phrase-making is not, for the moment, so much in

fashion as usual. Verlaine, Mallarmé, and Rimbaud
are dead, the symbolists have perished on the air, and
the days seem far distant when Belgians roamed in
conservatories under freezing moons. Most of the
better writers of verse and prose, in all countries, seek
more or less after precision, and have gained in truth
what they have perhaps lost in loveliness. Claptrap,
facile and inaccurate symbolism, the repetition of the
tag and the slogan, are to be found mainly just now
in third-rate literature, in popular speech, and in the
less educated press. In these places one finds, on a
lower plane, the same intention—the lazy and sentimental desire to convey an effect by using catchwords.

Allied with this desire is an impulse ever busily at
work on the English language, the instinct of prudery,
of evasion of some fact or object the mention of which
may possibly shock someone. Among the more obvious
and vulgar of the inaccurate substitutions which derive from this instinct is the curious use, noticeable
in newspapers and in courts of law, of the imbecile
phrase "in a certain condition" for "going to have a
child," and the lately prevalent and particularly fatuous "intimate." The fact that, apparently, everyone
concerned panders to and connives at this vulgar gen-
teelism on the part of learned counsels and others,
and answers them according to their folly, instead of
replying, "Everyone is always in a certain condition,"
or "Do you mean, were we lovers?" is evidence either
of the cynical and patient toleration with which we
regard the vagaries of the law, or of the wide existence
of that deeply rooted prudery for which Britons are
famed in Europe.

The instinct for evasion accounts, probably, for

more than these obvious inanities. Many a strange phrase strays about third-rate fiction to puzzle literal-minded readers. There is, for example, a remark often made, *he wiped his glasses*. This means that he felt emotion, and the implication is that the moisture which rose to the eyes in consequence of the emotion had settled on and dimmed the glasses. But I am informed by those who wear glasses that this is not what actually occurs, and that, when tears gather in the eyes, they do not spray out horizontally so as to wet the glasses, but either remain in the eye unfallen until reabsorbed, or roll vertically down the cheeks; nor do they give out steam or mist; therefore this process of wiping the glasses is not called for more at lachrymose moments than at others. If this is, as seems probable enough, the case, then either those who use this phrase do not know it, or knowing, they ignore it, and deliberately use the words *he wiped his glasses* as a convenient (because indirect) way of saying "tears were in his eyes." The impulse to do this is probably mixed; partly it is the instinct for evasion, a belief that masculine tears are not the thing (for it is usually male beings, such as colonels, doctors, lawyers, financiers, and the like stern men of affairs, who resort to this superfluous wiping process) and partly a desire to be faintly arch, to imply rather than to state, as in "There was something suspiciously like the sound of a kiss," and similar facetiæ (I use this word, of course, in its literal, not in its euphemistic booksellers' sense). Another common evasion of the fact of tears is a narration of how the nose was blown, but this, unlike the other, is a legitimate symbol.

Closely allied to the instinct for prudish evasion,

and also hard at work, is the tendency to see evil where no evil is. There are scores of words harmless in etymology and original meaning which are, to quote a frequent dictionary comment, "now used in a bad sense." Take *conspiracy*, for instance, and *conspire*. Dr. Johnson, who confined himself for the most part to meanings current and accepted at the time when he wrote, explains conspiracy as "a private agreement among several persons to commit some crime; a plot; a concerted treason. In law, an agreement of men to do anything; always taken in the evil part." The Oxford Dictionary, more historical in aim and scope, yet can, apparently, find in history no instance of men conspiring for good objects, and so we must assume that, from very early days, those who put their heads close and breathed together have been suspected of planning some evil.

Out of the many other harmless and neutral words thus degraded by the mind of man, *spinster* may be selected as a pathetic example. From meaning first a woman who spins, one of Shakespeare's "spinsters and knitters in the sun," then merely an unmarried girl or woman, it seems to have acquired (outside its legal use) some opprobrious cant sense, and to be used often with reference to some regrettable qualities, or to advanced age, or both. There is a tendency not to use it of unmarried girls; a tendency even not to use it of unmarried older women unless they fall, in the opinion of the speaker, into a certain temperamental category. *Bachelor* seems to have escaped, so far, similar opprobrious associations, so much so that the absurd and paradoxical phrase *bachelor woman,* or *bachelor girl,* has been coined to denote an unmarried female whom it would seem inapt, and perhaps harsh, to call a spinster. This impulse to degrade has produced so many cant uses of words and phrases that it must be counted one of the formative instincts in the language.

So, then, we have all these various psychological factors, and, doubtless, many more at which we might easily arrive by further thought, working side by side, towards the same ends of dark confusion. The human desire to magnify; the human instinct of evasion; the more obscure human preference for conveying meaning tactically, by a halo of vague associations, rather than by a precise statement; the desire to convey atmosphere by the hypnotism of phrases; the tendency to think evil; and ordinary unlettered human ignorance. And beyond all these, there is the heady human arrogance which makes us determine that words shall be our servants, not our masters, and causes us to dig as wide a gulf as may be between the meanings given them by our ancestors and those we have decided that they shall bear. After all, if you come to that, who were our ancestors that they should have the ordering of our speech? What they did (which was to set accepted meanings continually at defiance) we will in our turn do. Do dictionaries say that a word bears one meaning? We will cause it to bear another. It is, after all, our creature. Language should do anything it is told, undertake any job required, not be a stubborn, one-idead thing, like a household of servants who will each perform only his appointed task. To make each word a maid-of-all-work—here is a task worthy of our endeavours. But the convenience of such a result is a little counterbalanced by the inconvenience of having to expend a good deal of imagination and intuition on guessing at the particular work which has been assigned to any given word at the moment. The fate of language will, perhaps, ultimately depend largely on what proportion of its users object more to taking this trouble than to the rigidity of specialized service. Meanwhile, we have plenty of material for interesting speculation.

THE HOGARTH ESSAYS

HUNTING THE HIGHBROW

BY

LEONARD WOOLF

HUNTING THE HIGHBROW

THE highbrow is an extremely unpopular person. The hunt is up in the Press and in the atmosphere, which is used to convey through valves or crystals information, amusement, or strike news to so many happy homes. When I open a paper or listen-in I am continually told that we are all much better fellows—more honest, and clean, and happy, and wise, and English—for being lowbrows. Being, if not a highbrow, at any rate on the side of the highbrows, I am not cheered by the news. But the hunt is so persistent and vocal that it has led me to make certain investigations, of which this paper is the result. The paper might, perhaps, be more accurately called Notes on the Natural History of the Highbrow and on the Reasons for Hunting Him.

Let me begin from two attacks upon the unfortunate creature which fell into my hands in the same week, for they will give us an idea of what the quarry appears to be to the hunters. The first is by Mr. Gilbert Frankau, the famous novelist, and is entitled "An Author's Feelings on Publication Day." Mr. Frankau broadcasted his feelings, and they were subsequently circulated on paper to the Press. Mr. Frankau seems to define a highbrow as anyone who does not like the novels written by Mr. Frankau. That is not very illuminating, but he goes on to make the following general remarks:—

"If there are any highbrows listening to-night, I

suppose they will think that last sentence of mine a most terrible give-away. Highbrows, you see, are funny people. They do not believe there is any good in the great heart of the British public. They consider that the book or play or picture which entertains and educates and pleases and uplifts ninety people out of every hundred cannot possibly have any real artistic merit. They—the highbrows—think that literature is an exclusive thing—rather like one of those ugly statues, or still uglier pictures, which they are always telling us we ought to admire. But such beliefs are not mine. In fact, I am positive that if an author has a really good story to tell, and really interesting characters to put in it, and really interesting scenes to depict, it is his bounden duty to write his tale in such a way that it is comprehensible and entertaining and uplifting to the vast majority of his fellow-countrymen and countrywomen.

"I do not believe that literature, or any other art, can be the exclusive property of the few. I feel that a fine book must be the common property of everybody who can read. And I am quite sure that Homer and Virgil and Dante and Shakespeare and Charles Dickens —just to name a few of the world's greatest story-tellers—did not write for any little clique, or for any highbrow, but straight to the hearts of the majority of the people who could either read or listen to them in their day."

I will return to this extremely interesting view of the natural history of the highbrow in a moment, but before doing so I want to quote some extracts from an article by Mr. Robert Magill, which appeared in a Sunday paper in the same week in which Mr. Frankau broadcasted his opinions. After saying that nowadays it is extremely difficult to be a highbrow, "because good stuff is getting so well known," and "the grocer's boy dumps a pound of tea on the window-sill while he whistles an excerpt from Beethoven's Fourth Quartet," he proceeds:

"It would be well to examine what one means by a highbrow. The real highbrow, of course, is the man who prefers the appeal to his intellect rather than that solely to his senses. But as intellect is rare, and other people also have intellects, this doesn't always work. Therefore, in his disgust at finding somebody he regards as less intelligent than himself is capable of liking the stuff he likes, he retaliates by trying to persuade himself that he doesn't like it at all."

The scientific natural historian often finds that the sportsman has only a vague idea of the nature of the game which he hunts or shoots. The man with a gun includes under the name partridge or snipe, deer or elk, an enormous number of creatures which, the scientist knows, belong to different species or even genera. It will be obvious to anyone with scientific training that those mighty highbrow-hunters, Mr. Frankau and Mr. Magill, are doing the same thing with the highbrows. It is clear from their own words that they include under the name the following quite distinct species:—

1. *Altifrons altifrontissimus,* the original, primitive, and real highbrow or intellectual who, as Mr. Magill puts it, prefers the appeal to his intellect rather than that solely to his senses.

2. *Altifrons æstheticus* var. *severus,* the man who

only likes what is best in literature, art, and music, or, as Mr. Magill puts it, good stuff.

3. *Altifrons frankauensis,* the man who is not entertained and uplifted by the novels of Mr. Gilbert Frankau.

4. *Pseudaltifrons intellectualis,* the man who only likes what nobody else can understand.

5. *Pseudaltifrons æstheticus,* the man who, in literature, art, and music, only likes the latest thing or the oldest thing or the thing which the majority dislikes.

This rough and preliminary classification already teaches us something important about the natural history of the highbrow. Speaking broadly, there are two distinct families, species, or genera of this animal, and not only is each of these species subdivided into a considerable number of subspecies, but to each has attached itself a parasitic species of pseudo-highbrow which has been forced by the struggle for social existence or distinction to mimic the true highbrow. The chief characteristic of the one species is a marked development of or attachment to the intellect, of the other a peculiar development of æsthetic appreciation.

Both Mr. Frankau and Mr. Magill confuse the intellectual with the æsthetic highbrow, but it is most important for scientific purposes to keep them distinct. For they are not the same animal. It is true that not all male highbrows are impotent or female highbrows sterile, and therefore you occasionally come across a hybrid highbrow, who has all the characteristics of both species. But there is no necessary connection between the intellect and æsthetic appreciation, and therefore there are dozens of intellectual highbrows who are not æsthetic, and dozens of æsthetic highbrows who are not intellectual. Aristotle, William Godwin, Jeremy Bentham are typical examples of the pure *altifrons altifrontissimus* uncrossed with *æstheticus;* poets (Swinburne, for example), artists, and musicians will provide you with many examples of *altifrons æstheticus* uncrossed with *altifrontissimus.*

The distinction between the two species is important because, although the hunters are not always themselves fully conscious of the fact, each is hunted for a different reason. I propose to deal with the case of *æstheticus* first. Mr. Frankau and Mr. Magill between them make it quite clear why the æsthetic highbrow is unpopular. Mr. Magill, who is very fair and sportsmanlike, implies that the genuine æsthetic highbrow only likes what is æsthetically "good stuff." But the main charge against him is that he does not like what the great public likes ,and Mr. Frankau, in summing up and passing sentence on him, lets fall the *obiter dictum* that only what the great public likes can really be good stuff.

The quarrel between the æsthetic highbrow and his hunters is, in fact, concerned with a difference in standards, and it raises æsthetic and psychological problems of considerable intricacy and obscurity. Even Mr. Frankau could not deny that the following is not an unusual occurrence in the history of literature or art. The highbrows of a certain generation hail a new writer, painter, or composer as an artist of eminence, while the great heart of the public of that generation refuses to be entertained, educated, pleased, or uplifted by him. Controversy rages and dies down; a new generation of highbrows and Frankaus and great public arises; and behold the new generation of

Frankaus and great public is entertained, educated, pleased, and uplifted by those very works of art which the highbrow of the previous generation was derided and hunted for praising. It is true that some writers and composers who become classics go at once to the great heart of the public, but in the majority of cases before a great work of art is accepted generally as such, it is accepted by a few highbrows and rejected by the general public. I do not know whether it is necessary to give instances, because anyone who has lived forty years in the world has himself seen so many. When I was twenty, you were still thought a highbrow if you liked Browning and Meredith better than Stephen Phillips and Hall Caine. Samuel Butler, Conrad, and W. H. Hudson were read and appreciated by only a very small number of highbrows. Certainly, what the highbrows thought then about these writers, popular novelists and the great public say to-day. And then, again, I am unfortunately old enough to remember the year 1912, when for many hours I watched the great public roar with laughter at the "still uglier" pictures of Cézanne and Van Gogh, which it was then unsuccessfully being asked to admire by the highbrows, and which it is now buying at enormous prices for its private and public art collections.

The process is a very mysterious one by which a book, picture, or piece of music either passes into oblivion or becomes a classic, and even more mysterious is the part played in that process by the highbrow and the great heart of the public respectively. Take the five writers mentioned by Mr. Frankau. His words make it clear that the *Iliad,* the *Æneid,* the *Divine Comedy, King Lear,* and *Martin Chuzzlewit*

are all accepted as classics by the anti-highbrows, and
are certified as going straight to the hearts of the
majority of the people. But it is also clear that of two,
at least, of these writers Mr. Frankau, the spokesman
of the public, has never read a word. No one who had
ever read a line of the *Æneid* could possibly say that it
has a really good story, or that it has really interesting characters, or that it has really interesting scenes.
To call Virgil one of the world's greatest story-tellers
is just about as true as to call Aristotle one of the
world's greatest poets. The idea that the *Æneid* could
be comprehensible, entertaining, and uplifting to the
vast majority of the Romans of the Augustan age is
ludicrous. The number of people who have understood
and enjoyed that difficult, boring, absurd, and magnificent book since it was first written some 2000 years
ago probably has not yet equalled the number of
people who are entertained and uplifted to-day by a
popular novel in the first week after publication. And
ninety-nine per cent. of the people who understand
and enjoy Virgil are highbrows, for if there was ever
a highbrow poet who wrote for highbrows it was the
man who wrote the *Æneid*. Yet here is a highbrow,
who can only be understood and appreciated by highbrows and is only read by highbrows, accepted by
the highbrow-hunters as a classic, quoted as an example of a popular writer, and miraculously metamor-
phosed into a popular novelist. Surely a strange
phenomenon!

What I have said of Virgil, I believe to be even
more true of Dante. Personally, like Mr. Frankau, I
have never read Dante, but I have often looked at him,
and have always decided to reserve him as a book to be

read in old age when the evenings will be long and
time will move slowly. But I have opened him sufficiently often to see that he is not a great story-teller,
that he does not go straight to the heart of the ordinary
Fascist, and that you have to have a pretty high brow
even to understand him.

Let me sum up the position to which my investigations of the habits of *altifrons æstheticus* have brought
me. This animal is attracted by objects which it calls
works of art. It professes to like only what Mr. Magill
calls "good stuff," and it does not seem to enjoy contemporary popular authors, Royal Academy pictures,
or the music played by the Savoy Havana Band. It
occasionally announces that a contemporary writer, let
us say, is producing "good stuff," and this is the point
at which its behaviour is scientifically interesting. I
should say that in the vast majority of cases a writer
who is pronounced by *altifrons æstheticus* var. *severus*
to be a great writer is not accepted as such for an
appreciable time by the general public, and that a
very large proportion of new writers who are pronounced by contemporary highbrows to be great writers
are eventually recognized as such by the great public.
You have, then, this curious result, that those who are
hunted and derided for their opinions as highbrows
are more often than not in the end justified by the
opinions of their hunters.

To investigate and explain this phenomenon would
involve a long discussion of the relation between artistic value and popular appreciation. I must confine
myself to a few disjected suggestions. I suggest, first,
that the highbrow is genuinely attracted by elements
in literature, let us say, which may conveniently be

called æsthetic, and which are not primarily interesting
or attractive to the great public. I deny that the qualities which make the *Æneid*, or *King Lear*, or the
Iliad, or *War and Peace*, or *Paradise Lost*, or *Madame
Bovary*, or *Emma* good stuff have anything to do with
such things as really good and uplifting stories, interesting characters, and interesting scenes, though I agree
that what the general public primarily wants from a
book is a good story and certain amount of uplift. The
highbrow is therefore in literature one of those unpleasant persons whose standards are different from
the majority, and that is a very good reason for hunting him.

But that it is not the most interesting point. The
really curious problem is why in the end the standards
of æsthetic highbrowism should prevail with the general
public. It is indisputable that by far the greater number
of books which live and become classics and are uni-
versally recognized as masterpieces are books which
are good stuff by the standards of highbrows, not by
those of the great public. Mr. Frankau, when he
wanted to think of a masterpiece, thought of the
Æneid, not of *Two Little Wooden Shoes,* which years
ago went straight to the great heart of a nation; Mr.
Magill, when he wanted to think of some musical good
stuff, thought of Beethoven's Fourth Quartet (whatever exactly that may be), not of "The Lost Chord,"
or even "Tararaboomdeay." Every ten years or so
tens of thousands of novels, poems, biographies, essays
are produced which go straight to the great heart of
the world's public; there for a publishing season of six
months they flourish luxuriantly, pouring, I hope, a
shower of golden blossoms into the lap of the author

and publisher; but at the end of each publishing season 999 out of every 1000 have died, and at the end of ten years probably not even the name of one of them survives in the memory of anyone except their own authors, while at the end of fifty years even that has perished with the authors. Meanwhile, one or two or three highbrows productions which, with difficulty, sold 1000 copies to struggle into a second edition after two or three years, will have taken firm root in the heart of the ordinary man, so that at the end of fifty years they are ripe for sanctification in the Temple Classics or Everyman's Library.

I do not pretend that I can give any convincing psychological explanation of this curious phenomenon, but there are one or two points which are worth considering. One of the most obscure points connected with the immortality of highbrow and the mortality of popular literature is this. Why should the good story which goes straight to the heart of one generation practically never go to the heart of any subsequent generation? The highbrow of 1926 reads the *Æneid,* Dante, *Paradise Lost,* Keats, *Crotchet Castle,* Meredith, and *Erewhon* with considerable pleasure; the reader of Mr. Frankau's novels would never dream of reading *The Romance of the Forest* (Mrs Radcliffe, 7th ed. 1806), *The Doctor's Wife* (Miss Braddon, 7th ed. 1866), or *Lord Oakburn's Daughters* (Mrs. Wood, 1st ed. 1864, 12th 1888). I cannot find any explanation of this fact which really satisfies me. The obvious explanation is that a book which has to make its appeal only through its story and characters and scenes has to be topical. Manners and customs change, and what is a good story in 1806, 1866, or 1888 may well seem simply silly in 1926. There is, of course, some truth in this, but it is certainly not a complete explanation. The *Iliad* and *Odyssey* are still good stories, and so are *Pride and Prejudice, Villette* and *Wuthering Heights*. I am inclined to think that there must be dozens of dead best-sellers which, if they were republished, might be best-sellers again. Perhaps the terrible infantile mortality among best-sellers is connected with the exigencies of the supply rather than with the tastes of the consumers. A high birth-rate is inevitably accompanied by a high death-rate. People who produce books which are comprehensible, entertaining, and uplifting to the vast majority of their fellow-countrymen and countrywomen tend to produce one at least every twelve months, and often go on doing this for twenty or thirty years. If all of them remained best-sellers all the time, the rest of the world would very soon have to spend every hour of the day reading best-sellers in order to keep up with the supply. The only solution is to kill off the old in order to make room for the new. On the other hand, the highbrow is a very slow-breeding animal; he is rarely prolific; he is often in favour of and practises birth control; and there are not very many of him who are actually writing books in any generation. The problems of over-population do not, therefore, apply to highbrow literature. The highbrow considers himself fortunate if one book as good as *Crotchet Castle* appears in twenty years, or one as good as *War and Peace* in a century. The consequence is that it is not necessary to kill *Paradise Lost* in order to find time to read Proust.

The most interesting problems are, however, connected with the process by which works which have real artistic merit, according to the standards of æsthetic highbrows, seem eventually to go to the heart of the public and receive the frozen immortality accorded to recognized classics. It should be said at once that Mr. Frankau is certainly mistaken on one point. I claim to have as intimate an acquaintance as he has with the modern *altifrons æstheticus,* and it is certainly untrue that this creature holds that the book, play, or picture which appeals to ninety-nine people out of a hundred cannot possibly have artistic merit. Nearly every modern highbrow, for instance, would say that Dickens was a writer of genius, and it is notorious that his novels have always gone straight to the great heart of the British public. It is true that some very severe æsthetic highbrows would maintain that the qualities which make a book or a picture a great work of art are never those which make it appeal to ninety-nine out of every hundred people. But that is a very different thing from saying that a work which is popular cannot have artistic merit.

You have, therefore, to consider two theories which are at the opposite poles to one another. One is that of the most highbrow highbrows, which I have just stated; the other is that of people who believe with Mr. Frankau that nothing can be a great work of art which cannot be understood and appreciated by practically all ordinary people. Personally, I incline to think that the truth is too complicated to be covered by such simple and sweeping formulæ, and that it lies somewhere between the two extremes.

Mr. Frankau's statement is obviously absurd. The *Æneid* is indisputably a great poem, but however

educated the world might be, it would always exas-
perate and bore the vast majority of its inhabitants,
and in this case I should always number myself among
the majority, for in literature often *video meliora
proboque,* but, with ninety-nine people out of a hundred, *deteriora sequor.* The *Phædrus* is, to my mind,
a greater work of art than the *Æneid,* but it is certain
that not one per thousand of the Athenians could have
understood and appreciated it when it was written.
How many people out of every hundred could truthfully say that they understand and are entertained by
Urn Burial, or Donne's poems, or *Paradise Lost,* or
Tristram Shandy, or La Bruyère, or Wordsworth's
Prelude, or *The Brothers Karamazov,* or Proust? And
how many people will be prepared to deny that these
are great works of literature? No, the idea that
popularity is a test of artistic merit is merely the day-
dream of a popular writer. Most great literature is not
easy to read or understand; it is often extremely boring; it is very rarely entertaining or amusing. That is
why it is rarely read for or with pleasure by the great
public and why, when it first appears, it is frequently
condemned as mere highbrow stuff by ninety-nine out
of every hundred people.

On the other hand, I doubt the statement that the
qualities which make a book a great work of art never
appeal to the vast majority of people. It is probably
true that when a book is both a work of art and
popular, the qualities which give it æsthetic merit are
not those which have most to do with its popularity—
but that is a very different thing. Let me give an example. Mr. Frankau says that Shakespeare is one of
the world's greatest story-tellers, and in a sense this is

true. Shakespeare does sometimes have a good story to tell (though sometimes he has a very bad and muddled one). As a character drawer he is superb, and his scenes, both tragic and comic, are often magnificent. Now I am ready to agree with Mr. Frankau that, speaking generally, it is the story and the characters which appeal to the majority of people. But it is absurd to pretend that *King Lear* is one of the greatest, if not the greatest, play ever written because of its story and characters. If you look upon *King Lear* as a story it is really silly, and even the characters are not particularly interesting. The æsthetic merits of the play are in fact very little connected with the story, plot, characters, and scenes. In other words, the æsthetic qualities of Shakespeare are not those which primarily appeal to the majority of people.

One is still left with the question why, in that case, Shakespeare, and not Miss Dell or Mr. Hutchinson, is recognized by the public as the greatest of English writers? Partly, of course, it is snobbery. The highbrow is abused and hunted and his standards are derided, but the incorrigible snobbery of the human race brings it about that his æsthetic opinions and standards are adopted by his hunters. It is simply not true that the majority of ordinary people understand and appreciate and read Shakespeare; he bores them, and he bores them because he is an intellectual and æsthetic highbrow writing for intellectual and æsthetic highbrows. And what is true of Shakespeare is infinitely more true of most other great writers.

Nevertheless, I do not believe that the æsthetic qualities which make a book a great work of art never appeal to the public. For one has to face the fact that it is not merely the highbrows who keep the great corpus of classics in all languages alive. The really popular writers of each generation die, the great writers live, and they live to some extent at any rate in the hearts and speech of the public. Chaucer and Shakespeare and Sterne and Fielding and Jane Austen may not be very widely read, but they are English literature to the non-highbrow as well as to the highbrow. Mrs. Radcliffe, Miss Braddon, and Mrs. Wood are nothing at all; they are simply dead and buried together with Gower, Thompson, and Southey. That, I think, is a very remarkable fact—not a single non-highbrow second-rate popular writer slips through the highbrow sieve of immortality to be enshrined by the great public as a great writer in the teeth of the highbrows.

I cannot believe that this is due merely to the æsthetic dictatorship of the highbrow, or to undiluted snobbery of the non-highbrow. Surely, if that were the case, the ordinary man would have occasionally asserted himself, and we should find that one or two really popular writers, who only write good stories and go straight to the great heart of the public, had crept into immortality. But where are they? I cannot see a single one of them, though I could name dozens of pure highbrows, whom the ordinary man numbers among the world's great writers. The reason must, I think, be that real artistic merit does have, at any rate to a limited extent, some popular appeal. And if one examines the ordinary non-highbrow attitude towards the classics, ancient and modern, one can see something of the way in which this works.

I suggest first that æsthetic qualities, when combined

with non-æsthetic qualities which are popular, produce
an effect which the ordinary man feels and recognizes
as something different from and better than that of
popular and ephemeral literature. Thus no first-class
novelist is ever as popular as a really bad novelist,
because the æsthetic necessities involved in good novel-
writing make it impossible for the writer to concentrate his attention on producing a good story and interesting characters, something which will immediately be
understood and appreciated by ninety-nine out of a
hundred persons. But where a great artist can also
produce a good story, he will obtain a modified
popularity which is quite distinct from that of the
mere best-sellers, because his æsthetic qualities have
their effect. I believe that thousands of non-highbrows
appreciate Scott and Jane Austen in a way in which they
do not appreciate Mr. Hutchinson or Mr. Frankau.
They get more undiluted pleasure from Mr. Hutchinson and Mr. Frankau, but from Scott and Jane Austen
they get something besides the pleasure of day-dream-
ing through a good story; they get, in fact, some of that
purely æsthetic pleasure which is what appeals to the
highbrow. And the non-highbrow quite consciously
recognizes the distinction; he calls Scott and Jane
Austen good stuff. What applies to the novelist also
applies to the poet and the essayist. Tennyson was
never as popular as Ella Wheeler Wilcox, but in his
sentiments and sentimentality he had some of the
qualities which have sold *Poems of Passion* by the hundred thousand. Those are the qualities which made him
a second-class best-seller among poets. But he was also
an æsthetic highbrow poet, and as such he is recognized
by the non-highbrows; he is good stuff, but Ella

Wheeler Wilcox isn't. Considerable numbers of the
great public will read and thrill to "Tears, idle tears, I
know not what they mean" a hundred years after it
was written, but already the other day I saw Mrs.
Wilcox sinking into oblivion when I bought one of
her books reduced to threepence on Smith's bookstall
at Polegate station in Sussex.

There is another reason which makes me think that
æsthetic merit can accord an author a modified popularity, at any rate if he be dead. It is obvious that
new writers, painters, and musicians of great æsthetic
originality are not only not appreciated, but are frequently actively disliked by the public when they first
appear. A generation later they will apparently be
appreciated by hundreds of people who are not highbrows. There was an element in Keats, Wagner, and
Cézanne, for instance, an æsthetic element with an immediate appeal to a few highbrows, which at first
aroused in ordinary people a genuine and instinctive
aversion. Fifty years later the same element produces
no such hostile reaction; on the contrary, it appears to
give to a considerable number of the public much of
the same kind of pleasure as was originally confined
to the highbrow. It seemed to me unreasonable to believe that the original hostile reaction was genuine and
the later pleasure unreal or mere snobbery. The more
probable explanation is this: In works of art the qualities which are primarily attractive to the ordinary man
are generally not æsthetic. But when he is given sufficient time to grow accustomed to and understand the
æsthetic methods and intentions of an artist or a school,
the æsthetic merits have their effect upon and their
appeal to him. The non-highbrow who has just begun

to understand and appreciate Wordsworth or Beethoven finds himself up against something new and
disturbing, which he does not primarily want, when
Keats or Wagner swims into his ken—his first reaction
is annoyance, and he shows it by deriding any highbrow
who may tell him that Keats is a great poet or Wagner
a great composer. But give him a little time, and after
quarter or half a century he will have grown accustomed to the new rhythms and new methods and will
allow them to have their proper, pleasurable effect on
him.

I do not know that there is very much more to say
about *altifrons æstheticus,* and I still have to deal with
altifrons altifrontissimus. Before doing so, however, I
suppose that I ought to give a word or two to *pseudaltifrons æstheticus.* This is not a very interesting animal,
whom we have all come across from time to time lurk-
ing in the undergrowth of Cambridge, Oxford, Chelsea,
Bloomsbury, and other favourable localities. He is
really a cross between two genera widely dispersed
over the world's surface, the bore and the snob. Highbrow hunters, who, like all sportsmen, are more interested in killing their game than knowing its habits, always confuse the *altifrons æstheticus* with the *pseudaltifrons æstheticus.* They are also mistaken about the
numbers and habits of this animal. *Pseudaltifrons
æstheticus* is not, in my fortunate experience, very common. The study of great works of art entails so much
tedious labour that bores and snobs usually find other
more fruitful fields for their talents and activities.
But there are a certain number of hybrid bore-snobs
who have fastened upon literature, art, and music as
their peculiar habitat. It is not, however, really true

that even they, as people like Mr. Frankau believe, consider that literature is written for little cliques or is the exclusive property of the few. What is true of them is that, having, with justice, no reliance on their own æsthetic judgments, they are always after the latest thing either in antiquity or modernity—in fact, they are apt to run off with the crumbs which fall from the table of *altifrons æstheticus*. And there I propose to leave them.

Altifrons altifrontissimus, whom I now have to deal with, is a most formidable animal, very different from the mild-mannered and often charming *altifrons æstheticus*. He is the intellectual proper, the man who has a passion for the intellect. The reason for hating and hunting him is obvious. Ordinarily an innocuous and slightly ridiculous animal, he may at any moment and in any department of life become a terrible menace.

In ordinary times we very rarely think, and the use of the intellect, except for the purpose of finding reasons to support our passions and prejudices, is painful and distasteful to us. But the spectacle of another man using his intellect is much more painful and distasteful to us. By the time that we have arrived at the age of twenty-five most of our opinions are comfortably fixed, but they have not been fixed by reason. They are either prejudices which we have accepted from our surroundings or as reactions against our surroundings, or, if we are clever enough, they are reasons which we have invented in order to prove to ourselves and other people that we are right to do what we want to do. The use of the intellect for any other purposes tends, therefore, to be a very disturbing process, rubbing our prejudices the wrong way and thoroughly upsetting our equanimity. Modern civilization has devised various extremely effective methods for prescribing rigid limits to the use of the intellect. The most effective of all methods is education. The object of education seems to be partly to teach children and young people that to think is a dreary and laborious process. In my days education in schools and universities impressed upon us the conviction that the intellect should be used as sparingly as possible, but if used at all, should be exercised exclusively upon such useless subjects as dead languages, or upon subjects like Euclid, which were both untrue and completely unconnected with anything real.

Not only the educational system, but the Press, our party system in politics, the theory of the British Constitution, our legal system, the doctrines of religion and patriotism are all ingeniously calculated to make the use of the intellect suspect and unpopular. Oddly enough, the use of the intellect is really extraordinarily pleasant. The solving of a difficult problem or the working out of an intricate train of thought to a successful conclusion is accompanied by a pleasurable feeling which for intensity of thrill cannot unjustly be compared to that which the ordinary person gets from Miss Dell's novels or Mr. Magill's grocer's-boy is now said to get from the Fourth Quartet of Beethoven. That the non-highbrow is capable of this pleasure is shown by the popularity of the cross-word puzzle and the acrostic, and by the large number of retired colonels who play chess.

Altifrons altifrontissimus, or the highbrow intellectual, is an animal in whom this faculty for enjoying the use of his intellect is abnormally developed. Sometimes he is content to confine the exercise of his intellect to safe subjects, and then, if his mind be of a very high order, you get a chess champion like Dr. Lasker, or a mathematician like Newton, or a philosopher like Aristotle. But there have always been a certain number of highbrows who insist upon applying the intellect to all subjects and all departments of life—and then the trouble begins. If you begin to think about religion, or the relation of the sexes, or the party system, or education, or patriotism, you are lost, but, what is much more serious, they are lost too. They are the superstructures of illusions and prejudices, and as soon as reason is applied to their foundations they come down with a crash.

Hence the real intellectual is deservedly one of the most unpopular animals in the world. And he is, as I said, unlike the æsthetic highbrow—who is a poor, soft, gentle, long-haired creature—a dangerous and savage beast. In ordinary time, it is true, we usually succeed in cutting his claws and in making him harmless. We do this by the simple method of making him ridiculous. It is not difficult to do. An intellectual in politics, a man who applies his intellect to the doctrines of patriotism and puts his principles into practice, a schoolmaster who taught his pupils only what was true and according to the dictates of reason—these people would all simply make fools of themselves. The man who in the ordinary and actual world of to-day appeals to the intellect naturally suffers the fate which would overtake a drunken man who wandered by accident into a meeting of a Temperance Society, or a lunatic who entered a conference of mental specialists.

But the intellectual highbrow is deservedly hated

and hunted with an intensity which the hunters of æsthetic highbrows never feel. For, in the first place, *altifrons altifrontissimus,* when brought to bay, is able to defend himself. Even that is not the worst. Although, in normal times he is or appears to be ridiculous, at rare intervals in the world's history periods occur in which he becomes an extremely dangerous and powerful animal. This is due to the efficacy of human suffering. In ordinary times, as I have said, people do not think, and either naturally or through education dislike thought. But if you can make people miserable enough, you can eventually induce them to think about the causes of their misery. The whole of history shows both that you have to make people in large bodies extraordinarily miserable before this happens and that if communal misery gets beyond a certain point it does happen. But nothing is so dangerous as thought applied to the structure of society, for once people begin to think, you let in the highbrow, and anything may happen.

It is at such periods that the intellectual highbrow becomes a powerful and dangerous animal. At the end of the eighteenth century, and again during the Great War, the sum of human misery reached the point at which quite a large number of people began to think about the causes of their misery and the political and social structure. Naturally that was the opportunity for the intellectual highbrow, who had never been doing anything else and had made himself ridiculous by doing it. The hunted suddenly became a hunter, and President Wilson and Lenin, two magnificent specimens of *altifrons altifrontissimus,* were, for the moment at least, as powerful as the Tsar, the Kaiser,

M. Clemenceau, Mr. Lloyd George, or Mr. Bottomley. It is true that the moment is never a long one. The difficulty of suddenly changing a world based on prejudice and passion into a world based on reason, the vested interests in unreason, the weight of tradition against reason and the enormous mass of people who have grown up in that tradition—all these things make it inevitable that there is a pretty rapid return to what a famous statesman called a healthy state of affairs— every one for himself and God for us all. The power of the intellectual highbrow therefore soon vanishes, but the memory of him as a formidable animal, the consciousness that there are always those latent and dangerous possibilities in him, remain. He is very properly hunted with some ferocity and vindictiveness.

One's judgment of the intellectual highbrow must depend, I think, very much upon one's estimate of how far and how widely it is possible that mankind may be induced to apply reason to the arrangement of their communal affairs. If human psychology is such that men in groups will never act rationally towards one another, and will allow no permanent place to reason and intellect in the practical organization of society, then the sooner *altifrons altifrontissimus* is exterminated the better for the world. For under such circumstances he is usually a nuisance and at times a positive curse. It is much better that a man should be drunk all the time than that he should be sober for only a few hours once every six months, for during those few hours he will probably behave like a suicidal and homicidal maniac, whereas, if he is perpetually drunk, he will merely be asleep or soddenly stupid. So with society, the administration of minute doses of reason into its constitution is only a useless irritant, and the sudden injection every century or two of large doses completely upsets its balance. On the other hand, if there be any real possibility that man may become a rational, political, and social animal, I should be in favour of preserving and even encouraging the intellectual highbrow. For I remain convinced that if men would allow intellect and reason rather than passion and prejudice to have a say in their communal affairs, a good deal of the sordid ugliness and misery would disappear from society.

I have no space in which to deal further with *altifrons altifrontissimus*, though there are a good many other interesting questions connected with him. I should have liked, for instance, to say something of the curious process by which the ideas of intellectual highbrows are usually, when new and alive, fiercely rejected by the majority, but, when they are safely dead, are accepted as the last word in social and political wisdom. The process is oddly similar to that by which eventually the standards of the æsthetic highbrow are adopted even by his hunters.

As for *pseudaltifrons intellectualis*, nothing much need be said about him. The pseudo-intellectual highbrow bears to the intellectual highbrow the same relation as the pseudo-æsthetic highbrow to the æsthetic. He is a parasite, a hybrid between the bore and the snob, who attaches himself to intellectual things and to *altifrons altifrontissimus*. I expect that he is rather more numerous than the pseudo-æsthetic highbrow. I doubt whether he does much harm; the worst thing about him is that he often writes books which other people are unfortunately compelled to review. Indeed, personally, I prefer him to some of the subspecies of real highbrow. For instance, there is *altifrons altifrontissimus* var. *adelphicus*. This is a curious small subspecies which has made its appearance in recent times. An extraordinarily highbrow highbrow, it runs about all over the place attracting attention by proclaiming itself to be just an ordinary man, and how much better Life is than Intellect, and how deplorable highbrows are. But I must stop, for if once one begins on the subspecies of highbrow there is no end to it.

THE HOGARTH ESSAYS

THE FUTURE OF THE ART OF POETRY

BY

ROBERT GRAVES

To L. R. G.

THE FUTURE OF THE ART OF POETRY

MR. ROBERT TREVELYAN has forestalled me in his little book *Thamyris, or Is There a Future for Poetry?* But I find his judgments for the most part so parochial, and his style so unadventurous, that in spite of the wide applause he has won from the elder critics, I am not deterred from signing a minority report at variance with his. Mr. J. B. S. Haldane also, in his *Dædalus; or the Future of Science,* has a few lines to spare for the future of Poetry; and it would be well to treat of the views of both these writers before making an independent forecast.

Now, Mr. Trevelyan and Mr. Haldane are both writing not of poetry itself, but of the art and technique of poetry: and I am about to do the same. Poetry itself happens so rarely and is so rarely discerned as such when it does happen that I prefer not to discuss its future or past.

Mr. Trevelyan's chief concern is the change that has come over the art of poetry since it ceased to be chanted or sung, and began a new life as the spoken, written, or printed line. Now these are important changes if not particularly new ones. The regular chanting or singing element had already begun to disappear in mediæval times, and except as a small and somewhat extravagant cult no longer survives, because it has been discovered that speech, particularly under emotion, though it does not employ the pure diatonic scale, has a music of its own which can be as agreeable as it is complex; and the chanting of modern poetry, so far from giving it richer life, has in my experience the exact opposite effect: the chant is seldom more than a self-conscious and lugubrious drone. The change from the chanted or spoken to the written or printed line is also no novelty, dating back as it does behind the invention of printing to the great copying schools of the ancient world; which circulated books far more freely among the cultured classes than is now realized. But the effects of this change on the art of poetry grow yearly more apparent. Books get cheaper and more numerous, public recitations fewer; the Victorian habit of reading aloud in the home is dying; poetic drama is on its last legs theatrically; so that the spoken line is temporarily overshadowed by the printed line. True, poetry will never become a purely printed art, for the poet is too fond of the sound of his voice; but unless new developments of broadcasting or a great simplification and improvement of the gramophone make it possible to listen to poems with as great ease as one picks up a book of verse, the art of writing verse for the eye and the inner ear will progress, to the disadvantage of poetry composed for the outer ear. It is not enough to advise, as Mr. Trevelyan does, that we should read with this inward ear and give the lines the same *tempo* as if they were being spoken. For poems, when printed or written, have a unique character; though we may owe it to our ear to translate typography into sound, the importance of the first visual impact must not be sentimentally discounted for the sake of the singing tradition.

There are startling variations in the acceptability of

a poem, according to the style in which it is set down on the page. A poem typewritten almost always looks unattractive. The conventions of setting down poems are, as it were, the corridor through which we pass to the garden of imagination. If that corridor is white-tiled like the entrance to a public baths, or stuffy like the entrance to a museum, or postered like the entrance to a tube station, we usually enter the garden in the wrong frame of mind. The typewriter is, in my experience, still too commercial to serve as a proper introduction to the receptive imaginative mood, except in a commercial context.

On the other hand, the original manuscript of a poem, to any reader who is at all sensitive to handwriting, will often give so much inside information as to the character and habits of the poet (far more than could be got by hearing the poet read the piece in question) that the oppression of personality in the handwriting may actually make it impossible to concentrate on the particular poem itself. There remains printing. But there is printing *and* printing. The habit, for instance, of printing English poems in Italian types, or modern poems in old-English types, has a most confusing effect on the reader; and there is no poem that cannot be made more dignified than it ever was before, or more vulgar than anyone could expect it had the power of being, by judicious choice of print and printer and paper.

A small matter like the convention which gives a capital letter and a new line to every line of a poem is of immense importance. I never discovered that Mr. Sacheverell Sitwell's poems were any good until he had consented to use the initial capital letter, after two books in which the lower case was used. And then spelling. Who will deny that Milton's *On a Solemn Musick,* or Webster's *The White Divel,* or Blake's *The Tyger* get a powerful hold on our imaginations before we have even begun to read the poems? Or who could read Keats' *St. Agnes' Eve* in "simplifyd speling," and still be entranced? These startling effects do not correspond with any change of tone or accent in the spoken line, and there are therefore many who will protest that these effects have nothing to do with the poems themselves. But this is to insist sentimentally on the absolute priority of the spoken line. The fact is, poetry read silently and poetry spoken aloud are divergent arts; and we may summarize their different characters as follows:

In the first place, the outward ear has a far shorter memory than the conjunction of eye and inward ear. It readily forgets end-rhymes separated by more than three intervening lines, unusual words recurring at a longish interval, and structural sign-posts of various kinds; but it has a far greater sensitivity to the variation of vowel and consonant, to internal rhyme, and to awkward concurrence of consonants (technically called "syzygy"). I notice in Mr. Turner's recent *Landscape of Cytherea* more than a few awkwardnesses of syzygy in contexts where a harmonious flow is intended. "Sun's shadow," "soul's gullies strewn," "frost's cascade," "these shadows shone," "rocks spring," occur on a single page; and there are rhymes separated by nine and ten lines. In the case of poems for silent reading, both these irregularities are quite legitimate; the inward ear can and naturally does slur over its syzygal difficulties, and as the eye reads faster than the voice speaks, the rhyme-echo does not die away so quickly: but spoken poems would be severely handicapped by these methods.

The next obvious difference is that a poem of simple content can become very significant when spoken. The same poem, printed, is intellectually negligible, and one is tempted to say, "My ear deceived me"; whereas a poem of highly concentrated content is impossible to hear with enjoyment until it has been read and thoroughly digested by the eye. The eye is a very summary, shrewd, supercilious organ, as it were the Enquiries Clerk of the Mind, and cannot be bothered with a visiting poem that has no air of immediate distinction to commend it; and the beauty of a poem may lie for the reader—quite adventitiously, the Eye will claim—in the inflections of voice intended by the poet, inflections for which the printer has not yet discovered even an approximate notation. The ear is a much simpler and sympathetic official, and once buttonholed will often commend to the management what the eye would call a most undeserving case, for though the ear may be wilfully blind, the eye is inclined to deafness. The ear can never properly appreciate a difficult poem of remote reference, intricate structure, and unusual diction. For when a poem is printed it is always possible to refer back, to pause and puzzle, and still keep the continuity of the rhyme alive. In the spoken poem there is no such licence; once a spoken poem begins, its rhyme-echoes and the rhyme of its parts are quite destroyed by any puzzling or interruption.

The ear and eye are both fallible in their interpretations of the poet's intentions, but in different ways. The ear may mishear words such as "all together" or "in deed," as if they were "altogether" and "indeed," and make even wilder mistakes, particularly with proper names, and cannot readily distinguish, say, between *discreet* and *discrete;* whereas the eye can go even farther astray, particularly in the mistaking of rhythm. A regular two-stress line like Swinburne's *Hertha* can be read as a four-stress line, or *vice versa.* Even the careful examination of the context sometimes prevents the poet's intention if it be, say, ironic or playful, from coming through, and I recall an instance of a passage in a Shakespeare comedy:—

> Passed there a buck this way?
> No, but two does,

being mistaken by the eye for an intentionally absurd *non-sequitur* where "does" was read as a verb and not as a substantive.

The future of the Art of Poetry then will be concerned for a start with the problem how the outward ear, which carries with it the inward eye, and the outward eye, which carries with it the inward ear, may be satisfied by the same poem equally. It is a problem partly of word-mechanics and partly of psychology. On the whole, the adjustment tends at present to be unfair to the ear. A striking exception is Mr. Nicholas Vachel Lindsay, the American, whose verses are all primarily intended for recitation. They have a very bare look in print, and a directness of statement which the Enquiries Clerk finds positively rustic; but as Mr. Lindsay himself recites them, they are strangely effective. A fair adjustment between the arts of written or spoken poetry is, I believe, possible once the demands of each are fully and equally realized. For instance, it may be desirable in the ear's interest to allow time for a mental adjustment after, and even before, the use of an unusual word or one highly charged with reference. In Shakespeare's

> It would rather
> The multitudinous seas incarnadine,

there is a distinct pause made after "the multitudinous" by the concurrence of two *s's,* and between "seas" and "incarnadine" there is again a tendency to give a slight pause, owing perhaps to the displacement of "would" from the word it governs.

So also a modern poet, Mr. Bertram Higgins, in his poem *Ulysses in Ithaca,* writes:

> Robbed of its element of wet,
> And discrete on a dune,

where the unusual word "discrete," which has to be distinguished from "discreet," is given an introducing pause by the necessity of separating the *d* of "and" and the *d* of "discrete," and a following pause by the tendency to avoid putting a heavy stress on the word "on." It must be noticed that these pauses, which have the effect almost of inverted commas, do to some extent help the ears to recognize, uninformed by the eye, that it is not the ordinary "discreet" which is being used. The details of this adjustment we may leave future poets to settle; and if ever they re-introduce, with a difference, the Alexandrian tricks of shaping poems in the form of wings, crosses, pyramids, and so on, and burying acrostics in them solely for the ingenious delight of the eye; or if they write poems solely for public declamation, that is no concern of ours. Eye poetry and ear poetry are both worthy arts, if distinguished. At this point it must be observed that though the subsidiary senses—smell, touch, taste—are not the direct means by which we take in poems, as inward senses they are most important vehicles of thought, and must be used to give completeness to the poetic life.

To return to Mr. Trevelyan: he conducts an enquiry into the future of verse forms, and comes to the conclusion that anything may happen—but he sincerely hopes that it won't. Several of his statements puzzle me a good deal—for instance, this: "Blank verse is the oldest of our verse forms," which is wildly unhistorical, even if, as Mr. Trevelyan suggests oddly enough, Chaucer's rhymed couplet can be so regarded. And again, "The conscious principle according to which English verse has been written from the time of Chaucer until recent years has been that of syllable counting"; this is only true of one of the main strands of English poetry. It is true that this has been the principle of the cultured prosody imposed on English from the Continent; but the earlier native prosody, which takes small stock of syllables, reckoning instead musically by the stress-centres of the line and the time interval between them, has never been driven from popular poetry, and has frequently been adopted by poets of culture. The readiest examples of native prosody are to be found in nursery rhyme and country ballad:

> Misty, moisty was the morn,
>   Chilly was the weather;
> There I met an old man,
>   Dressed all in leather,
> Dressed all in leather
>   Against the wind and rain.

It was, how do you do? and how do you do?
And how do you do? again.

At Wednesbury there was a cocking,
  A match between Newton and Scroggin;
The colliers and nailers left work
  And all to old Spittle's went jogging.
To see this noble sport
  Many noblemen resorted,
And though they had but little money
  Yet that little they freely sported.

Though the syllables in both cases number most ir-
regularly, nobody can deny that the pieces scan.

In the earliest English verse these stress-centres (for
often the stress is not on one syllable but, as in *how do
you do?* and *how do you do?* spread over two or three)
are marked clearly by alliteration. Anglo-Saxon verse
is all alliterative and stressed, its syllables are un-
counted. In the fourteenth century came William Lang-
land, a contemporary of Chaucer's. Though the most
famous of the middle English poets to revive the
Anglo-Saxon alliterative metre, he was by no means
the only one. In the sixteenth century John Skelton, in
my opinion one of the three or four outstanding English
poets, though reducing the alliteration, adding rhyme,
and even using the lineal arrangement of rhyme-royal,
wrote in the native style as often as in the Continental.
In the seventeenth century, Shakespeare, who had been
dominated at his first visit to London by the Continental prosody in vogue at the theatres, gradually re-
discovered his popular inheritance, and developed the
foppish blank verse that Surrey and Wyatt had brought
from Italy into a metre in which both principles, native
and Continental, interacted; it was a metre capable at
times of stresses as turbulent as those in *Beowulf*,

while at others it would still strut syllabically like a fine gentleman.

The two principles of prosody correspond in a marked way with contrary habits of life, with political principles: the Continental, with the classical principle of preordained structure, law and order, culture spreading downwards from the educated classes—the feudal principle; the native English, with what Mr. John Ransom calls the Gothic principle, one of organic and unforeseen growth, warm blood, impulsive generosity and frightful error—the communal principle, threatening the classic scheme from below. The rare poets who have contrived to reconcile the two principles have always had, like Skelton and Shakespeare, one foot firmly planted in the aristocratic set and the other equally firmly in the crowd. The future of English prosody depends enormously on the political outcome of the present class warfare. A Red victory would bring with it, I believe, a renewal of the native prosody in a fairly pure form, as the White domination of the eighteenth century made for pure Classicism, and kept it dominant until the Romantic Revival, intimately connected with the French Revolution, re-introduced stress-prosody.

Dr. Scripture has made one very important point about classical prosody: that it is tinged with what he calls the typographical fallacy, namely, that the space between printed letters and the space between printed words represent an actual time-interval, or at least that it is possible to divide a verse up into feet by driving wedges between syllables; whereas, excepting definite long pauses for ease or emphasis, verse as spoken is really one continuous flow of the voice-

stream, and when a sensitive instrument is set to record it, there is nothing of a regular rise and fall in
the resultant wavy line drawn to indicate either syllables or feet; that most of English classical verse,
while conforming typographically to the syllable-
counting principle and to the rigid dualism of "short
or long?" that goes with it, gets its quality from a far
subtler musical scheme than that of an ordered sequence
of approximately identical feet, iambs, dactyls and
what not; that, in fact, the musical delight we derive
from, say, Gray's *Elegy* is not and never was one of
elementary arithmetic, but is based really on the variance of distance, pitch, and sonority between what cus-
tom arithmetically marks off as identical feet. This is
not to deny the legitimacy of thinking in syllables. A
syllable is a useful convention, and its adoption in classical verse has led to the calming and slowing down of
rhythm, suitable for grave and reflective thought. Its
neglect, in the prosody of stress-centres, has made for
fury and ecstasy.

This brings us to Mr. Trevelyan's account of *vers
libre*. He writes "success of 'free verse' is in proportion
to the degree in which we are made aware of a fixed
metrical base underlying the irregularities. But what
are we to think of this kind of thing?—

> "Come, my songs, let us express our baser passions.
> Let us express our envy for the man with a steady
>   job and no worry about the future."

He comments: "But it would almost seem that at
times free verse is no more than an excuse for utter-
ing futilities and ineptitudes that we should not have
dared to express in honest prose." Honest prose in-

deed: an appeal to prejudice! And what about the enormous amount of futile and inept verse in traditional dress? And why "*fixed* metrical base"?

One of the most remarkable developments of modern music has been the constant changing of time and idiom in the course of even a short piece; at each change it is the listener's obligation no less than the musician's to be aware of the change. So with poems, to limit them to a fixed metrical base is asking for trouble. The monstrous effect of standardizing the rhythm of even so ancient a piece as *The Holy Land of Walsinghame* to a fixed metrical base will readily be admitted.

The claim of free verse is that actually each line, not only each stanza or passage, may be subject to a new musical change. Then if the reader does not recognize this change, it is his fault as much as it is the poet's. Admitted, few poets who write free verse have any great sense of musical unity; they cannot often relate the changes to any appreciable unity of structure. But this can be and has been done; and the failure to get more than an episodic interest in a poem is just as marked in poems written in stanzas or couplets as in free verse. Local rhythmic felicities in English poems are, comparatively, far more numerous than poems whose general rhythmic structure commends itself without remarkable local excitements.

Ezra Pound's couplet that Mr. Trevelyan holds out for scorn seems to me clear enough: the long second line expresses admirably the rhythm of a man, in fact, with a steady job and no worries about the future. And again, all "honest prose" is capable of reduction to verse by the simple expedient of letting it fall into short

lines, each capable of a rhythm. Most sermons can be
readily reduced to fairly regular blank verse. Con-
versely, all traditional verse can be written and read
as prose; rhymes, "poetical" inversions, and archaisms
are the only ingredients that give it away at all easily.
But the fact is, that in reading prose or in reading
verse quite a different attitude is adopted by the
reader, and it is this attitude more than the intrinsic
quality of the writing that logically decides whether it
is prose or verse that is being read. Of this I shall
shortly treat.

Meanwhile let us turn from Mr. Trevelyan to Mr.
J. B. S. Haldane, our second prophet. In his remarkable essay on the *Future of Science,* Mr. Haldane,
while lavish of his quotations from poets living and
dead, takes a gloomy view of the poetic scene. He holds
that the decay of Poetry to-day is due to the de-
fective education of the poets; the poet must understand his subject-matter. He affirms that at present not
a single competent poet understands industrial life,
that no poet since Shelley has been up to date in chem-
ical knowledge, and that if we want poets to interpret
physical science, which is, says Mr. Haldane, vastly
more stimulating to the imagination than are the Classics, we must see that our possible poets are instructed
in science and economics.

"Not until our poets are once more drawn from the
educated classes (I speak as a scientist) will they
appeal to the average man by showing him that beauty
in his own life, as Homer and Virgil appealed to the
street urchins who scrawled their verses on the walls
of Pompeii."

There is a wonderful amount of loose thinking

in this short paragraph; the last sentence particularly is brimful of mischief and mis-statement. It reads as a challenge; but accepting it as a professional poet, I must allow Mr. Haldane choice of weapons, which will of course be the scientific method. Then to isolate his facts or assumptions, test them critically in turn, tabulating them with (a), (b), and (c).

(a) *Poetry is in decay because Poetry has lost touch with Science: and Science is the chief interest of the average Englishman to-day.*

My comment is that decay pre-supposes a prime; but Poetry even in its public aspect has never had a prime in which it has been in touch with the *average man,* except in societies where the poet has not yet specialized as a bard, and which are so homogeneous that all duties and pastimes are interchangeable; or in advanced societies where, in a common calamity or triumph, the distinction of class, education, occupation, and so on temporarily disappear, and the consequent poetry has an appeal as wide as it is intense. Decay and prime then are purely local phenomena, occurring in different levels of society, which as highbrow, low-brow, and mezzo-brow have no discoverable literary contact; and even so they are not absolute terms, as one may talk of the prime and decay of roses, or of the human body. Shakespeare's *Tempest* in one sense is the prime of English imaginative drama; but if the prime is to be put at Marlowe's *Tamburlaine* or Kidd's *Spanish Tragedy,* the *Tempest* must be admitted to show signs of the decay of those elements which made the former plays admirable.

Moreover, Science itself is not the interest of the average Englishman any more than Poetry. There is a high-brow science class really interested in its developments, a mezzo-brow science class grateful for the comfort it provides, and a low-brow class more or less indifferent to it, except as its development affects wages and labour. And even within the limits of brow-classification, what does "average" mean? Until a cerebral index can be arranged to decide intelligence as readily as a cephalic index decides race, and until poems can be subjected to a critical analysis as readily as physical substances are to spectral analysis, we cannot scientifically assume that an average can in either case be struck.

(b) *There has been no poet up to date in chemistry since Shelley; our competent poets are also uneducated in the science of economics, and unacquainted with industrial life.*

I don't know in the least what "competent" means to Mr. Haldane. Professional scientists, he says, have no perception of literary form; and since he admits that he is now talking as a scientist, the only meaning that he can rightly attach to "competent" is "well spoken of in literary circles"—and literary circles are notoriously fallible and fickle. Mr. Haldane is sadly misinformed about the education of living English poets. Among the most competent of these, according to the contemporary highbrow valuation, are to be found an architect, a mining engineer, an economic expert, a navvy, a scavenger, a senator, a natural historian, a museum official, a professional soldier, a clerk in the Standard Oil Company, a tramp, a dog-breeder, a peer, a seaman, and a metaphysician. This may be confirmed by the short biographies given in Mr. Louis Untermeyer's *Modern British Poets.* For a poet who has been up to date in Science since Shelley, what about Francis Thompson? At one time it was his chief interest.

> (c) *Really competent poets interpret life: therefore well-educated poets of the future will achieve great poetry chiefly by interpreting Science and Industry, which are the only forms of life at present not suffering from decay.*

When a scientist talks about interpretation then difficulties begin. The nearest he can get to interpretation is a simplification of technical language into something rudely resembling unlearned speech: "Einstein Made Easy," "Mendelism at a Glance." These are interpretations, but they differ from poetic interpretation in respecting the original structure of thought, at any rate, in outline. The scientific method is consistently one of accurate equations and reasonable cross-references, *e.g.,* "The sum of the squares on the smaller sides of a right-angled triangle is equal to the square on the hypotenuse side"; or "water is formed of two parts hydrogen gas to one part of oxygen"; or "the negroid races may be readily distinguished by black skin, broad lips, and curly black hair." When therefore a scientist speaks of a poet "interpreting" industrial life he expects the interpretation to be as simple as Pythagoras' interpretation of the two sides of the right-angled triangle in terms of the hypotenuse, or any other interpretative formula of the physicist or anthropologist. Now, while it may be maintained that legitimate cross references can be made between the images or rhythms of a poem, and the physical and imaginative context in which the poet was when the poem found its form, the scientist cannot expect even in traditional (let alone modern) poems to find any equational formula constant between the poem and its context. The scientific mind gets a rude shock when it learns, for instance, that whereas the original *Royal George* actually did go down, as Thomas Campbell relates, with Admiral Kempenfeldt and his twice four hundred men on board, the original "schooner Hesperus" was not really wrecked at all, but reached Boston harbour with a damaged bowsprit only; the *female lashed to a mast,* which Longfellow noted in his diary of the same storm, belonged to a vessel whose fate was never "interpreted." Again Longfellow's phrase about the old moon having the young moon on her arm is salvage, so to speak, from yet another wreck altogether, that of Sir Patrick Spens' ship on its return from "Norraway over the faem." And Sir Patrick Spens himself, if it comes to that, had historically speaking nothing whatever to do with either of the two voyages which, fused together as one, form the subject of "Sir Patrick Spens," the ballad.

That Mr. Haldane is unaware how well educated many of our "competent poets" are is probably due to their refusal to interpret scientific or industrial experience in the way he intends; and the fact is, purely literary poets are those which appeal most to scientists, as Mr. Haldane's own quotations prove. I don't imagine he would have much use for a modern *Purple Island* in physiology, a *Loves of the Plants* in botany, or a *Polyolbion* in geography; and I haven't noticed him rushing into print with a retraction of his statements on Mr. Noyes' account, whose recent accomplished epic, *The Torch-bearers,* purports to give a history of the triumphs of Science throughout the ages.

But we are forgetting those urchins of Pompeii: Were they really so entranced with the *Iliad* that they could not contain themselves when they saw a blank wall? Surely a simpler explanation would be that they were airing their calligraphic accomplishments, and the first things that occurred to them to put down were lines of verse that had been beaten into them that day at school. On the nursery wall next day as I write is the inspiring reflection in chalk:

> Dame Trot was an old woman with kind blue
> eyes and a white . . .

for I have two urchins learning to read and write, and their School Primer opens with this tale of Dame Trot. And does Mr. Haldane remember the Greek epigram of the doctor who objected to his son learning Homer? He complained that the boy came home with a rigmarole about one Achilles, who sent many valiant souls down to Hades. "What good does that stuff do him? Why, I myself, in the course of my profession, have done as much as Achilles." That doctor anticipated (by two thousand years) Mr. Haldane's view that the Classics were played out, but he was powerless to prevent a number of competent poets who have come since, including Virgil—whose works also the urchins scrawled on the Pompeian walls,—from sucking rich life from even the dry bones of Homer.

What, however, is the state of the verse market today? Among the low-brow public very little verse is read. John Oxenham has had a success, but minute

in proportion with his potential public. The causes
are not obscure. This is the public created by elementary education; elementary education has been a by-
product of industrialism, and is aimed not at a
humaner culture, but at raising the industrial and civic
efficiency of the masses. "Poetry" as it has been taught
in the elementary schools in years gone by has, therefore, not encouraged many children on leaving school
to continue their acquaintance with it; but novels
and stories have formed no part of the curriculum,
and can therefore be read without prejudice. The
mezzo-brow public has had usually two or three years
of schooling more than the low-brow public, and reads
more reputably; it corresponds closely with the middle
class, and is educated for the higher commercial groups
of industrialism.

Open any one of the better monthly magazines of
fiction: each story, though it falls short of literature
with a capital L, is thoroughly workmanlike. It has
a definite point to which it moves easily and economically; the characters, unless the story is definitely a
farce, are convincing; the local colour is carefully
applied. In two cases out of three a considerable
demand is made on the reader's observation and
memory for slight clues to the dénouement occurring
in the first page of the story; and even when the dénouement comes, it comes quietly, perhaps in a single
word, a mere gesture, by which the reader who has
not cultivated the "short-story sense" will be completely baffled. But whereas the art of the short-story
has advanced enormously in the course of the last
thirty years, and the intelligence of the short-story
reader with it, the general run of verse that we find

occasionally sandwiched between short stories in these magazines is as banal, nerveless, and amateur as could well be imagined.

Now the difference is, there is a genuine and sincere demand for the short story on its own account. The question "is it literature?" does not arise. There is no such demand for verse. Its appearance at all in a shilling magazine is only a survival from the days before modern education and the short-story boom when verse was really read and enjoyed by the upper middle classes, the days when crowds queued up for a new canto of *Don Juan,* and a publisher could offer Thomas Moore 3000 guineas advanced royalties for *Lalla Rookh.* The publishing of verse in volume form is similarly a mere window-dressing, a graceful tribute to the past, a sop to literature; but not a business proposition. The mezzo-brow attitude towards the poet has since the boom days become a most unhealthy one; it is like that of modern youth towards its parents, a sentiment that has gradually changed, after a series of disappointments and misunderstandings, from affectionate respect to scorn and indifference.

It is, again, largely because of an educational system which links "poetry" up with geometry and French as a "subject to be done"—and to be "done" in school is to be "done for" in private life—that verse is viewed with as great suspicion by the intelletual middle classes as by their social inferiors. The pulpit has assisted in deepening this suspicion. The poet always, it is thought, has a sinister design on the reader. Either he is trying to put over a spiritual or historical message of some dry sort, or he is claiming genius and its anti-social privileges. In any case he is drawing the reader from the quiet paths of enjoyable reading to the stern mountain of literature, a region from which one customarily returns jaded, if improved, to impress other travellers with a satchel full of poetic specimens, chipped from the hard rocks and carefully ticketed. This mistrust of the poet ensures that, dead poets only being "done" in schools and universities, living poets cannot economically practise the art for a livelihood. Patronage is dead these two hundred years, and the high-brow public is not large enough to support its poets by casual purchase of their wares. The result is that the writing of verse is now largely in the hands of gifted young amateurs, who publish a single book, and then undertake the more serious and remunerative work of prose; of idlers with money who want a literary reputation, and find a series of lyrics less fatiguing to produce than a novel; and of retired judges, ambassadors and heads of colleges and such, who crown their career with a volume of graceful verse,—people, in fact, who encourage rather than dispel the lack of confidence in poetry; so that it is next to impossible for a serious practising poet to get a hearing from the middle-class public, which is numerically large enough to support dozens of poets, and still less from the low-brow public, which could afford to make them all men of wealth.

The public that is acquiring a short-story sense and a film sense and a fast-traffic sense and a radio sense is not a dull public; as it is not a dull public, neither is it a lazy public. The enthusiasm for the cross-word puzzle and for home-made radio sets proves that. The theory that because industrial, commercial, or professional life weighs so heavy, poems, to make any appeal at all, must be narcotic, can no longer stand. On the contrary, the daily round is so routine-ridden that, except where the standard of living is definitely below the poverty line, any stimulant to thought of an adventurous kind is most welcome, though indeed the adventure is bound by economic, ethical, religious, and educational limits. The poetry sense has not been correspondingly cultivated with these other new senses largely because poetry is likely to make demands at variance with the utilitarian system of education and life. As a marketable commodity verse is in a vicious circle: the less it is wanted the duller it gets, and the duller it gets the less it is wanted. A young workman cannot afford to apprentice himself to the poetry trade, which is suffering sadly from inefficiency and dilution. In the short-story trade wages are high. Though the goods are machine-cut, he has the satisfaction of knowing that they meet a genuine demand. The models improve in speed and finish yearly.

But it would be the greatest mistake to push this metaphor farther, to regard poetry as a sort of perpetual coach-building, and fiction as a sort of motor-car industry. True, language and conditions of life have changed so completely in the last fifty years that the greater part of traditional English verse is utterly out of date except to scholars; what was once the pride of the roads we now think of as a lumbering coach. But there is no reason why modern verse should not become to modern prose what the airplane is to the motor-car. Properly handled, poetry has certain mechanical advantages over prose: prose can never rise off the ground; it must keep to the roads or the open country.

The low-brow, mezzo-brow, and the backward part even of the high-brow public does not realize this, and will demand an explanation of mechanical theory, if not a demonstration of practice.

Simply put, the intrinsic virtues of verse are these: its rhythms, rhymes, and texture have an actual toxic effect on the central nervous system. In the resulting condition the imaginative powers are quickened and strengthened, voices are heard, images are called up, and various emotions felt of a far greater intensity than in normal life. This toxic effect is of greater or less strength according to the level of mental functioning obtaining which varies between the more or less sedate thought and the monstrosities of trance or a deep sleep. The soup tablet firm that puts its advertisement into a rough rhyme —

> Why does the Huntsman devour the fox so?
> Because there is nothing for dinner but Broxo,

and the student who masters his lists of facts by help of a rhymed *memoria technica*—"In 1492, Columbus sailed the ocean blue"—are alike aware of this physiological effect verse has on mental receptivity. But besides the greater vividness of image and strengthening of music, the heightening of receptivity and sensitivity that verse properly handled brings, there is another great contribution: that is the awaredness of a whole region of hidden association and implication behind phrases that in prose would be accepted at their face value.

For instance, the adjective "pettifogging" would in prose be construed merely as the conventional insult for a lawyer. If the same adjective were to be used

in poetry qualifying, say a philosopher, there would
be an increased vitality in the word, which there-
upon, for those aware of its etymology, would recall
its connection with Fugger, the great continental mer-
chant banker whose minions, the little fuggers, were
so sly at their trade. The philosopher would thus be
accused of having a commercial mind, and the same
attachment to verbal formula and ancient authority
as a lawyer. At the same time the "fog" syllable would
take on a life of its own; "pettiness" and "fogginess,"
though conceptions not originally bound up with "pettifogging," would colour the lines in which they occurred,
and mate with the hidden associations of the other
words there contained. One of the chief powers of the
poet is in his ability to control these hidden or forgotten associations of words while remaining in the toxic
condition of which I have spoken, so that they interact
in a sense distinct from the face-value of the poem, a
sense which cannot be understood except by those in the
same condition of heightened sensibility. The poet is
able to use both the method of logic and the method
of fantastic thought, which is *sensorial hieroglyphic;*
and what cannot be expressed by either of these means
can be conveyed in the musical side of poetry, the
rhythm, rhyme, and texture, which have not of course
fulfilled their function merely by inducing and maintaining the toxic condition.

This briefly is the power of the art of Poetry as I
understand it; but whether, and if so how soon, the
poetry-sense will appear in a wide circle of readers
is another question. I cannot foresee any immediate
social or political change that will produce it. A great
deal of verse that has been popularly admired in times

past has been admired for reasons unconcerned with the peculiar powers that I have just outlined; it has been admired merely for the elegance of the stories it told, or the morality of its sentiments, or the divine character it professed; and it is doubtful whether, in Europe at least, there has ever been widely spread a poetry-sense which, once the added receptivity induced by verse has been taken into account, has been distinguishable from a prose-sense. Perhaps if there is ever to be a widespread poetry-sense some economic solution should first appear, ending the financial obsession which colours all human relations and qualities to-day. The difficulties of keeping supplies in circulation are now largely smoothed over by standardization of goods, and by standardization of the consumers' minds by education and the press. If supplies became more plentiful, and decentralization of industry and therefore of standardized mentality became possible, poetry of a greater variety, freedom, and intensity might result. For the standardization of mind has achieved the practical result that the immediate and formal characteristics of any matter under examination, usually recognized in terms of value or efficiency, are alone discerned; other latent characteristics, spiritual or personal, are generally suppressed as contributing nothing to the mechanical purpose of life.

Meanwhile there is a small part of society which, being more or less independent of economic fashions, is at liberty to think for itself, and to have adventures in Poetry and Art beyond the bounds which enclose the middle class. This is not to say that the advanced poet is a man of wealth—or even that he is always born into the independent classes; but certainly any support he

gets will be from men of independent means, and if
he wishes to consolidate any success that naïveté has
won for him, he must learn to speak the language of
that class, and become as free from social prejudice as
any of its members; he must become aware of the
history of the art he practises, and in the light of this
history must discover what is strong in his own work
and remain unabashed by the riches of his new experience. This advanced art is a very small part of the
whole artistic output, and if the greatest immediate
good of the greatest numbers is to be considered, cannot be justified. Its practicians are not, as I have said,
paid a living wage, and direct patronage is dead; that
they manage to live at all and find time for their work
is usually due to a certain amount of indirect patronage
enabling them to keep in touch with this independent
society. But this art, freed from any retrograde temptations by the broken market for poetry in the backward
part of society, is alone worth serious discussion, and
has indeed begun to make as great a revolution in the
technique of poetry as, for instance, the one that
came shortly after the Norman Conquest.

Poetry has, in a word, begun to "go round the
corner." The straight street in which English bards
have for centuries walked is no longer so attractive,
now that a concealed turning has been found opening
up a new street or network of streets whose existence
tradition hardly suspected. Traditionalists will even
say of the adventurers: "They have completely disappeared; they are walking in the suburbs of poetry
called alternatively Nonsense or Madness." But it dis-
turbs these traditionalists that the defections from
the highway are numerous, and that the poets con-

cerned cannot be accused of ignorance of the old ways, of mental unbalance in other departments of life, or of insincerity. As a well-dyed traditionalist once myself, I can recall my anger and impatience when reading advanced verse, which seemed to me utterly unlovely and meaningless; anger and impatience still occasionally arise in me when I read, but for a different reason: I dislike poems which, while discarding the old usages, do not make effective use of the new methods at their disposal, and I would be the last to deny that in the present transitional and experimental stage there are writers who have attempted to get notoriety by innovations and obscurities in which they do not themselves believe; but I do not believe that they are very numerous.

This new departure can best be illustrated by an analogy from painting, because painting began the round-the-corner movement before poetry. The traditional view of portrait-painting in England has been that the likeness must be as nearly as possible photographic, and the colours similarly must imitate the natural colours of the body; the pose and dress and background are also expected to be informative of the conditions and circumstances of the character depicted. But portrait-painting, owing largely to the competition of the camera, has taken a new turn; a modern portrait represents hardly anything of what we may call the formal history and geography of the sitter. The rest is a new experience based on the relationship between painter and sitter. Whatever traits of character or circumstance in the sitter have impressed themselves most strongly on the painter form the nucleus of the design—sensorial hieroglyph again—

and the design is harmonious with an untranslatable but none the less effective statement in terms of colour, texture, and form. Statement of what? Of a unique experience to which the painter and sitter equally contribute. Traditional painting assumes that a speaking likeness of the thing painted, the likeness that a smooth pool of water or a good mirror would give, provided that the thing painted is a reputable object and properly posed, is the final goal of art. Traditional poems similarly are, in intention at least, concerned with the translation into smooth verse, direct or allegorical, of selected and not always historical episodes in history, of selected slices of geography, and of idealized moods and characters.

Modern poems and modern paintings do not set out to translate or interpret in the traditional sense, but to provide an independent experience, to which indeed formal history and geography are pre-requisites, and from which they may even be psychologically deduced, but in which they are not important interests in themselves. In giving this new experience it is found necessary to dispense with a great deal of grammatic, logical, and photographic convention; with prejudices about the absolute and permanent value of particular kinds of truth, beauty, virtue, and harmony; and with the restriction order under which caprice, error, and unsolved conflict have hitherto been debarred from giving poems the same reality as life.

I can overhear the comment: "Better that poetry should perish utterly than lose its idealistic character." So recently a pretty quarrel has been picked over an unidealistic though not particularly outrageous public monument in Hyde Park. It is fitting that obscene mutilations should have been committed on it by a party of law students who would stand politically for tradition and photographically idealistic accuracy. It is possible that this particular panel is definitely anti-traditional in conception and invites positive reprisals; but there is this about much unidealistic modern art, that, though untraditional in its technique, character, and end, so it is for the most part untraditional in not claiming superiority for itself over all existing forms. The new methods are not claimed as absolutely better, as all new schools hitherto have been; they are only claimed as different, and as more suited to the moods of the party that professes them. Traditionalism and the new method (which, being a cousin of mathematic Relativity, may therefore borrow the name) do not deny each other any more than post-Euclidian geometry denies the local truth and coherence of Euclidian geometry. The arts or advanced and traditional poetry can live side by side, and the same poet can employ both methods alternatively without self-contradiction.

I may conclude with a few particular statements about this new poetic Relativity. In subject—but to speak of the subject is to speak in terms of translation—so let us say in atmosphere and experience, it has no obvious bounds other than those to which the human mind is always subject.

It adopts the syntactical convention of the thought-level on which it is staged. This may be regular enough, but if the mood reaches a point in fantasia where grammar becomes frayed and snaps, then it can dispense with grammar. In structure it is Protean; there is no architectural preconception; the growth is organic.

In imagery it is only bound by the preference of the individual author for imagery of a particular kind, as that of touch, sound, motion, colour, shape or measurement, and by the conjectural intuition of the reader for remote allusions. One of the most remarkable traits of recent verse has been the qualification of the experience of one sense by that of another. So Miss Sitwell speaks of "clucking flowers," meaning flowers bent down so that they seem like hens clucking; and of "early light creaking down," meaning light moving uncertainly in the early morning, out in angles and squares as it streams across a house, getting such a wooden quality that in its slow movement it may be almost said to creak; "shrill grass," meaning grass so young and green that you would credit it with the piping voice of a fledgling or a child. In diction the mood determines the vocabulary: literary, exotic, archaic, commercial, homely, learned, or disgusting: and, as in Mr. Eliot's *The Waste Land,* each of these vocabularies contributes in turn. In rhyme, rhythm, and texture it is evolving a music as complex and free as instrumental music. In implication, it draws freely on modern psychological research for the exploitation of the hidden symbolism and associations of words employed. In literary allusion it assumes an intimacy with the better-known imaginative writers in all languages. It makes severe demands upon the reader; but the theory that the poet should do all the work and spoon-feed his reader is perhaps one of the greatest weaknesses of traditional verse.

It is at present coloured by the mood of sceptic irony in which the society which approves these new methods lives: irony is the state which succeeds revolt

and despair, as revolt and despair succeed complac-
ency and certainty. But irony is not at all a final mood,
it is more negative than positive in character, and must
yield eventually to a richer and more constructive
life. The art of Poetry is moving into this new life
more slowly than the graphic arts or music, because
it is the art embracing all arts (in the same way Philosophy is the science of sciences; and until mathematics,
theology, biology, and psychology have made and con-
solidated their separate advances, cannot take up its
position in support). Perhaps the reason why advanced
poems are often so confusing to the student to-day
is that in few cases have the musical, the pictorial, and
the intellectual forces kept proper alignment in the
general advance. And as a great many so-called philosophic systems are not strictly philosophy at all, but
generalizations from psychological, theological, and
mathematical or economic theory, so poems self-styled
that specialize in thought, in music, or in imagery, but
in each case to the neglect of the other departments,
are not strictly poems. The actual technique and direction of the art of poetry may suffer the most astounding changes, but to keep its name and continuity it
must always remain a unique art, harmonizing its
contributory arts, and raising no one of these to the
magistracy of its fellows.

THE HOGARTH ESSAYS

HOMAGE TO JOHN DRYDEN

THREE ESSAYS ON POETRY
OF THE SEVENTEENTH
CENTURY

BY

T. S. ELIOT

To George Saintsbury

HOMAGE TO JOHN DRYDEN

PREFACE

THE three essays composing this small book were written several years ago for publication in the "*Times* Literary Supplement," to the editor of which I owe the encouragement to write them, and now the permission to reprint them. Inadequate as periodical criticism, they need still more justification in a book. Some apology, therefore, is required.

My intention had been to write a series of papers on the poetry of the seventeenth and eighteenth centuries: beginning with Chapman and Donne, and ending with Johnson. This forbidden fruit of impossible leisure might have filled two volumes. At best, it would not have pretended to completeness; the subjects would have been restricted by my own ignorance and caprice, but the series would have included Aurelian Townshend and Bishop King, and the authors of "Cooper's Hill" and "The Vanity of Human Wishes," as well as Swift and Pope. That which dissipation interrupts, the infirmities of age come to terminate. One learns to conduct one's life with greater economy: I have abandoned this design in the pursuit of other policies. I have long felt that the poetry of the seventeenth and eighteenth centuries, even much of that of inferior inspiration, possesses an elegance and a dignity absent from the popular and pretentious verse of the Romantic Poets and their successors. To have urged this claim persuasively would have led me indirectly into consideration of politics, education, and theology which I no longer care to approach in this way. I hope that these three papers may in spite of and partly because of their defects preserve in cryptogram certain notions which, if expressed directly, would be destined to immediate obloquy, followed by perpetual oblivion.

T. S. Eliot.

I. JOHN DRYDEN

IF THE prospect of delight be wanting (which alone justifies the perusal of poetry) we may let the reputation of Dryden sleep in the manuals of literature. To those who are genuinely insensible of his genius (and these are probably the majority of living readers of poetry) we can only oppose illustrations of the following proposition: that their insensibility does not merely signify indifference to satire and wit, but lack of perception of qualities not confined to satire and wit and present in the work of other poets whom these persons feel that they understand. To those whose taste in poetry is formed entirely upon the English poetry of the nineteenth century—to the majority—it is difficult to explain or excuse Dryden: the twentieth century is still the nineteenth, although it may in time acquire its own character. The nineteenth century had, like every other, limited tastes and peculiar fashions; and, like every other, it was unware of its own limitations. Its tastes and fashions had no place for Dryden; yet Dryden is one of the tests of a catholic appreciation of poetry.

He is a successor of Jonson, and therefore the descendant of Marlowe; he is the ancestor of nearly all that is best in the poetry of the eighteenth century. Once we have mastered Dryden—and by mastery is meant a full and essential enjoyment, not the enjoyment of a private whimsical fashion—we can extract

whatever enjoyment and edification there is in his contemporaries—Oldham, Denham, or the less remunerative Waller; and still more his successors—not only
Pope, but Phillips, Churchill, Gray, Johnson, Cowper,
Goldsmith. His inspiration is prolonged in Crabbe and
Byron; it even extends, as Mr. van Doren cleverly
points out, to Poe. Even the poets responsible for the
revolt were well acquainted with him: Wordsworth
knew his work, and Keats invoked his aid. We cannot fully enjoy or rightly estimate a hundred years
of English poetry unless we fully enjoy Dryden; and to
enjoy Dryden means to pass beyond the limitations of
the nineteenth century into a new freedom.

> All, all of a piece throughout!
> Thy Chase had a Beast in View;
> Thy Wars brought nothing about;
> Thy Lovers were all untrue.
> 'Tis well an Old Age is out,
> And time to begin a New.

> .   .   .

> The world's great age begins anew,
> The golden years return,
> The earth doth like a snake renew
> Her winter weeds outworn:
> Heaven smiles, and faiths and empires gleam
> Like wrecks of a dissolving dream.

The first of these passages is by Dryden, the second by
Shelley; the second is found in the "Oxford Book of
English Verse," the first is not; yet we might defy
anyone to show that the second is superior on intrin-
sically poetic merit. It is easy to see why the second
should appeal more readily to the nineteenth, and what
is left of the nineteenth under the name of the twentieth, century. It is not so easy to see propriety in an

image which divests a snake of "winter weeds"; and
this is a sort of blemish which would have been noticed
more quickly by a contemporary of Dryden than by a
contemporary of Shelley.

These reflections are occasioned by an admirable
book on Dryden which has appeared at this very turn
of time, when taste is becoming perhaps more fluid
and ready for a new mould.* It is a book which every
practitioner of English verse should study. The consideration is so thorough, the matter so compact, the appreciation so just, temperate, and enthusiastic, and
supplied with such copious and well-chosen extracts
from the poetry, the suggestion of astutely placed
facts leads our thought so far, that there only remain
to mention, as defects which do not detract from its
value, two omissions: the prose is not dealt with, and
the plays are somewhat slighted. What is especially
impressive is the exhibition of the very wide range of
Dryden's work, shown by the quotations of every
species. Everyone knows "MacFlecknoe," and parts
of "Absalom and Achitophel"; in consequence, Dryden
has sunk by the persons he has elevated to distinction
—Shadwell of Settle, Shaftesbury, and Buckingham.
Dryden was much more than a satirist; to dispose of
him as a satirist is to place an obstacle in the way of
our understanding. At all events, we must satisfy ourselves of our definition of the term "satire"; we must
not allow our familiarity with the word to blind us
to differences and refinements; we must not assume
that satire is a fixed type, and fixed to the prosaic,
suited only to prose; we must acknowledge that satire

---

*Mark van Doren, "John Dryden" (New York: Harcourt, Brace
& Howe.

is not the same thing in the hands of two different writers of genius. The connotations of "satire" and of "wit," in short, may be only prejudices of nineteenth-century taste. Perhaps, we think, after reading Mr. van Doren's book, a juster view of Dryden may be given by beginning with some other portion of his work than his celebrated satires; but even here there is much more present, and much more that is poetry, than is usually supposed.

The piece of Dryden's which is the most fun, which is the most sustained display of surprise after surprise of wit from line to line, is "MacFlecknoe." Dryden's method here is something very near to parody; he applies vocabulary, images, and ceremony which arouse epic associations of grandeur, to make an enemy helplessly ridiculous. But the effect, though disastrous for the enemy, is very different from that of the humour which merely belittles, such as the satire of Mark Twain. Dryden continually enhances: he makes his object great, in a way contrary to expectation; and the total effect is due to the transformation of the ridiculous into poetry. As an example may be taken a fine passage plagiarized from Cowley, from lines which Dryden must have marked well, for he quotes them directly in one of his prefaces. Here is Cowley:—

> Where their vast courts the mother-waters keep,
> And undisturbed by moons in silence sleep. . . .
> Beneath the dens where unfledged tempests lie,
> And infant winds their tender voices try.

In "MacFlecknoe" this becomes:—

> Where their vast courts the mother-strumpets keep,
> And undisturbed by watch, in silence sleep.
> Near these, a nursery erects its head,
> Where queens are formed, and future heroes bred;

Where unfledged actors learn to laugh and cry,
Where infant punks their tender voices try,
And little Maximins the gods defy.

The passage from Cowley is by no means despicable
verse. But it is a commonplace description of com-
monly poetic objects; it has not the element of *surprise*
so essential to poetry, and this Dryden provides. A
clever versifier might have written Cowley's lines;
only a poet could have made what Dryden made of
them. It is impossible to dismiss his verses as "prosaic";
turn them into prose and they are transmuted, the
fragrance is gone. The reproach of the prosaic, levelled
at Dryden, rests upon a confusion between the emotions considered to be poetic—which is a matter allowing considerable latitude of fashion—and the
result of personal emotion in poetry; and, in the third
place, there is the emotion *depicted* by the poet in
some kinds of poetry, of which the "Testaments" of
Villon is an example. Again, there are the intellect, the
originality and independence and clarity of what we
vaguely call the poet's "point of view." Our valuation
of poetry, in short, depends upon several considerations, upon the permanent and upon the mutable and
upon the transitory. When we try to isolate the essentially poetic, we bring our pursuit in the end to something insignificant; our standards vary with every poet
whom we consider. All we can hope to do, in the attempt to introduce some order into our preferences,
is to clarify our reasons for finding pleasure in the
poetry that we like.

With regard to Dryden, therefore, we can say this
much. Our taste in English poetry has been largely
founded upon a partial perception of the value of

Shakespeare and Milton, a perception which dwells upon sublimity of theme and action. Shakespeare had a great deal more; he had nearly everything to satisfy our various desires for poetry. The point is that the depreciation or neglect of Dryden is not due to the fact that his work is not poetry, but to a prejudice that the material, the feelings, out of which he built is not poetic. Thus Matthew Arnold observes, in mentioning Dryden and Pope together, that "their poetry is conceived and composed in their wits, genuine poetry is conceived in the soul." Arnold was, perhaps, not altogether the detached critic when he wrote this line; he may have been stirred to a defence of his own poetry, conceived and composed in the soul of a mid-century Oxford graduate. Pater remarks that Dryden—

"Loved to emphasize the distinction between poetry and prose, the protest against their confusion coming with somewhat diminished effect from one whose poetry was so prosaic."

But Dryden was right, and the sentence of Pater is cheap journalism. Hazlitt, who had perhaps the most uninteresting mind of all our distinguished critics, says—

"Dryden and Pope are the great masters of the artificial style of poetry in our language, as the poets of whom I have already treated—Chaucer, Spenser, Shakespeare, and Milton—were of the natural."

In one sentence Hazlitt has committed at least four crimes against taste. It is bad enough to lump Chaucer, Spenser, Shakespeare, and Milton together under the denomination of "natural"; it is bad to commit

Shakespeare to one style only; it is bad to join Dryden and Pope together; but the last absurdity is the contrast of Milton, our greatest master of the *artificial* style, with Dryden, whose *style* (vocabulary, syntax, and order of thought) is in a high degree natural. And what all these objections come to, we repeat, is a repugnance for the material out of which Dryden's poetry is built.

It would be truer to say, indeed, even in the form of the unpersuasive paradox, that Dryden is distinguished principally by his *poetic* ability. We prize him, as we do Mallarmé, for what he made of his material. Our estimate is only in part the appreciation of ingenuity: in the end the result *is* poetry. Much of Dryden's unique merit consists in his ability to make the small into the great, the prosaic into the poetic, the trivial into the magnificent. In this he differs not only from Milton, who required a canvas of the largest size, but from Pope, who required one of the smallest. If you compare any satiric "character" of Pope with one of Dryden, you will see that the method and intention are widely divergent. When Pope alters, he diminishes; he is a master of miniature. The singular skill of his portrait of Addison, for example, in the "Epistle to Arbuthnot," depends upon the justice and reserve, the apparent determination not to exaggerate. The genius of Pope is not for caricature. But the effect of the portraits of Dryden is to transform the object into something greater, as were transformed the verses of Cowley quoted above.

> A fiery soul, which working out its way,
> Fretted the pigmy body to decay:
> And o'er informed the tenement of clay.

These lines are not merely a magnificent tribute. They create the object which they contemplate; the poetry is purer than anything in Pope except the last lines of the "Dunciad." Dryden is in fact much nearer to the master of comic creation than to Pope. As in Jonson, the effect is far from laughter; the comic is the material, the result is poetry. The Civic Guards of Rhodes—

> The country rings around with loud alarms,
> And raw in fields the rude militia swarms;
> Mouths without hands; maintained at vast expense,
> In peace a charge, in war a weak defence;
> Stout once a month they march, a blust'ring band,
> And ever, but in times of need, at hand;
> This was the morn, when issuing on the guard,
> Drawn up in rank and file they stood prepared
> Of seeming arms to make a short essay,
> Then hasten to be drunk, the business of the day.

Sometimes the wit appears as a delicate flavour to the magnificence, as in "Alexander's Feast":—

> Sooth'd with the sound the king grew vain;
> Fought all his battles o'er again;
> And thrice he routed all his foes, and thrice he slew the slain.

The great advantage of Dryden over Milton is that while the former is always in control of his ascent, and can rise or fall at will (and how masterfully, like his own Timotheus, he directs the transitions!), the latter has elected a perch from which he cannot afford to fall, and from which he is in danger of slipping.

> food alike those pure
> Intelligential substances require
> As doth your Rational; and both contain
> Within them every lower faculty

> Of sense, whereby they hear, see, smell, touch, taste,
> Tasting concoct, digest, assimilate,
> And corporeal to incorporeal turn.

Dryden might have made poetry out of that; his translation from Lucretius is poetry. But we have an ingenious example, on which to test our contrast of Dryden and Milton: it is Dryden's "Opera," called "The State of Innocence and Fall of Man," of which Nathaniel Lee neatly says in his preface:—

> Milton did the wealthy mine disclose,
> And rudely cast what you could well dispose:
> He roughly drew, on an old-fashioned ground,
> A chaos, for no perfect world were found,
> Till through the heap, your mighty genius shined.

In the author's preface Dryden acknowledges his debt generously enough:—

"The original being undoubtedly, one of the greatest, most noble, and most sublime poems, which either this age or nation has produced."

The poem begins auspiciously:—

Lucifer: Is this the seat our conqueror has given?
> And this the climate we must change for Heaven?
> These regions and this realm my wars have got;
> This mournful empire is the loser's lot:
> In liquid burnings, or on dry to dwell,
> Is all the sad variety of hell.

It is an early work; it is on the whole a feeble work; it is not deserving of sustained comparison with "Paradise Lost." But "all the sad variety of hell"! Dryden is already stirring; he has assimilated what he could from Milton; and he has shown himself capable of producing as splendid verse.

The capacity for assimilation, and the consequent extent of range, are conspicuous qualities of Dryden. He advanced and exhibited his variety by constant translation; and his translations of Horace, of Ovid, of Lucretius, are admirable. His gravest defects are supposed to be displayed in his dramas, but if these were more read they might be more praised. From the point of view of either the Elizabethan or the French drama they are obviously inferior; but the charge of inferiority loses part of its force if we admit that Dryden was not quite trying to compete with either, but was pursuing a direction of his own. He created no character; and although his arrangements of plot manifest exceptional ingenuity, it is the pure magnificence of diction, of poetic diction, that keeps his plays alive :—

> How I loved
> Witness ye days and nights, and all ye hours,
> That danced away with down upon your feet,
> As all your business were to count my passion.
> One day passed by, and nothing saw but love;
> Another came, and still 'twas only love:
> The suns were wearied out with looking on,
> And I untired with loving.
> I saw you every day and all the day;
> And every day was still but as the first:
> So eager was I still to see you more . . .
>
> While within your arms I lay,
> The world fell mould'ring from my hands each hour.

Such language is pure Dryden: it sounds, in Mr. van Doren's phrase, "like a gong." "All for Love," from which the lines are taken, is Dryden's best play, and this is perhaps the highest reach. In general, he is best in his plays when dealing with situations which do not demand great emotional concentration; when his situation is more trivial, and he can practise his art of making the small great. The back-talk between the Emperor and his Empress Nourmahal, in "Aurungzebe," is admirable purple comedy:—

Emperor: Such virtue is the plague of human life:
A virtuous woman, but a cursèd wife.
In vain of pompous chastity y'are proud:
Virtue's adultery of the tongue, when loud.
I, with less pain, a prostitute could bear,
Than the shrill sound of virtue, virtue hear,
In unchaste wives—
There's yet a kind of recompensing ease:
Vice keeps 'em humble, gives 'em care to please:
But against clamourous virtue, what defence?
It stops our mouths, and gives your noise pretence . . .

What can be sweeter than our native home?
Thither for ease, and soft repose, we come;
Home is the sacred refuge of our life:
Secure from all approaches but a wife.
If thence we fly, the cause admits no doubt:
None but an inmate foe could force us out.
Clamours, our privacies uneasy make:
Birds leave their nests disturbed, and beasts their haunts forsake.

But drama is a mixed form; pure magnificence will not carry it through. The poet who attempts to achieve a play by the single force of the word provokes comparison, however strictly he confine himself to his capacity, with poets of other gifts. Corneille and Racine do not attain their triumphs by magnificence of this sort; they have concentration also, and, in the midst of their phrases, an undisturbed attention to the human soul as they knew it.

Nor is Dryden unchallenged in his supreme ability to make the ridiculous, or the trivial, great.

> Avez-vous observé que maints cercueils de vieilles
> Sont presque aussi petits que celui d'un enfant?

Those lines are the work of a man whose verse is as magnificent as Dryden's, and who could see profounder possibilities in wit, and in violently joined images, than ever were in Dryden's mind. For Dryden, with all his intellect, had a commonplace mind. His powers were, we believe, wider, but no greater, than Milton's; he was confined by boundaries as impassable, though less strait. He bears a curious antithetical resemblance to Swinburne. Swinburne was also a master of words, but Swinburne's words are all suggestions and no denotation; if they suggest nothing, it is because they suggest too much. Dryden's words, on the other hand, are precise, they state immensely, but their suggestiveness is almost nothing.

> That short dark passage to a future state;
> That melancholy riddle of a breath,
> That something, or that nothing, after death.

is a riddle, but not melancholy enough, in Dryden's splendid verse. The question, which has certainly been waiting, may justly be asked: Whether, without this which Dryden lacks, verse can be poetry? What is man to decide what poetry is? Dryden's use of language is not, like that of Swinburne, weakening and demoralizing. Let us take as a final test his elegy upon Oldham, which deserves not to be mutilated:—

Farewell, too little and too lately known,
Whom I began to think and call my own;
For sure our souls were near allied, and thine
Cast in the same poetic mould with mine.
One common note on either lyre did strike,
And knaves and fools we both abhorred alike.
To the same goal did both our studies drive;
The last set out the soonest did arrive.
Thus Nisus fell upon the slippery place,
Whilst his young friend performed and won the race.
O early ripe! to thy abundant store
What could advancing age have added more?
It might (what nature never gives the young)
Have taught the numbers of thy native tongue.
But satire needs not those, and wit will shine
Through the harsh cadence of a rugged line.
A noble error, and but seldom made,
When poets are by too much force betrayed.
Thy generous fruits, though gathered ere their prime,
Still showed a quickness; and maturing time
But mellows what we write to the dull sweets of rhyme.
Once more, hail, and farewell; farewell, thou young,
But ah, too short, Marcellus of our tongue!
Thy brows with ivy and with laurels bound;
But fate and gloomy night encompass thee around.

From the perfection of such an elegy we cannot detract; the lack of nebula is compensated by the satisfying completeness of the statement. Dryden lacked what his master Jonson possessed, a large and unique view of life; he lacked insight, he lacked profundity. But where Dryden fails to satisfy, the nineteenth century does not satisfy us either; and where that century has condemned him, it is itself condemned. In the next revolution of taste it is possible that poets may turn to the study of Dryden. He remains one of those who have set standards for English verse which it is desperate to ignore.

II. THE METAPHYSICAL POETS

By collecting these poems* from the work of a generation more often named than read, and more often read
than profitably studied, Professor Grierson has rendered a service of some importance. Certainly the reader
will meet with many poems already preserved in other
anthologies, at the same time that he discovers poems
such as those of Aurelian Townshend or Lord Herbert
of Cherbury here included. But the function of such an
anthology as this is neither that of Professor Saintsbury's admirable edition of Caroline poets nor that of
the "Oxford Book of English Verse." Mr. Grierson's
book is in itself a piece of criticism, and a provocation of criticism; and we think that he was right in
including so many poems of Donne, elsewhere (though
not in many editions) accessible, as documents in the
case of "metaphysical poetry." The phrase has long
done duty as a term of abuse, or as the label of a quaint
and pleasant taste. The question is to what extent the
so-called metaphysicals formed a school (in our own
time we should say a "movement"), and how far this
so-called school or movement is a digression from the
main current.

Not only is it extremely difficult to define metaphysical poetry, but difficult to decide what poets practise
it and in which of their verses. The poetry of Donne
(to whom Marvell and Bishop King are sometimes
nearer than any of the other authors) is late Elizabethan, its feeling often very close to that of Chapman.

---

*"Metaphysical Lyrics and Poems of the Seventeenth Century":
Donne to Butler. Selected and edited, with an Essay, by Herbert J. C.
Grierson (Oxford: Clarendon Press. London: Milford.).

The "courtly" poetry is derivative from Jonson, who borrowed liberally from the Latin; it expires in the next century with the sentiment and witticism of Prior. There is finally the devotional verse of Herbert, Vaughan, and Crashaw (echoed long after by Christina Rossetti and Francis Thompson); Crashaw, sometimes more profound and less sectarian than the others, has a quality which returns through the Elizabethan period to the early Italians. It is difficult to find any precise use of metaphor, simile, or other conceit, which is common to all the poets and at the same time important enough as an element of style to isolate these poets as a group. Donne, and often Cowley, employ a device which is sometimes considered characteristically "metaphysical"; the elaboration (contrasted with the condensation) of a figure of speech to the farthest stage to which ingenuity can carry it. Thus Cowley develops the commonplace comparison of the world to a chessboard through long stanzas ("To Destiny"), and Donne, with more grace, in "A Valediction," the comparison of two lovers to a pair of compasses. But elsewhere we find, instead of the mere explication of the content of a comparison, a development by rapid association of thought which requires considerable agility on the part of the reader.

> On a round ball
> A workeman that hath copies by, can lay
> An Europe, Afrique, and an Asia,
> And quickly make that, which was nothing, *All,*
>   So doth each teare,
>   Which thee doth weare,
> A globe, yea world by that impression grow,
> Till thy tears mixt with mine doe overflow
> This world, by waters sent from thee, my heaven dissolved so.

Here we find at least two connexions which are not
implicit in the first figure, but are forced upon it by the
poet: from the geographer's globe to the tear, and
the tear to the deluge. On the other hand, some of
Donne's most successful and characteristic effects are
secured by brief words and sudden contrasts—

> A bracelet of bright hair about the bone,

where the most powerful effect is produced by the
sudden contrast of associations of "bright hair" and
of "bone." This telescoping of images and multiplied
association is characteristic of the phrase of some of
the dramatists of the period which Donne knew: not
to mention Shakespeare, it is frequent in Middleton,
Webster, and Tourneur, and is one of the sources of
the vitality of their language.

Johnson, who employed the term "metaphysical
poets," apparently having Donne, Cleveland, and
Cowley chiefly in mind, remarks of them that "the
most heterogeneous ideas are yoked by violence together." The force of this impeachment lies in the failure of the conjunction, the fact that often the ideas are
yoked but not united; and if we are to judge of styles
of poetry by their abuse, enough examples may be
found in Cleveland to justify Johnson's condemnation.
But a degree of heterogeneity of material compelled
into unity by the operation of the poet's mind is omni-
present in poetry. We need not select for illustration
such a line as—

> Notre âme est un trois-mâts cherchant son Icarie;

we may find it in some of the best lines of Johnson himself ("The Vanity of Human Wishes") :—

His fate was destined to a barren strand,
A petty fortress, and a dubious hand;
He left a name at which the world grew pale,
To point a moral, or adorn a tale,

where the effect is due to a contrast of ideas, different
in degree but the same in principle, as that which
Johnson mildly reprehended. And in one of the finest
poems of the age (a poem which could not have been
written in any other age), the "Exequy" of Bishop
King, the extended comparison is used with perfect
success: the idea and the simile become one, in the
passage in which the Bishop illustrates his impatience
to see his dead wife, under the figure of a journey:—

Stay for me there; I will not faile
To meet thee in that hollow Vale.
And think not much of my delay;
I am already on the way,
And follow thee with all the speed
Desire can make, or sorrows breed.
Each minute is a short degree,
And ev'ry houre a step towards thee.
At night when I betake to rest,
Next morn I rise nearer my West
Of life, almost by eight houres sail,
Than when sleep breath'd his drowsy gale. . . .
But heark! My Pulse, like a soft Drum
Beats my approach, tells *Thee* I come;
And slow howere my marches be,
I shall at last sit down by *Thee*.

(In the last few lines there is that effect of terror
which is several times attained by one of Bishop King's
admirers, Edgar Poe.) Again, we may justly take these
quatrains from Lord Herbert's Ode, stanzas which

would, we think, be immediately pronounced to be of
the metaphysical school :—

> So when from hence we shall be gone,
>   And be no more, nor you, nor I,
>   As one another's mystery,
> Each shall be both, yet both but one.
>
> This said, in her up-lifted face,
>   Her eyes, which did that beauty crown,
>   Were like two starrs, that having faln down,
> Look up again to find their place:
>
> While such a moveless silent peace
>   Did seize on their becalmed sense,
>   One would have thought some influence
> Their ravished spirits did possess.

There is nothing in these lines (with the possible exception of the stars, a simile not at once grasped, but
lovely and justified) which fits Johnson's general ob-
servations on the metaphysical poets in his essay on
Cowley. A good deal resides in the richness of association which is at the same time borrowed from and
given to the word "becalmed"; but the meaning is
clear, the language simple and elegant. It is to be
observed that the language of these poets is as a rule
simple and pure; in the verse of George Herbert this
simplicity is carried as far as it can go—a simplicity
emulated without success by numerous modern poets.
The *structure* of the sentences, on the other hand, is
sometimes far from simple, but this is not a vice; it is
a fidelity to thought and feeling. The effect, at its best,
is far less artificial than that of an ode by Gray. And
as this fidelity induces variety of thought and feeling,
so it induces variety of music. We doubt whether, in

the eighteenth century, could be found two poems in
nominally the same metre, so dissimilar as Marvell's
"Coy Mistress" and Crashaw's "Saint Teresa"; the
one producing an effect of great speed by the use of
short syllables, and the other an ecclesiastical solemnity
by the use of long ones :—

> Love, thou art absolute sole lord
> Of life and death.

If so shrewd and sensitive (though so limited) a
critic as Johnson failed to define metaphysical poetry
by its faults, it is worth while to inquire whether we
may not have more success by adopting the opposite
method: by assuming that the poets of the seventeenth
century (up to the Revolution) were the direct and
normal development of the precedent age; and, without prejudicing their case by the adjective "metaphysical," consider whether their virtue was not something permanently valuable, which subsequently disappeared, but ought not to have disappeared. Johnson
has hit, perhaps by accident, on one of their peculiarities, when he observes that "their attempts were always
analytic"; he would not agree that, after the dissociation, they put the material together again in a new
unity.

It is certain that the dramatic verse of the later
Elizabethan and early Jacobean poets expresses a degree of development of sensibility which is not found
in any of the prose, good as it often is. If we except
Marlowe, a man of prodigious intelligence, these
dramatists were directly or indirectly (it is at least a
tenable theory) affected by Montaigne. Even if we
except also Jonson and Chapman, these two were

notably erudite, and were notably men who incorpor-
ated their erudition into their sensibility: their mode
of feeling was directly and freshly altered by their
reading and thought. In Chapman especially there is a
direct sensuous apprehension of thought, or a recreation of thought into feeling, which is exactly what we
find in Donne :—

> in this one thing, all the discipline
> Of manners and of manhood is contained;
> A man to join himself with th' Universe
> In his main sway, and make in all things fit
> One with that All, and go on, round as it;
> Not plucking from the whole his wretched part,
> And into straits, or into nought revert,
> Wishing the complete Universe might be
> Subject to such a rag of it as he;
> But to consider great Necessity.

We compare this with some modern passage :—

> No, when the fight begins within himself,
> A man's worth something. God stoops o'er his head,
> Satan looks up between his feet—both tug—
> He's left, himself, i' the middle; the soul wakes
> And grows. Prolong that battle through his life!

It is perhaps somewhat less fair, though very tempting
(as both poets are concerned with the perpetuation of
love by offspring), to compare with the stanzas already quoted from Lord Herbert's Ode the following
from Tennyson :—

> One walked between his wife and child,
> With measured footfall firm and mild,
> And now and then he gravely smiled.
>   The prudent partner of his blood
>   Leaned on him, faithful, gentle, good,
>   Wearing the rose of womanhood.

And in their double love secure,
The little maiden walked demure,
Pacing with downward eyelids pure.
    These three made unity so sweet,
    My frozen heart began to beat,
    Remembering its ancient heat.

The difference is not a simple difference of degree between poets. It is something which had happened to the
mind of England between the time of Donne or Lord
Herbert of Cherbury and the time of Tennyson and
Browning; it is the difference between the intellectual
poet and the reflective poet. Tennyson and Browning
are poets, and they think; but they do not feel their
thought as immediately as the odour of a rose. A
thought to Donne was an experience; it modified his
sensibility. When a poet's mind is perfectly equipped
for its work, it is constantly amalgamating disparate
experience; the ordinary man's experience is chaotic,
irregular, fragmentary. The latter falls in love, or
reads Spinoza, and these two experiences have nothing
to do with each other, or with the noise of the typewriter or the smell of cooking; in the mind of the
poet these experiences are always forming new wholes.

We may express the difference by the following
theory:—The poets of the seventeenth century, the
successors of the dramatists of the sixteenth, possessed
a mechanism of sensibility which could devour any
kind of experience. They are simple, artificial, difficult, or fantastic, as their predecessors were; no less
nor more than Dante, Guido Cavalcanti, Guinizelli,
or Cino. In the seventeenth century a dissociation of
sensibility set in, from which we have never recovered;
and this dissociation, as is natural, was due to the influence of the two most powerful poets of the century,

Milton and Dryden. Each of these men performed certain poetic functions so magnificently well that the
magnitude of the effect concealed the absence of others.
The language went on and in some respects improved;
the best verse of Collins, Gray, Johnson, and even
Goldsmith satisfies some of our fastidious demands
better than that of Donne or Marvell or King. But
while the language became more refined, the feeling
became more crude. The feeling, the sensibility, expressed in the "Country Churchyard" (to say nothing
of Tennyson and Browning) is cruder than that in the
"Coy Mistress."

The second effect of the influence of Milton and
Dryden followed from the first, and was therefore slow
in manifestation. The sentimental age began early in
the eighteenth century, and continued. The poets re-
volted against the ratiocinative, the descriptive; they
thought and felt by fits, unbalanced; they reflected.
In one or two passages of Shelley's "Triumph of
Life," in the second "Hyperion," there are traces of
a struggle toward unification of sensibility. But Keats
and Shelley died, and Tennyson and Browning rumi-
nated.

After this brief exposition of a theory—too brief,
perhaps, to carry conviction—we may ask, what would
have been the fate of the "metaphysical" had the current of poetry descended in a direct line from them, as
it descended in a direct line to them? They would not,
certainly, be classified as metaphysical. The possible
interests of a poet are unlimited; the more intelligent
he is the better; the more intelligent he is the more
likely that he will have interests: our only condition is
that he turn them into poetry, and not merely medi-

tate on them poetically. A philosophical theory which
has entered into poetry is established, for its truth or
falsity in one sense ceases to matter, and its truth in
another sense is proved. The poets in question have,
like other poets, various faults. But they were, at best,
engaged in the task of trying to find the verbal equivalent for states of mind and feeling. And this means
both that they are more mature, and that they wear
better, than later poets of certainly not less literary
ability.

It is not a permanent necessity that poets should be
interested in philosophy, or in any other subject. We
can only say that it appears likely that poets in our
civilization, as it exists at present, must be *difficult*.
Our civilization comprehends great variety and complexity, and this variety and complexity, playing upon
a refined sensibility, must produce various and complex
results. The poet must become more and more comprehensive, more allusive, more indirect, in order to
force, to dislocate if necessary, language into his meaning. (A brilliant and extreme statement of this view,
with which it is not requisite to associate oneself, is
that of M. Jean Epstein, "La Poésie d'aujourd-hui.")
Hence we get something which looks very much like
the conceit—we get, in fact, a method curiously similar to that of the "metaphysical poets," similar also
in its use of obscure words and of simple phrasing.

> Ô géraniums diaphanes, guerroyeurs sortilèges,
> Sacrilèges monomanes!
> Emballages, dévergondages, douches! Ô pressoirs
> Des vendanges des grands soirs!
> Layettes aux abois,
> Thyrses au fond des bois!

Transfusions, représailles,
Relevailles, compresses et l'éternel potion,
Angélus! n'en pouvoir plus
De débâcles nuptiales! de débâcles nuptiales!

The same poet could write also simply :—

Elle est bien loin, elle pleure,
Le grand vent se lamente aussi . . .

Jules Laforgue, and Tristan Corbière in many of his
poems, are nearer to the "school of Donne" than any
modern English poet. But poets more classical than
they have the same essential quality of transmuting
ideas into sensations, of transforming an observation
into a state of mind.

Pour l'enfant, amoureux de cartes et d'estampes,
L'univers est égal à son vaste appétit.
Ah, que le monde est grand à la clarté des lampes!
Aux yeux du souvenir que le monde est petit!

In French literature the great master of the seventeenth century—Racine—and the great master of the
nineteenth—Baudelaire—are more like each other
than they are like anyone else. The greatest two
masters of diction are also the greatest two psychologists, the most curious explorers of the soul. It is
interesting to speculate whether it is not a misfortune
that two of the greatest masters of diction in our language, Milton and Dryden, triumph with a dazzling
disregard of the soul. If we continued to produce Mil-
tons and Drydens it might not so much matter, but as
things are it is a pity that English poetry has remained
so incomplete. Those who object to the "artificiality"

of Milton or Dryden sometimes tell us to "look into our hearts and write." But that is not looking deep enough; Racine or Donne looked into a good deal more than the heart. One must look into the cerebral cortex, the nervous system, and the digestive tracts.

May we not conclude, then, that Donne, Crashaw, Vaughan, Herbert and Lord Herbert, Marvell, King, Cowley at his best, are in the direct current of English poetry, and that their faults should be reprimanded by this standard rather than coddled by antiquarian affection? They have been enough praised in terms which are implicit limitations because they are "metaphysical" or "witty," "quaint" or "obscure," though at their best they have not these attributes more than other serious poets. On the other hand, we must not reject the criticism of Johnson (a dangerous person to disagree with) without having mastered it, without having assimilated the Johnsonian canons of taste. In reading the celebrated passage in his essay on Cowley we must remember that by wit he clearly means something more serious than we usually mean to-day; in his criticism of their versification we must remember in what a narrow discipline he was trained, but also how well trained; we must remember that Johnson tortures chiefly the chief offenders, Cowley and Cleveland. It would be a fruitful work, and one requiring a substantial book, to break up the classification of Johnson (for there has been none since) and exhibit these poets in all their difference of kind and of degree, from the massive music of Donne to the faint, pleasing tinkle of Aurelian Townshend—whose "Dialogue between a Pilgrim and Time" is one of the few regrettable omissions from this excellent anthology.

III. ANDREW MARVELL

THE tercentenary of the former member for Hull
deserves not only the celebration proposed by that
favoured borough, but a little serious reflection upon
his writing. That is an act of piety, which is very different from the resurrection of a deceased reputation.
Marvell has stood high for some years; his best poems
are not very many, and not only must be well known,
from the "Golden Treasury" and the "Oxford Book
of English Verse," but must also have been enjoyed by
numerous readers. His grave needs neither rose nor
rue nor laurel; there is no imaginary justice to be done;
we may think about him, if there be need for thinking,
for our own benefit, not his. To bring the poet back
to life—the great, the perennial, task of criticism—is
in this case to squeeze the drops of the essence of two
or three poems; even confining ourselves to these, we
may find some precious liquor unknown to the present
age. Not to determine rank, but to isolate this quality,
is the critical labour. The fact that of all Marvell's
verse, which is itself not a great quantity, the really
valuable part consists of a very few poems indicates
that the unknown quality of which we speak is probably a literary rather than a personal quality; or, more
truly, that it is a quality of a civilization, of a traditional habit of life. A poet like Donne, or like
Baudelaire or Laforgue, may almost be considered the
inventor of an attitude, a system of feeling or of
morals. Donne is difficult to analyse: what appears at
one time a curious personal point of view may at an-

other time appear rather the precise concentration of
a kind of feeling diffused in the air about him. Donne
and his shroud, the shroud and his motive for wearing
it, are inseparable, but they are not the same thing.
The seventeenth century sometimes seems for more
than a moment to gather up and to digest into its art
all the experience of the human mind which (from the
same point of view) the later centuries seem to have
been partly engaged in repudiating. But Donne would
have been an individual at any time and place; Marvell's best verse is the product of European, that is to
say Latin, culture.

Out of that high style developed from Marlowe
through Jonson (for Shakespeare does not lend himself to these genealogies) the seventeenth century separated two qualities: wit and magniloquence. Neither
is as simple or as apprehensible as its name seems to
imply, and the two are not in practice antithetical;
both are conscious and cultivated, and the mind which
cultivates one may cultivate the other. The actual
poetry, of Marvell, of Cowley, of Milton, and of
others, is a blend in varying proportions. And we must
be on guard not to employ the terms with too wide a
comprehension; for like the other fluid terms with
which literary criticism deals, the meaning alters with
the age, and for precision we must rely to some degree
upon the literacy and good taste of the reader. The
wit of the Caroline poets is not the wit of Shakespeare,
and it is not the wit of Dryden, the great master of
contempt, or of Pope, the great master of hatred, or
of Swift, the great master of disgust. What is meant
is something which is a common quality to the songs in

"Comus" and Cowley's Anacreontics and Marvell's Horatian Ode. It is more than a technical accomplishment, or the vocabulary and syntax of an epoch; it is, what we have designated tentatively as wit, a tough reasonableness beneath the slight lyric grace. You cannot find it in Shelley or Keats or Wordsworth; you cannot find more than an echo of it in Landor; still less in Tennyson or Browning; and among contemporaries Mr. Yeats is an Irishman and Mr. Hardy is a modern Englishman—that is to say, Mr. Hardy is without it and Mr. Yeats is outside of the tradition altogether. On the other hand, as it certainly exists in Lafontaine, there is a large part of it in Gautier. And of the magniloquence, the deliberate exploitation of the possibilities of magnificence in language which Milton used and abused, there is also use and even abuse in the poetry of Baudelaire.

Wit is not a quality that we are accustomed to associate with "Puritan" literature, with Milton or with Marvell. But if so, we are at fault partly in our conception of wit and partly in our generalizations about the Puritans. And if the wit of Dryden or of Pope is not the only kind of wit in the language, the rest is not merely a little merriment or a little levity or a little impropriety or a little epigram. And, on the other hand, the sense in which a man like Marvell is a "Puritan" is restricted. The persons who opposed Charles I and the persons who supported the Commonwealth were not all of the flock of Rabbi Zeal-of-the-land Busy or the United Grand Junction Ebenezer Temperance Association. Many of them were gentlemen of the time who merely believed, with considerable show of reason, that government by a Parliament of gentlemen was better than government by a Stuart; though they were, to that extent, Liberal Practitioners, they could hardly foresee the tea-meeting and the Dissidence of Dissent. Being men of education and culture, even of travel, some of them were exposed to that spirit of the age which was coming to be the French spirit of the age. This spirit, curiously enough, was quite opposed to the tendencies latent or the forces active in Puritanism; the contest does great damage to the poetry of Milton; Marvell, an active servant of the public, but a lukewarm partisan, and a poet on a smaller scale, is far less injured by it. His line on the statue of Charles II, "It is such a King as no chisel can mend," may be set off against his criticism of the Great Rebellion: "Men . . . ought and might have trusted the King." Marvell, therefore, more a man of the century than a Puritan, speaks more clearly and unequivocally with the voice of his literary age than does Milton.

This voice speaks out uncommonly strong in "The Coy Mistress." The theme is one of the great traditional commonplaces of European literature. It is the theme of "O mistress mine," of "Gather ye rosebuds," of "Go, lovely rose"; it is in the savage austerity of Lucretius and the intense levity of Catullus. Where the wit of Marvell renews the theme is in the variety and order of the images. In the first of the three paragraphs Marvell plays with a fancy which begins by pleasing and leads to astonishment.

> Had we but world enough and time,
> This coyness, lady, were no crime,
> 　　　　. . . I would
> Love you ten years before the Flood,

> And you should, if you please, refuse
> Till the conversion of the Jews;
> My vegetable love should grow
> Vaster than empires and more slow. . . .

We notice the high speed, the succession of concentrated images, each magnifying the original fancy.
When this process has been carried to the end and
summed up, the poem turns suddenly with that surprise
which has been one of the most important means of
poetic effect since Homer :—

> But at my back I always hear
> Time's wingèd chariot hurrying near,
> And yonder all before us lie
> Deserts of vast eternity.

A whole civilization resides in these lines :—

> Pallida Mors æqua pulsat pede pauperumb tabernas,
> Regumque turris. . . .

And not only Horace but Catullus himself :—

> Nobis, cum semel occidit brevis lux,
> Nox est perpetua una dormienda.

The verse of Marvell has not the grand reverberation
of Catullus's Latin; but the image of Marvell is certainly more comprehensive and penetrates greater
depths than Horace's.

A modern poet, had he reached the height, would
very likely have closed on this moral reflection. But the
three strophes of Marvell's poem have something like
a syllogistic relation to each other. After a close approach to the mood of Donne,

> then worms shall try
> That long-preserved virginity . . .
> The grave's a fine and private place,
> But none, I think, do there embrace,

the conclusion,

> Let us roll all our strength and all
> Our sweetness up into one ball,
> And tear our pleasures with rough strife,
> Through the iron gates of life.

It will hardly be denied that this poem contains wit; but it may not be evident that this wit forms the crescendo and diminuendo of a scale of great imaginative power. The wit is not only combined with, but fused into, the imagination. We can easily recognize a witty fancy in the successive images ("my *vegetable* love," "till the conversion of the Jews"), but this fancy is not indulged, as it sometimes is by Cowley or Cleveland, for its own sake. It is structural decoration of a serious idea. In this it is superior to the fancy of "L'Allegro," "Il Penseroso," or the lighter and less successful poems of Keats. In fact, this alliance of levity and seriousness (by which the seriousness is intensified) is a characteristic of the sort of wit we are trying to identify. It is found in

> Le squelette était invisible
> Au temps heureux de l'art païen!

of Gautier, and in the *dandysme* of Baudelaire and Laforgue. It is in the poem of Catullus which has been quoted, and in the variation by Ben Jonson :—

> Cannot we deceive the eyes
> Of a few poor household spies?

> 'Tis no sin love's fruits to steal,
> But that sweet sin to reveal,
> To be taken, to be seen,
> These have sins accounted been.

It is in Propertius and Ovid. It is a quality of a sophisticated literature; a quality which expands in English literature just at the moment before the English mind altered; it is not a quality which we should expect Puritanism to encourage. When we come to Gray and Collins, the sophistication remains only in the language, and has disappeared from the feeling. Gray and Collins were masters, but they had lost that hold on human values, that firm grasp of human experience, which is a formidable achievement of the Elizabethan and Jacobean poets. This wisdom, cynical perhaps but untired (in Shakespeare, a terrifying clairvoyance), leads toward, and is only completed by, the religious comprehension; it leads to the point of the *Ainsi tout leur a craqué dans la main* of Bouvard and Pécuchet.

The difference between imagination and fancy, in view of this poetry of wit, is a very narrow one. Obviously, an image which is immediately and unintentionally ridiculous is merely a fancy. In the poem "Upon Appleton House," Marvell falls in with one of these undesirable images, describing the attitude of the house toward its master:—

> Yet thus the laden house does sweat,
> And scarce endures the master great;
> But, where he comes, the swelling hall
> Stirs, and the square grows spherical;

which, whatever its intention, is more absurd than it was intended to be. Marvell also falls into the even commoner error of images which are over-developed or distracting; which support nothing but their own misshapen bodies:—

> And now the salmon-fishers moist
> Their leathern boats begin to hoist;
> And, like Antipodes in shoes,
> Have shod their heads in their canoes.

Of this sort of image a choice collection may be found in Johnson's "Life of Cowley." But the images in "The Coy Mistress" are not only witty, but satisfy the elucidation of Imagination given by Coleridge:—

> "This power . . . reveals itself in the balance or reconcilement of opposite or discordant qualities: of sameness, with difference; of the general, with the concrete; the idea with the image; the individual with the representative; the sense of novelty and freshness with old and familiar objects; a more than usual state of emotion with more than usual order; judgment ever awake and steady self-possession with enthusiasm and feeling profound or vehement. . . ."

Coleridge's statement applies also to the following verses, which are selected because of their similarity, and because they illustrate the marked caesura which Marvell often introduces in a short line:—

> The tawny mowers enter next,
> Who seem like Israelites to be
> Walking on foot through a green sea.
>
> And now the meadows fresher dyed,
> Whose grass, with moister colour dashed,
> Seems as green silks but newly washed.
>
> He hangs in shades the orange bright,
> Like golden lamps in a green night.

> Annihilating all that's made
> To a green thought in a green shade.
>
> Had it lived long, it would have been
> Lilies without, roses within.

The whole poem, from which the last of these quotations is drawn ("The Nymph and the Fawn"), is built upon a very slight foundation, and we can imagine what some of our modern practitioners of slight themes would have made of it. But we need not descend to an invidious contemporaneity to point the difference. Here are six lines from "The Nymph and the Fawn":—

> I have a garden of my own,
> But so with roses overgrown
> And lilies, that you would it guess
> To be a little wilderness;
> And all the spring-time of the year
> It only lovèd to be there.

And here are five lines from "The Nymph's Song to Hylas" in the "Life and Death of Jason," by William Morris:—

> I know a little garden close
> Set thick with lily and red rose.
> Where I would wander if I might
> From dewy dawn to dewy night,
> And have one with me wandering.

So far the resemblance is more striking than the difference, although we might just notice the vagueness of allusion in the last line to some indefinite person, form, or phantom, compared with the more explicit reference of emotion to object which we should expect from Marvell. But in the latter part of the poem Morris divaricates widely:—

Yet tottering as I am, and weak,
Still have I left a little breath
To seek within the jaws of death
An entrance to that happy place;
To seek the unforgotten face
Once seen, once kissed, once reft from me
Anigh the murmuring of the sea.

Here the resemblance, if there is any, is to the latter
part of "The Coy Mistress." As for the difference, it
could not be more pronounced. The effect of Morris's
charming poem depends upon the mistiness of the feeling and the vagueness of its object; the effect of Marvell's upon its bright, hard precision. And this precision is not due to the fact that Marvell is concerned
with cruder or simpler or more carnal emotions. The
emotion of Morris is not more refined or more spiritual; it is merely more vague: if anyone doubts whether
the more refined or spiritual emotion can be precise, he
should study the treatment of the varieties of discar-
nate emotion in the "Paradiso." A curious result of the
comparison of Morris's poem with Marvell's is that
the former, though it appears to be more serious, is
found to be the slighter; and Marvell's "Nymph and
the Fawn," appearing more slight, is the more serious.

So weeps the wounded balsam; so
The holy frankincense doth flow;
The brotherless Heliades
Melt in such amber tears as these.

These verses have the suggestiveness of true poetry;
and the verses of Morris, which are nothing if not an
attempt to suggest, really suggest nothing; and we
are inclined to infer that the suggestiveness is the aura
around a bright clear centre, that you cannot have the

aura alone. The day-dreamy feeling of Morris is essentially a slight thing; Marvell takes a slight affair, the feeling of a girl for her pet, and gives it a connection with that inexhaustible and terrible nebula of emotion which surrounds all our exact and practical passions and mingles with them. Again, Marvell does this in a poem which, because of its formal pastoral machinery, may appear a trifling object:—

> *Clorinda*: Near this, a fountain's liquid bell
> Tinkles within the concave shell.
>
> *Damon:* Might a soul bathe there and be clean,
> Or slake its drought?

where we find that a metaphor has suddenly rapt us to the image of spiritual purgation. There is here the element of *surprise,* as when Villon says:—

> Necessité faict gens mesprendre
> Et faim saillir le loup des boys,

the surprise which Poe considered of the highest importance, and also the restraint and quietness of tone which make the surprise possible. And in the verses of Marvell which have been quoted there is the making the familiar strange, and the strange familiar, which Coleridge attributed to good poetry.

The effort to construct a dream-world, which alters English poetry so greatly in the nineteenth century, a dream-world utterly different from the visionary realities of the Vita Nuova or of the poetry of Dante's contemporaries, is a problem of which various explanations may no doubt be found; in any case, the result makes a poet of the nineteenth century, of the

same size as Marvell, a more trivial and less serious
figure. Marvell is no greater personality than William
Morris, but he had something much more solid behind
him: he had the vast and penetrating influence of Ben
Jonson. Jonson never wrote anything so pure as Marvell's Horatian Ode; but this ode has that same quality
of wit which was diffused over the whole Elizabethan
product and concentrated in the work of Jonson. And,
as was said before, this wit which pervades the poetry
of Marvell is more Latin, more refined, than anything
that succeeded it. The great danger, as well as the
great interest and excitement, of English prose and
verse, compared with French, is that it permits and
justifies an exaggeration of particular qualities to the
exclusion of others. Dryden was great in wit, as Milton
in magniloquence; but the former, by isolating this
quality and making it by itself into great poetry, and
the latter, by coming to dispense with it altogether,
may perhaps have injured the language. In Dryden
wit becomes almost fun, and thereby loses some contact with reality; becomes pure fun, which French wit
almost never is.

> The midwife placed her hand on his thick skull,
> With this prophetic blessing: *Be thou dull.*

> A numerous host of dreaming saints succeed,
> Of the true old enthusiastic breed.

This is audacious and splendid; it belongs to satire
beside which Marvell's Satires are random babbling;
but it is perhaps as exaggerated as—

> Oft he seems to hide his face,
> But unexpectedly returns,
> And to his faithful champion hath in place

> Bore witness gloriously; whence Gaza mourns,
> And all that band them to resist
> His uncontrollable intent.

How oddly the sharp Dantesque phrase "whence Gaza mourns" springs out from the brilliant but ridiculous contortions of Milton's sentence!

> Who from his private gardens, where
> He lived reservèd and austere,
>   (As if his highest plot
>   To plant the bergamot)

> Could by industrious valour climb
> To ruin the great work of Time,
>   And cast the kingdoms old
>   Into another mold;

> .   .   .   .

> The Pict no shelter now shall find
> Within his parti-coloured mind,
>   But, from this valour sad,
>   Shrink underneath the plaid:

There is here an equipoise, a balance and proportion of tones, which, while it cannot raise Marvell to the level of Dryden or Milton, extorts an approval which these poets do not receive from us, and bestows a pleasure at least different in kind from any they can often give. It is what makes Marvell a classic; or classic in a sense in which Gray and Collins are not; for the latter, with all their accredited purity, are comparatively poor in shades of feeling to contrast and unite.

We are baffled in the attempt to translate the quality indicated by the dim and antiquated term "wit" into the equally unsatisfactory nomenclature of our own time. Even Cowley is only able to define it by negatives:—

> Comely in thousand shapes appears;
>   Yonder we saw it plain; and here 'tis now,
>   Like spirits in a place, we know not how.

It has passed out of our critical coinage altogether, and no new term has been struck to replace it; the quality seldom exists, and is never recognized.

> In a true piece of Wit all things must be
>   Yet all things there agree;
> As in the Ark, join'd without force or strife,
> All creatures dwelt, all creatures that had life.
>   Or as the primitive forms of all
>   (If we compare great things with small)
> Which, without discord or confusion, lie
> In that strange mirror of the Deity.

So far Cowley has spoken well. But if we are to attempt even no more than Cowley, we, placed in a retrospective attitude, must risk much more than anxious generalizations. With our eye still on Marvell, we can say that wit is not erudition; it is sometimes stifled by erudition, as in much of Milton. It is not cynicism, though it has a kind of toughness which may be confused with cynicism by the tender-minded. It is confused with erudition because it belongs to an educated mind, rich in generations of experience; and it is confused with cynicism because it implies a constant inspection and criticism of experience. It involves, probably, a recognition, implicit in the expression of every experience, of other kinds of experience which are possible, which we find as clearly in the greatest as in poets like Marvell. Such a general statement may seem to take us a long way from "The Nymph and the Fawn," or even from the Horatian Ode; but it is perhaps justified by the desire to account for that precise taste of

Marvell's which finds for him the proper degree of
seriousness for every subject which he treats. His
errors of taste, when he trespasses, are not sins against
this virtue; they are conceits, distended metaphors and
similes, but they never consist in taking a subject too
seriously or too lightly. This virtue of wit is not a
peculiar quality of minor poets, or of the minor poets
of one age or of one school; it is an intellectual quality
which perhaps only becomes noticeable by itself, in the
work of lesser poets. Furthermore, it is absent from
the work of Wordsworth, Shelley, and Keats, on whose
poetry nineteenth-century criticism has unconsciously
been based. To the best of their poetry wit is irrelevant :—

> Art thou pale for weariness
> Of climbing heaven and gazing on the earth,
> Wandering companionless
> Among the stars that have a different birth,
> And ever changing, like a joyless eye,
> That finds no object worth its constancy?

We should find it difficult to draw any useful comparison between these lines of Shelley and anything by
Marvell. But later poets, who would have been the
better for Marvell's quality, were without it; even
Browning seems oddly immature, in some way, beside
Marvell. And nowadays we find occasionally good
irony, or satire, which lack wit's internal equilibrium,
because their voices are essentially protests against
some outside sentimentality or stupidity; or we find
serious poets who are afraid of acquiring wit, lest they
lose intensity. The quality which Marvell had, this
modest and certainly impersonal virtue—whether we
call it wit or reason, or even urbanity—we have pat-

ently failed to define. By whatever name we call it, and however we define that name, it is something precious and needed and apparently extinct; it is what should preserve the reputation of Marvell. *C'était une belle âme, comme on ne fait plus à Londres.*

THE HOGARTH ESSAYS

HENRY JAMES AT WORK

BY

THEODORA BOSANQUET

HENRY JAMES AT WORK

I

I KNEW nothing of Henry James beyond the revelation of his novels and tales before the summer of 1907. Then, as I sat in a top-floor office near Whitehall one August morning, compiling a very full index to the Report of the Royal Commission on Coast Erosion, my ears were struck by the astonishing sound of passages from *The Ambassadors* being dictated to a young typist. Neglecting my Blue-book, I turned round to watch the operator ticking off sentences which seemed to be at least as much of a surprise to her as they were to me. When my bewilderment had broken into a question, I learnt that Henry James was on the point of coming back from Italy, that he had asked to be provided with an amanuensis, and that the lady at the typewriter was making acquaintance with his style. Without any hopeful design of supplanting her, I lodged an immediate petition that I might be allowed the next opportunity of filling the post, supposing she should ever abandon it. I was told, to my amazement, that I need not wait. The established candidate was not enthusiastic about the prospect before her, was even genuinely relieved to look in another direction. If I set about practising typewriting on a Remington machine at once, I could be interviewed by Henry James as soon as he arrived in London. Within an hour I had begun work on the typewriter. By the time he was ready to interview me, I could tap out paragraphs of *The Ambassadors* at quite a fair speed.

He asked no questions at that interview about my speed on a typewriter or about anything else. The friend to whom he had applied for an amanuensis had told him that I was sufficiently the right young woman for his purpose and he relied on her word. He had, at the best, little hope of any young woman beyond docility. We sat in armchairs on either side of a fireless grate while we observed each other. I suppose he found me harmless and I know that I found him overwhelming. He was much more massive than I had expected, much broader and stouter and stronger. I remembered that someone had told me he used to be taken for a sea-captain when he wore a beard, but it was clear that now, with the beard shaved away, he would hardly have passed for, say, an admiral, in spite of the keen gray eyes set in a face burned to a colourable sea-faring brown by the Italian sun. No successful naval officer could have afforded to keep that sensitive mobile mouth. After the interview I wondered what kind of impression one might have gained from a chance encounter in some such observation cell as a railway carriage. Would it have been possible to fit him confidently into any single category? He had reacted with so much success against both the American accent and the English manner that he seemed only doubtfully Anglo-Saxon. He might perhaps have been some species of disguised cardinal, or even a Roman nobleman amusing himself by playing the part of a Sussex squire. The observer could at least have guessed that any part

he chose to assume would be finely conceived and generously played, for his features were all cast in the
classical mould of greatness. He might very well have
been a merciful Cæsar or a benevolent Napoleon, and
a painter who worked at his portrait a year or
two later was excusably reminded of so many illustrious makers of history that he declared it to be a
hard task to isolate the individual character of the
the model.

If the interview was overwhelming, it had none of
the usual awkwardness of such curious conversations.
Instead of critical angles and disconcerting silences,
there were only benign curves and ample reassurances.
There was encouraging gaiety in an expanse of bright
check waistcoat. He invited me to ask any questions
I liked, but I had none to ask. I wanted nothing but
to be allowed to go to Rye and work his typewriter.
He was prepared, however, with his statements and,
once I was seated opposite to him, the strong, slow
stream of his deliberate speech played over me without
ceasing. He had it on his mind to tell me the conditions of life and labour at Rye, and he unburdened
himself fully, with numberless amplifications and quali-
fications but without any real break. It would be a dull
business, he warned me, and I should probably find Rye
a dull place. He told me of rooms in Mermaid Street,
"very simple, rustic and antique—but that is the case
for everything near my house, and this particular little
old house is very near mine, and I know the good
woman for kind and worthy and a convenient cook
and in short——." It was settled at once that I should
take the rooms, that I should begin my duties in
October.

II

Since winter was approaching, Henry James had begun to use a panelled, green-painted room on the upper floor of Lamb House for his work. It was known simply as the green room. It had many advantages as a winter workroom, for it was small enough to be easily warmed and a wide south window caught all the morning sunshine. The window overhung the smooth, green lawn, shaded in summer by a mulberry tree, surrounded by roses and enclosed behind a tall, brick wall. It never failed to give the owner pleasure to look out of this window at his charming English garden where he could watch his English gardener digging the flower-beds or mowing the lawn or sweeping up fallen leaves. There was another window for the afternoon sun, looking towards Winchelsea and doubly glazed against the force of the westerly gales. Three high bookcases, two big writing-desks and an easy chair filled most of the space in the green room, but left enough clear floor for a restricted amount of the pacing exercise that was indispensable to literary composition. On summer days Henry James liked better to work in the large "garden room" which gave him a longer stretch for perambulation and a window overlooking the cobbled street that curved up the hill past his door. He liked to be able to relieve the tension of a difficult sentence by a glance down the street; he enjoyed hailing a passing friend or watching a motor-car pant up the sharp little slope. The sight of one of these vehicles could be counted on to draw from him a vigorous outburst of amazement, admiration, or horror for the complications of an age that produced such efficient monsters for gobbling protective distance.

The business of acting as a medium between the spoken and the typewritten word was at first as alarming as it was fascinating. The most handsome and expensive typewriters exercise as vicious an influence as any others over the spelling of the operator, and the new pattern of a Remington machine which I found installed offered a few additional problems. But Henry James's patience during my struggles with that baffling mechanism was unfailing—he watched me helplessly, for he was one of the few men without the smallest pretension to the understanding of a machine—and he was as easy to spell from as an open dictionary. The experience of years had evidently taught him that it was not safe to leave any word of more than one syllable to luck. He took pains to pronounce every pronounceable letter, he always spelt out words which the ear might confuse with others, and he never left a single.punctuation mark unuttered, except sometimes that necessary point, the full stop. Occasionally, in a low "aside" he would interject a few words for the enlightenment of the amanuensis, adding, for instance, after spelling out "The Newcomes," that the words were the title of a novel by one Thackeray.

The practice of dictation was begun in the nineties. By 1907 it was a confirmed habit, its effects being easily recognizable in his style, which became more and more like free, involved, unanswered talk. "I know," he once said to me, "that I'm too diffuse when I'm dictating." But he found dictation not only an easier but a more inspiring method of composing than writing with his own hand, and he considered that the gain in expression more than compensated for any loss of concision. The spelling out of the words, the indication of commas, were scarcely felt as a drag on the movement of his thought. "It all seems," he once explained, "to be so much more effectively and unceasingly *pulled* out of me in speech than in writing." Indeed, at the time when I began to work for him, he had reached a stage at which the click of a Remington machine acted as a positive spur. He found it more difficult to compose to the music of any other make. During a fortnight when the Remington was out of order he dictated to an Oliver typewriter with evident discomfort, and he found it almost impossibly disconcerting to speak to something that made no responsive sound at all. Once or twice when he was ill and in bed I took down a note or two by hand, but as a rule he liked to have the typewriter moved into his bedroom for even the shortest letters. Yet there were to the end certain kinds of work which he was obliged to do with a pen. Plays, if they were to be kept within the limits of possible performance, and short stories, if they were to remain within the bounds of publication in a monthly magazine, must be written by hand. He was well aware that the manual labour of writing was his best aid to a desired brevity. The plays—such a play as *The Outcry,* for instance— were copied straight from his manuscript, since he was too much afraid of "the murderous limits of the English theatre" to risk the temptation of dictation and embroidery. With the short stories he allowed himself a little more freedom, dictating them from his written draft and expanding them as he went to an extent which inevitably defeated his original purpose. It is almost literally true to say of the sheaf of tales collected in *The Finer Grain* that they were all written in response to a single request for a short story for *Harper's Monthly Magazine.* The length was to be about 5,000 words and each promising idea was cultivated in the optimistic belief that it would produce a flower too frail and small to demand any exhaustive treatment. But even under pressure of being written by hand, with dictated interpolations rigidly restricted, each in turn pushed out to lengths that no chopping could reduce to the word limit. The tale eventually printed was *Crapy Cornelia,* but, although it was the shortest of the batch, it was thought too long to be published in one number and appeared in two sections, to the great annoyance of the author.

III

The method adopted for full-length novels was very different. With a clear run of 100,000 words or more before him, Henry James always cherished the delusive expectation of being able to fit his theme quite easily between the covers of a volume. It was not until he was more than half way through that the problem of space began to be embarrassing. At the beginning he had no questions of compression to attend to, and he "broke ground," as he said, by talking to himself day by day about the characters and construction until the persons and their actions were vividly present to his inward eye. This soliloquy was of course recorded on the type-writer. He had from far back tended to dramatize all the material that life gave him, and he more and more prefigured his novels as staged performances, arranged in acts and scenes, with the characters making their observed entrances and exits. These scenes he worked out until he felt himself so thoroughly possessed of the action that he could begin on the dictation of the book itself—a process which has been incorrectly described by one critic as re-dictation from a rough draft. It was nothing of the kind. Owners of the volumes containing *The Ivory Tower* or *The Sense of the Past* have only to turn to the Notes printed at the end to see that the scenario dictated in advance contains practically none of the phrases used in the final work. The two sets of Notes are a different and a much more interesting literary record than a mere draft. They are the framework set up for imagination to clothe with the spun web of life. But they are not bare framework. They are elaborate and abundant. They are the kind of exercise described in *The Death of the Lion* as "a great gossiping eloquent letter—the overflow into talk of an artist's amorous design." But the design was thus mapped out with the clear understanding that at a later stage and at closer quarters the subject might grow away from the plan. "In the intimacy of composition pre-noted proportions and arrangements do most uncommonly insist on making themselves different by shifts and variations, always improving, which impose themselves as one goes and keep the door open always to something *more* right and *more* related. It is subject to that constant possibility, all the while, that one does pre-note and tentatively sketch."*

The preliminary sketch was seldom consulted after the novel began to take permanent shape, but the same method of "talking out" was resorted to at difficult points of the narrative as it progressed, always for the

The Ivory Tower (Collins, 1917), p. 341.

sake of testing in advance the values of the persons involved in a given situation, so that their creator should
ensure their right action both for the development of
the drama and the truth of their relations to each other.
The knowledge of all the conscious motives and con-
cealments of his creatures, gained by unwearied observation of their attitudes behind the scenes, enabled
Henry James to exhibit them with a final confidence
that dispensed with explanations. Among certain stum-
bling blocks in the path of the perfect comprehension of
his readers is their uneasy doubt of the sincerity of the
conversational encounters recorded. Most novelists
provide some clue to help their readers to distinguish
truth from falsehood, and in the theatre, although husbands and wives may be deceived by lies, the audience
is usually privy to the plot. But a study of the Notes to
The Ivory Tower will make it clear that between the
people created by Henry James lying is as frequent as
among mortals and not any easier to detect.

For the volumes of memories, *A Small Boy and
Others, Notes of a Son and Brother,* and the uncom-
pleted *Middle Years,* no preliminary work was needed.
A straight dive into the past brought to the surface
treasure after treasure, a wealth of material which became embarrassing. The earlier book was begun in
1911, after Henry James had returned from a year
in the United States, where he had been called by his
brother's fatal illness. He had come back, after many
seasons of country solitude, to his former love of the
friendly London winter, and for the first few months
after his return from America he lodged near the Re-
form Club and came to the old house in Chelsea where
I was living and where he had taken a room for his

work. It was a quiet room, long and narrow and rather dark—he used to speak of it as "my Chelsea cellar." There he settled down to write what, as he outlined it to me, was to be a set of notes to his brother William's early letters, prefaced by a brief account of the family into which they were both born. But an entire volume of memories was finished before bringing William to an age for writing letters, and *A Small Boy* came to a rather abrupt end as a result of the writer's sudden decision that a break must be made at once if the flood of remembrance was not to drown his pious intention.

It was extraordinarily easy for him to recover the past; he had always been sensitive to impressions and his mind was stored with records of exposure. All he had to do was to render his sense of those records as adequately as he could. Each morning, after reading over the pages written the day before, he would settle down in a chair for an hour or so of conscious effort. Then, lifted on a rising tide of inspiration, he would get up and pace up and down the room, sounding out the periods in tones of resonant assurance. At such times he was beyond reach of irrelevant sounds or sights. Hosts of cats—a tribe he usually routed with shouts of execration—might wail outside the window, phalanxes of motor-cars bearing dreaded visitors might hoot at the door. He heard nothing of them. The only thing that could arrest his progress was the escape of the word he wanted to use. When that had vanished he broke off the rhythmic pacing and made his way to a chimney-piece or book-case tall enough to support his elbows while he rested his head in his hands and audibly pursued the fugitive.

IV

In the autumn of 1907, when I began to tap the Remington typewriter at Henry James's dictation, he was engaged on the arduous task of preparing his Novels and Tales for the definitive New York edition, published in 1909. Since it was only between breakfast and luncheon that he undertook what he called "inventive" work, he gave the hours from half-past ten to half-past one to the composition of the prefaces which are so interesting a feature of the edition. In the evenings he read over again the work of former years, treating the printed pages like so many proof-sheets of extremely corrupt text. The revision was a task he had seen in advance as formidable. He had cultivated the habit of forgetting past achievements almost to the pitch of a sincere conviction that nothing he had written before about 1890 could come with any shred of credit through the ordeal of a critical inspection. On a morning when he was obliged to give time to the selection of a set of tales for a forthcoming volume, he confessed that the difficulty of selection was mainly the difficulty of reading them at all. "They seem," he said, "so bad until I *have* read them that I can't force myself to go through them except with a pen in my hand, altering as I go the crudities and ineptitudes that to my sense deform each page." Unfamiliarity and adverse prejudice are rare advantages for a writer to bring to the task of choosing among his works. For Henry James the prejudice might give way to half reluctant appreciation as the unfamiliarity passed into recognition, but it must be clear to every reader of the prefaces that he never lost the sense of being paternally responsible for two distinct families. For the earlier brood, acknowledged fruit of his alliance with Romance, he claimed indulgence on the ground of their youthful spontaneity, their confident assurance, their rather touching good faith. One catches echoes of a plea that these elderly youngsters may not be too closely compared, to their inevitable disadvantage, with the richly endowed, the carefully bred, the highly civilized and sensitized children of his second marriage, contracted with that wealthy bride, Experience. Attentive readers of the novels may perhaps find the distinction between these two groups less remarkable than it seemed to their writer. They may even wonder whether the second marriage was not rather a silver wedding, with the old romantic mistress cleverly disguised as a woman of the world. The different note was possibly due more to the substitution of dictation for pen and ink than to any profound change of heart. But whatever the reason, their author certainly found it necessary to spend a good deal of time working on the earlier tales before he considered them fit for appearance in the company of those composed later. Some members of the elder family he entirely cast off, not counting them worth the expense of completely new clothes. Others he left in their place more from a necessary, though deprecated, respect for the declared taste of the reading public than because he loved them for their own sake. It would, for instance, have been difficult to exclude *Daisy Miller* from any representative collection of his work, yet the popularity of the tale had become almost a grievance. To be acclaimed as the author of *Daisy Miller* by persons blandly unconscious of *The Wings of the Dove* or *The Golden Bowl* was a reason among many for Henry James's despair of intelligent comprehension. Confronted repeatedly with *Daisy*, he felt himself rather in the position of some *grande dame* who, with a jewel-case of sparkling diamonds, is constrained by her admirers always to appear in the simple string of moonstones worn at her first dance.

From the moment he began to read over the earlier tales, he found himself involved in a highly practical examination of the scope and limits of permissible revision. Poets, as he pointed out, have often revised their verse with good effect. Why should the novelist not have equal license? The only sound reason for not altering anything is a conviction that it cannot be improved. It was Henry James's profound conviction that he could improve his early writing in nearly every sentence. Not to revise would have been to confess to a loss of faith in himself, and it was not likely that the writer who had fasted for forty years in the wilderness of British and American misconceptions without yielding a scrap of intellectual integrity to editorial or publishing tempters should have lost faith in himself. But he was well aware that the game of revision must be played with a due observance of the rules. He knew that no novelist can safely afford to repudiate his fundamental understanding with his readers that the tale he has to tell is at least as true as history and the figures he has set in motion at least as independently alive as the people we see in offices and motor-cars. He allowed himself few freedoms with any recorded appearances or actions, although occasionally the temptation to correct a false gesture, to make it "right," was too strong to be resisted. We have a pleasant instance of this

correction in the second version of *The American*. At
her first appearance, the old Marquise de Bellegarde
had acknowledged the introduction of Newman by returning his handshake "with a sort of British positiveness which reminded him that she was the daughter of
the Earl of St. Dunstan's." In the later edition she be-
haves differently. "Newman came sufficiently near to
the old lady by the fire to take in that she would offer
him no handshake. . . . Madame de Bellegarde looked
hard at him and refused what she did refuse with a
sort of British positiveness which reminded him that
she was the daughter of the Earl of St. Dunstan's."
There were good reasons why the Marquise should
have denied Newman a welcoming handshake. Her attitude throughout the book was to be consistently hostile
and should never have been compromised by the signi-
ficantly British grip. Yet it is almost shocking to see her
snatching back her first card after playing it for so
many years. She was to perform less credible actions
than shaking hands with an innocent American, as her
progenitor knew very well. He invited his readers, in
the preface to *The American,* to observe the impossible behaviour of the noble Bellegarde family, but he
realized that since they had been begotten in absurdity
the Bellegardes could under no stress of revision
achieve a very solid humanity. The best he could do
for them was to let a faint consciousness flush the mind
of Valentin, the only detached member of the family.
In the first edition Valentin warned his friend of the
Bellegarde peculiarities with the easy good faith of the
younger Henry James under the spell of the magic
word "Europe." "My mother is strange, my brother
is strange, and I verily believe I am stranger than

either. Old trees have queer cracks, old races have odd secrets." To this statement he added in the revised version: "We're fit for a museum or a Balzac novel." A comparable growth of ironic perception was allowed to Roderick Hudson, whose comment on Rowland's admission of his heroically silent passion for Mary Garland, "It's like something in a novel," was altered to: "It's like something in a bad novel."

V

But the legitimate business of revision was, for Henry James, neither substitution nor re-arrangement. It was the demonstration of values implicit in the earlier work, the retrieval of neglected opportunities for adequate "renderings." "It was," as he explained in his final preface, "all sensibly, as if the clear matter being still there, even as a shining expanse of snow spread over a plain, my exploring tread, for application to it, had quite unlearned the old pace and found itself naturally falling into another, which might sometimes more or less agree with the original tracks, but might most often, or very nearly, break the surface at other places. What was thus predominantly interesting to note, at all events, was the high spontaneity of these deviations and differences, which become thus things not of choice but of immediate and perfect necessity: necessity to the end of dealing with the quantities in question at all." On every page the act of re-reading became automatically one with the act of re-writing, and the revised parts are just "those rigid conditions of re-perusal, registered; so many close notes, as who should say, on the particular vision of the matter itself

that experience had at last made the only possible one."
These are words written with the clear confidence of
the artist who, in complete possession of his "facul-
ties," had no need to bother himself with doubts as to
his ability to write better at the end of a lifetime of
hard work and varied experience than at the beginning.
He knew he could write better. His readers have not
always agreed with his own view. They have de-
nounced the multiplication of qualifying clauses, the
imposition of a system of punctuation which, although
rigid and orderly, occasionally fails to act as a guide
to immediate comprehension of the writer's intention, and the increasing passion for adverbial inter-
positions. "Adjectives are the sugar of literature and
adverbs the salt," was Henry James's reply to a criticism which once came to his ears.

It must be admitted that the case for the revised
version relies on other merits than simplicity or elegance to make its claim good. It is not so smooth, nor
so easy, nor, on the whole, so pretty as the older form.
But it is nearly always richer and more alive. Abstrac-
tions give place to sharp definite images, loose vague
phrases to close-locked significances. We can find a
fair example of this in *The Madonna of the Future,* a
tale first published in 1879. In the original version one
of the sentences runs: "His professions, somehow, were
all half professions, and his allusions to his work and
circumstances left something dimly ambiguous in the
background." In the New York Edition this has become: "His professions were practically somehow, all
masks and screens, and his personal allusions as to his
ambiguous background mere wavings of the dim lan-
tern." In some passages it would be hard to deny a

gain of beauty as well as of significance. There is, for instance, a sentence in the earlier account of Newman's silent renunciation of his meditated revenge, in the Cathedral of Notre Dame: "He sat a long time; he heard far-away bells chiming off, at long intervals, to the rest of the world." In the definitive edition of *The American* the passage has become: "He sat a long time; he heard far-away bells chiming off into space, at long intervals, the big bronze syllables of the Word."

A paragraph from *Four Meetings,* a tale worked over with extreme care, will give a fair idea of the general effect of the revision. It records a moment of the final Meeting, when the helplessly indignant narrator is watching poor Caroline ministering to the vulgar French cocotte who has imposed herself on the hospitality of the innocent little New Englander.

"At this moment," runs the passage of 1879, "Caroline Spencer came out of the house bearing a coffee pot on a little tray. I noticed that on her way from the door to the table she gave me a single quick vaguely appealing glance. I wondered what it signified; I felt that it signified a sort of half-frightened longing to know what, as a man of the world who had been in France, I thought of the Countess. It made me extremely uncomfortable. I could not tell her that the Countess was very possibly the runaway wife of a little hairdresser. I tried, suddenly, on the contrary, to show a high consideration for her."

The "particular vision" registered on re-perusal reveals states of mind much more definite than these wonderings and longings and vague appeals.

"Our hostess moreover at this moment came out of

the house, bearing a coffee-pot and three cups on a neat little tray. I took from her eyes, as she approached us, a brief but intense appeal—the mute expression, as I felt, conveyed in the hardest little look she had yet addressed me, of her longing to know what as a man of the world in general and of the French world in particular, I thought of these allied forces now so en-camped on the stricken field of her life. I could only 'act,' however, as they said at North Verona, quite impenetrably—only make no answering sign. I couldn't intimate, much less could I frankly utter, my inward sense of the Countess's probable past, with its measure of her virtue, value and accomplishments, and of the limits of consideration to which she could properly pretend. I couldn't give my friend a hint of how I my-self personally 'saw' her interesting pensioner—whether as the runaway wife of a too-jealous hair-dresser or of a too-morose pastry-cook, say; whether as a very small bourgeoise, in fine, who had vitiated her case beyond patching up, or even some character of the nomadic sort, less edifying still. I couldn't let in, by the jog of a shutter, as it were, a hard informing ray and then, washing my hands of the business, turn my back for ever. I could on the contrary but save the situation, my own at least, for the moment, by pulling myself together with a master hand and appear-ing to ignore everything but that the dreadful person between us *was* a 'grande dame.' "

Anyone genuinely interested in "the how and the whence and the why these intenser lights of experience come into being and insist on shining," will find it a profitable exercise to read and compare the old and the new versions of any of the novels or tales first pub-

lished during the 'seventies or 'eighties. Such a reader
will be qualified to decide for himself between the opinion of a bold young critic that "all the works have
been subjected to a revision which in several cases,
notably *Dasiy Miller* and *Four Meetings,* amounts to
their ruin," and their writer's confidence that "I
shouldn't have breathed upon the old catastrophes and
accidents, the old wounds and mutilations and disfigure-
ments wholly in vain. . . . I have prayed that the finer
air of the better form may sufficiently seem to hang
about them and gild them over—at least for readers,
however few, at all *curious* of questions of air and
form."

VI

Explanatory prefaces and elaborate revisions, short
stories and long memories, were far from being the
complete tale of literary labour during the last eight
years of Henry James's life. A new era for English
drama was prophesied in 1907. Led by Miss Horn-
iman, advocates of the repertory system were march-
ing forward, capturing one by one the intellectual
centres of the provinces. In London, repertory seasons
were announced in two West-end theatres. Actor-
managers began to ask for "non-commercial" plays and
when their appeal reached Henry James it met with a
quick response. The theatre had both allured and re-
pelled him for many years, and he had already been
the victim of a theatrical misadventure. His assertions
that he wrote plays solely in the hope of making money
should not, I think, be taken as the complete explanation of his dramas. It is pretty clear that he wrote
plays because he wanted to write them, because he was

convinced that his instinct for dramatic situations could find a happy outlet in plays, because writing for the stage is a game rich in precise rules and he delighted in the multiplication of technical difficulties, and because he lived in circles more addicted to the intelligent criticism of plays than to the intelligent criticism of novels. The plays he wrote in the early 'nineties are very careful exercises in technique. They are derived straight from the light comedies of the Parisian stage, with the difference that in the 'nineties, for all their advertised naughtiness, there were even stricter limits to the free representation of Parisian situations on English stages than there are to-day. In *The Reprobate,* a play successfully produced a few years ago by the Stage Society, the lady whose hair has changed from black to red and from red to gold is the centre of the drama, she holds the key to the position, but all her complicating effect depends upon the past— pasts being allowed on every stage comparative license of reference. The compromising evidence is all a matter of old photographs and letters, and the play loses in vividness whatever it may gain in respectability. Nobody knew better than the author that *The Reprobate* was not a good play. Terror of being cut forbade him to work on a subject of intrinsic importance. With another hour guaranteed, a playwright might attempt anything, but "he does not get his hour, and he will probably begin by missing his subjects. He takes, in his dread of complication, a minor one, and it's heavy odds that the minor one, with the habit of small natures, will prove thankless."

Other early plays had been converted into novels or tales and so published. One of these, written originally for Miss Ellen Terry but never produced by her, had appeared as an incongruous companion to *The Turn of the Screw* in the volume entitled *The Two Magics.* A few attentive readers had seen the dramatic possibilities of *Covering End,* and when it was suggested to Henry James that he should convert it into a three-act comedy for production by Mr. Forbes Robertson (as he was then) and Miss Gertrude Elliot, he willingly consented. Flying under a new flag, as *The High Bid,* the play was produced in London in February, 1909, but only for a series of matinées, the prodigious success of *The Passing of the Third Floor Back* precluding the possibility of an evening for any other production under the same management. Under the inspiration of the repertory movement, other material was re-cast for acting. *The Other House* was re-dictated as a tragedy. *Owen Wingrave* became *The Saloon,* a one-act play produced by Miss Gertrude Kingston in 1910. Finally an entirely new three-act comedy, *The Outcry,* was written round the highly topical subject of the sale of art treasures to rich Americans. It was not produced during Henry James's life. At the time when it should have been rehearsed he was ill and the production was postponed. On his recovery, he went to the United States for a year, and when he came back the day of repertory performances had died in a fresh night of stars.

When *The Outcry* was given by the Stage Society in 1917, it was evident that the actors were embarrassed by their lines, for by 1909, when the play was written, the men and women of Henry James could talk only in the manner of their creator. His own speech, assisted by the practice of dictating, had by

that time become so inveterately characteristic that
his questions to a railway clerk about a ticket or to a
fishmonger about a lobster, might easily be recognized
as coined in the same mint as his addresses to the
Academic Committee of the Royal Society of Literature. Apart from this difficulty of enunciating the lines,
The Outcry has all the advantages over the earlier
plays. The characters are real and they act from adequate motives. The solution of the presented problem, which requires, like most of the author's solutions,
a change of heart, is worked out with admirable art,
without any use of the mechanical shifts and stage
properties needed in *The Reprobate*. It is not very
difficult to believe that if Henry James had been encouraged twenty years earlier to go on writing plays
he might have made a name as a dramatist, but the
faithful may be forgiven for rejoicing that the playwright was sacrificed to the novelist and critic.

VII

Many men whose prime business is the art of writing find rest and refreshment in other occupations.
They marry or they keep dogs, they play golf or
bridge, they study Sanskrit or collect postage stamps.
Except for a period of ownership of a dachshund,
Henry James did none of these things. He lived a life
consecrated to the service of a jealous, insatiable, and
supremely rewarding goddess, and all his activities
had essential reference to that service. He had a great
belief in the virtues of air and exercise, and he was
expert at making a walk of two or three miles last for
as many hours by his habit of punctuating movement

with frequent and prolonged halts for meditation or conversation. He liked the exhilaration of driving in a motor-car, which gave him, he said, "a sense of spiritual adventure." He liked a communicative companion. Indeed the cultivation of friendships may be said to have been his sole recreation. To the very end of his life he was quick to recognize every chance of forming a friendly relation, swift to act on his recognition, and beautifully ready to protect and nourish the warm life of engendered affection. His letters, especially those written in his later years, are more than anything else great generous gestures of remembrance, gathering up and embracing his correspondents much as his talk would gather up his hearers and sweep them along on a rising flood of eloquence.

But that fine capacity for forming and maintaining a "relation" worked, inevitably, within definite limits. He was obliged to create impassable barriers between himself and the rest of mankind before he could stretch out his eager hands over safe walls to beckon and to bless. He loved his friends, but he was condemned by the law of his being to keep clear of any really entangling net of human affection and exaction. His contacts had to be subordinate, or indeed ancillary, to the vocation he had followed with a single passion from the time when, as a small boy, he obtained a report from his tutor as showing no great aptitude for anything but a felicitous rendering of La Fontaine's fables into English. Nothing could be allowed to interfere for long with the labour from which Henry James never rested, unless perhaps during sleep. When his "morning stint of inventive work" was over, he went forth to the renewed assault of the impressions that were always lying in wait for him. He was perpetually and mercilessly exposed, incessantly occupied with the task of assimilating his experience, freeing the pure workable metal from the base, remoulding it into new beauty with the aid of every device of his craft. He used his friends not, as some incompletely inspired artists do, as in themselves the material of his art, but as the sources of his material. He took everything they could give and he gave it back in his books. With this constant preoccupation, it was natural that the people least interesting to him were the comparatively dumb. To be "inarticulate" was for him the cardinal social sin. It amounted to a wilful withholding of treasures of alien experience. And if he could extract no satisfaction from contemplating the keepers of golden silence, he could gain little more from intercourse with the numerous persons he dismissed from his attention as "simple organisms." These he held to be mere waste of any writer's time, and it was characteristic that his constant appreciation of the works of Mrs. Wharton was baffled by the popularity of *Ethan Frome,* because he considered that the gifted author had spent her labour on creatures too easily comprehensible to be worth her pains. He greatly preferred *The Reef,* where, as he said, "she deals with persons really fine and complicated."

We might arrive at the same conclusion from a study of the prefaces to the New York Edition. More often than not, the initial idea for a tale came to Henry James through the medium of other people's talk. From a welter of anecdote he could unerringly pick out the living nucleus for a reconstructed and balanced work of art. His instinct for selection was ad-

mirable, and he could afford to let it range freely
among a profusion of proffered subjects, secure that it
would alight on the most promising. But he liked to
have the subjects presented with a little artful dis-
crimination, even in the first instance. He was dependent on conversation, but it must be educated and up to
a point intelligent conversation. There is an early letter
written from Italy in 1874, in which he complains of
having hardly spoken to an Italian creature in nearly
a year's sojourn, "save washerwomen and waiters.
This, you'll say, is my own stupidity," he continues,
"but granting this gladly, it proves that even a creature
addicted as much to sentimentalizing as I am over the
whole *mise en scène* of Italian life, doesn't find an easy
initiation into what lies behind it. Sometimes I am over-
whelmed with the pitifulness of this absurd want of
reciprocity between Italy itself and all my rhapsodies
about it." Other wanderers might have found more
of Italy in washerwomen and waiters, here guaranteed to be the true native article, than in all the
nobility of Rome or the Anglo-Americans of Venice,
but that was not Henry James's way. For him neither
pearls nor diamonds fell from the lips of waiters and
washerwomen, and princesses never walked in his
world disguised as goosegirls.

Friendships are maintained by the communication
of speech and letters. Henry James was a voluminous
letter-writer and exhaustively communicative in his
talk upon every subject but one, his own work, which
was his own real life. It was not because he was indifferent to what people thought of his books that he
evaded discussion about them. He was always touched
and pleased by any evidence that he had been intelli-

gently read, but he never went a step out of his way
to seek this assurance. He found it safest to assume
that nobody read him, and he liked his friends none
the worse for their incapacity. Meanwhile, the volumes of his published works—visible, palpable, read-
able proof of that unceasing travail of the creative
spirit which was always labouring behind the barrier
of his silence—piled themselves up year after year, to
be dropped on to the tables of booksellers and pushed
on to the shelves of libraries, to be bought and cherished by the faithful, ignored by the multitude, and
treated as a test of mental endurance by the kind of
person who organized the Browning Society. For-
tunately for literature, Henry James did not lend himself to exploitation by any Jacobean Society. Instead
of inventing riddles for prize students, he scattered
about his pages a number of pregnant passages containing all the clues that are needed for keeping up
with him. It was his theory that if readers didn't keep
up with him—as they admittedly didn't always—the
fault was entirely in their failure of attention. There
are revelations in his books, just as he declared them
to be in the works of Neil Paraday. "Extract the
opinion, disengage the answer—these are the real
acts of homage."

VIII

From his familiar correspondence we need not hope
to extract as considered an opinion or as definite an
answer as from the novels, but his letters are extraordinarily valuable as sidelights, helping us to see how
it happened that any man was able to progress along
so straight a path from one end of his life to another.

The two volumes of memories are clear evidence of the kind of temperamental make-up with which Henry James was gifted, the two volumes of letters show how his life contributed to preserve and enhance his rare capacity for taking and keeping impressions. They show him too as unusually impervious to everything which is not an impression of visual images or a sense of a human situation. He was very little troubled by a number of ideas which press with an increasing weight upon the minds of most educated persons. Not until the outbreak of the Great War was he moved to utter a forcible "opinion" about affairs outside his personal range. He was delightfully free from the common delusion that by grouping individuals in arbitrary classes and by twisting harmless adjectives into abstract nouns it is possible for us to think of more than one thing at a time and to conceive of qualities apart from their manifestation. What he saw he possessed; what he understood he criticized, but he never reckoned it to be any part of his business to sit in judgment on the deeds of men working in alien material for inartistic ends, or to speculate about the nature of the universe or the conflict or reconciliation of science with religion. He could let Huxley and Gladstone, the combatant champions of Darwinism and orthodox theology, enrich the pages of a single letter without any reference to their respective beliefs. "Huxley is a very genial, comfortable being . . . But of course my talk with him is mere amiable generalities." Of Gladstone there is a little more, but again the personal impression is the thing sought. "I was glad of a chance to feel the 'personality' of a great political leader—or as G. is now thought here even, I think, by his partisans,

ex-leader. That of Gladstone is very fascinating—his
urbanity extreme—his eye that of a man of genius—
and his apparent self-surrender to what he is talking
of without a flaw. He made a great impression on me."
One would like to know what the subject was to which
Gladstone had surrendered himself in his talk with
this entranced young American, who must surely, for
his part, have been as much reduced conversationally
to "mere amiable generalities" as on the occasion of
his meeting Huxley. It is difficult to think of a single
likely point of contact between the minds of Gladstone and Henry James. But that, for delicacy of reg-
istration, was an advantage. The recording instrument
could perform its work without the hindrance of any
distraction of attention from the man himself to the
matter of his speech, which did not presumably contain any germ for cultivation into fiction.

His nationality saved Henry James from the common English necessity of taking a side in the political
game; and in the United States nobody of his world
had expected him to be interested in politics. There is
a pleasant account in *The Middle Years* of his blank-
ness when he was asked at a London breakfast-table
for "distinctness about General Grant's first cabinet,
upon the formation of which the light of the newspaper happened then to beat." The question was embarrassing. "There were, it appeared, things of interest
taking place in America, and I had had, in this absurd
manner, to come to England to learn it: I had had
over there on the ground itself no conception of any
such matter—nothing of the smallest interest, by any
perception of mine, as I suppose I should still blush

to recall, had taken place in America since the War."
Nothing of any great public interest, by any perception
of his, was to take place in Europe until the outbreak
of another war at that time far beyond the range of
speculation. But if cabinets and parties and politics
were and remained outside the pale of his sensibility,
he was none the less charmed by the customs of a
country where Members of Parliament and Civil
Servants could meet together for a leisurely breakfast,
thus striking "the exciting note of a social order in
which everyone wasn't hurled straight, with the mo-
mentum of rising, upon an office or a store."

IX

Henry James came to England to admire. But his
early reverence for the men and women of an island
with so fine and ancient a historic tone as Great Britain
soon faded. He had forgotten, in the first passion of
acquaintance, that the English are born afresh in every
generation and are about as new as young Americans,
differing from them chiefly in having other forms of
domestic and ecclesiastical architecture and smoother
lawns to take for granted. He looked at old stone
castles and Tudor brickwork, at great hanging eaves
and immemorial gardens, and then he looked at the
heirs of this heritage and listened intently for their
speech. This was disappointing, partly because they
spoke so little. "I rarely remember," he wrote when
he had lived through several London months, "to
have heard on English lips any other intellectual ver-
dict (no matter under what provocation) than this

broad synthesis 'so immensely clever.' What exasper-
ates you is not that they can't say more but that they
wouldn't if they could."

How different was this inarticulate world from the
fine civilization of Boston, from the cultivated circle
that gathered round Charles Eliot Norton at Shady
Hill. To that circle he appealed for sympathy, com-
plaining that he was "sinking into dull British acceptance and conformity. . . . I am losing my standard—
my charming little standard that I used to think so
high; my standard of wit, of grace, of good manners,
of vivacity, of urbanity, of intelligence, of what makes
an easy and natural style of intercourse! And this in
consequence of having dined out during the past winter
107 times!" Great men, or at the least men with great
names, swam into his ken and he condemned them.
Ruskin was "weakness pure and simple." In Paris he
found that he could "easily—more than easily—see all
round Flaubert intellectually." A happy Sunday evening at Madame Viardot's provoked a curious reflection on the capacity of celebrated Europeans to behave
absurdly and the incapacity of celebrated Americans
to indulge in similar antics. "It was both strange and
sweet to see poor Turgenev acting charades of the
most extravagant description, dressed out in old
shawls, and masks, going on all fours, etc. The charades are their usual Sunday evening occupation and
the good faith with which Turgenev, at his age and
with his glories, can go into them is a striking example
of the truth of that spontaneity which Europeans have
and we have not. Fancy Longfellow, Lowell, or
Charles Norton doing the like and every Sunday evening!"

Whether or not all celebrated Americans behave with invariable decorum, the astonished spectator of Turgenev's performance had no temptation to "do the like." His appearance among a company of artists and writers gathered together in a country village during the late summer of 1886 has been characteristically recorded by Mr. Edmund Gosse. "Henry James was the only sedate one of us all—benign, indulgent, but grave, and not often unbending beyond a genial chuckle. . . . It is remembered with what affability he wore a garland of flowers at a birthday feast, and even, nobly descending, took part one night in a cake-walk. But mostly, though not much our senior, he was serious, mildly avuncular, but very happy and unupbraiding."

By that time Henry James was at his ease in England. The inhabitants were no longer either gods or imbeciles. Through the general British fog he had perceived gleams of intelligence shining on his bewilderment. He was no longer wholly dependent on Boston for refreshment. He could fall back upon the company of Mr. Edmund Gosse and he had found a friend in R. L. Stevenson. The little handful of Islanders possessed of a genuine interest in the art of letters and the criticism of life emerged from the obscurity, and he made out that, on the whole, there were perhaps about as many civilized people in England as in his native land. Yet he was a little troubled about his position. He wondered, while he reviewed the past, whether the path he had so carefully chosen for himself was the right one, whether he might not have missed more by leaving the United States than he had gained by coming to England. He lamented, in a letter written to his

brother William in 1899, that he had not had the kind
of early experience that might have attached him to his
own country. He earnestly advised a different treatment for his nephews. "What I most of all feel, and
in the light of it conjure you to keep doing for them,
is their being *à même* to contract local saturations and
attachments in respect to their *own* great and glorious
country, to learn, and strike roots into, its infinite
beauty, as I suppose, and variety. . . . Its being their
'own' will double their *use* of it."

It was only after a visit to America in 1904 that
he found, on his return to Rye, that he had a home
and a country. He was able after this discovery to
write to Mrs. Wharton that "your only drawback is
not having the homeliness and the inevitability and
the happy limitation and the affluent poverty, of a
Country of your Own (comme moi, par exemple!)";
and he could declare after taking the Oath of Alle-
giance to the King of England in 1915 that "I was
really too associated before for any nominal change to
matter. The process has only shown me what I virtually
was—so that it's rather disappointing in respect to
acute sensation. I *haven't* any." Associated he certainly was, allied by innumerable sympathies and affec-
tions to the adopted country. But he was never really
English or American or even Cosmopolitan. And it is
too difficult to suppose that even if he had passed all
his youth in New England and contracted all the local
saturations and attachments he urged for his nephews
he could ever have melted comfortably into American
uniformity. He, who took nothing in the world for
granted, could surely never have taken New England
for granted.

To-day, with the complete record before us—the novels, criticisms, biographies, plays, and letters—we can understand how little those international relations that engaged Henry James's attention mattered to his genius. Wherever he might have lived and whatever human interactions he might have observed, he would in all probability have reached much the same conclusion that he arrived at by the way of America, France, and England. When he walked out of the refuge of his study into the world and looked about him, he saw a place of torment, where creatures of prey perpetually thrust their claws into the quivering flesh of the doomed, defenceless children of light. He had the abiding comfort of an inner certainty (and perhaps he did bring that from New England) that the children of light had an eternal advantage; he was aware to the finest fibre of his being that the "poor sensitive gentlemen" he so numerously treated possessed a treasure that would outlast all the glittering paste of the world and the flesh; he knew that nothing in life mattered compared with spiritual decency.

We may conclude that the nationalities of his betrayed and triumphant victims are not an important factor. They may equally well be innocent Americans maltreated by odious Europeans, refined Europeans fleeced by unscrupulous Americans, or young children of any race exposed to evil influences. The essential fact is that wherever he looked Henry James saw fineness apparently sacrificed to grossness, beauty to avarice, truth to a bold front. He realized how constantly the tenderness of growing life is at the mercy of personal tyranny and he hated the tyranny of persons over each other. His novels are a repeated exposure of this wickedness, a reiterated and passionate plea for the fullest freedom of development, unimperilled by reckless and barbarous stupidity.

He was himself most scrupulously careful not to exercise any tyrannical power over other people. The only advice he ever permitted himself to offer to a friend was a recommendation to "let your soul live." Towards the end of his days his horror of interfering, or seeming to interfere, with the freedom of others became so overpowering that it was a misery for him to suspect that the plans of his friends might be made with reference to himself. Much as he enjoyed seeing them, he so disliked to think that they were undergoing the discomfort of voyages and railway journeys in order to be near him that he would gladly have prevented their start if he could. His Utopia was an anarchy where nobody would be responsible for any other human being but only for his own civilized character. His circle of friends will easily recall how finely Henry James had fitted himself to be a citizen of this commonwealth.

THE ARTIST AND PSYCHO-ANALYSIS

BY

ROGER FRY

THE ARTIST AND PSYCHO–ANALYSIS*

As I am no psychologist, my presumption in addressing a gathering of professional psychologists seems to call for apology. My defence is that of late years you have managed to make yourselves so interesting to the world at large that you have inevitably attracted the attention of outsiders. You have let off too many fireworks in your back garden to wonder that strangers have been looking over the wall.

Before the advent of Dr. Freud you worked for so long in a tranquil and almost deserted solitude that this invasion of your privacy may be a strange and disturbing experience. As an artist let me assure you that you will get accustomed to it, for we artists have always been absurdly interesting to the outside world, and are, a good many of us, by no means averse from these self-invited guests in our workshops. And to be perfectly frank psychologists are the latest disturbers of our rest and threaten to be not the least importunate.

That is one reason why I thought it might be profitable if we arranged together the terms on which you would be not only admitted, but welcomed. Those terms are very simple, they consist of one clause, namely, that before you tell us what we are doing and why we do it, we think you should take the trouble to understand what we think we are doing and why we think we do it. I know how impatient doctors are while

*A paper read to the British Psychological Society.

the patient is going through his symptoms but he does generally make that concession to human nature. If after that, you can show us that we have got a mistaken notion of our own activities, that we have unconsciously rationalized them and in doing so disguised their true significance, we will listen in all humility.

What I have to suggest to you to-night is rather complicated. I will therefore begin by summarizing briefly my main ideas.

(1) The words "art" and "artist" are simple enough, but alas they have no sharply defined usage. Artists are a group of people of very different temperments and some of them are actuated by quite different motives, and exercise quite different psychical activities, from others.

(2) I believe that two distinct aims and activities have got classed together under the word "art," and that the word "artist" is used of two distinct groups of men. One of these groups into which I would divide artists is mainly preoccupied with creating a fantasy-world in which the fulfilment of wishes is realized. The other is concerned with the contemplation of formal relations. I believe this latter activity to be as much detached from the instinctive life as any human activity that we know; to be in that respect on a par with science. I consider this latter the distinctive esthetic activity. I admit that to some extent these two aims may both appear in any given work of art but I believe them to be fundamentally different, if not in their origins, at least in their functions.

To begin with let us get clear about the question of origins. No doubt the question of the origin of any phenomenon is of great interest and importance, but it must always be borne in mind that the discovery of the origin is not an explanation of the phenomenon. Origins do not necessarily explain functions. The alimentary canal and the brain both have their origin in the epithelial tissue, but one would give an enquirer a strange idea of the functional importance of the brain in the economy of the body if one only stated that it was originally part of the skin.

So if you were to prove that art originated in the sexual feelings of man, that might be a very important and interesting discovery, but it would be no explanation of the significance of art for human life. Not what an organ came from, but what it has come to be, is the most important consideration, though what it came from, and the path it has taken in its progress, may throw a light on what it really is. As an instance take the case of language. Dr. Freud in his lectures quotes a theory of language which I am not qualified to criticize or approve but which sounds to me plausible—it is that when men began to work in groups at wood-cutting, building, or what not, they sweetened their toil by shouting together sounds that had a sexual significance and that gradually these sounds become dissociated from sex and associated with particular actions or objects, and thus the original roots of language came into being. Now to argue from this that language is merely a function of the sex instinct would be grotesque. Since it has come to be the vehicle for the whole discursive intellectual life of man—it has come to serve most of all precisely those activities which are most completely removed from the instinctive life. Indeed all human activities must presumably have their ultimate origins in some part of the purely animal and instinctive life of our earliest ancestors.

Science itself, the activity of the pure reflective intellect, no doubt comes from a gradual misapplication and distortion of what was once only a weapon in the struggle for life. What was once hardly more than the animal ingenuity, which enabled man to contrive elementary devices for protection or shelter, has become through that very process of misapplication the purely reflective and disinterested intellectual power of an Einstein or a Freud, and we can show almost every intermediate stage in this long process. Now if you wanted to investigate the real nature of this truth-seeking passion of scientific men, it might be important, no doubt, to discover when it first branched off from the instinctive ratiocination of animals, but you could say nothing about its significance unless you studied it beyond the point where it had lost all traces of its subservience to the instinctive life. To understand the scientific activity you must note that its essence is precisely this complete detachment from the instinctive life, its complete uselessness, its abiological nature, since it exists not to serve life but truth, and this is precisely why those who devote themselves to this activity are constantly in conflict with the mass of mankind which is deeply concerned with life and completely indifferent to truth.

Now one of the pleas I want to make to you is that, if you wish to discover something about the nature of artistic activity, you should study it at a stage where it has thrown off the traces of its origin, has run clear, as it were, of all these accessory accompaniments which surround and, perhaps, cloak it in its earlier stages.

There is such a thing as impure or useful science,
and, if you were to analyze that activity, you would
find all sorts of biological motives at work, although
the fundamental truth-seeking passion of pure science
is distinguished precisely by its independence of, and
its indifference to, biological necessity.

Similarly there is an impure and, perhaps, useful art
(though the use of impure art is not so easily demon-
strated as that of impure science) ; here too, analysis
would reveal a number of elements which really form
no part of the essential esthetic activity, and you will
make a serious mistake if, after such an analysis, you
declare these to be constituent parts of that phenomenon.

If you have a substance which you know to be
chemically pure it is clear that you have a right to say
that every element which you discover in that substance by analysis is a constituent part of it, but, if
you have any reason to suspect an impure mixture, you
know that any particular element which the analysis
reveals may be due to the impurity and form no part
of the substance which you are investigating.

Now that the esthetic activity does mix in various
degrees with a number of other activities is surely
evident. Take for instance advertisements: many of
these show no esthetic effort and do not even try to
afford esthetic pleasure; they merely convey more or
less inaccurate information about a particular object.
You can think of advertisements where not only are
the merits of the objects enumerated but the object,
let us say a bottle of Somebody's Beer, is depicted.
Every detail of the bottle and its label is given so that
we may recognize it when we see it in the bar, but

there is no sign that in the manner of representation any thought has been expended for our esthetic pleasure. On the other hand I take certain advertisements in American journals, where advertisements are taken seriously and romantically, and I find a very genuine effort, in the proportion and spacing of the letters, in the harmonious consistence of the forms, and in the exact presentation of the object, towards esthetic pleasure. None the less this esthetic appeal is mixed with all sorts of appeals to other feelings than the love of beauty—appeals to our sense of social prestige, to our avarice, to our desire for personal display, and so forth.

Or take again the case of dress—here no doubt there is often a considerable care for pure beauty of line and harmony of colour, but such considerations have continually to give place to far more pressing concerns connected with social rivalry, in fact to all the complicated mass of instincts which go to make up what we call snobbishness.

These, then, are cases of obvious mixtures, in which the esthetic impulse has a part—but you will say these belong to applied art; if we take pictures which subserve no ultimate use we shall surely be safe. But alas the vast majority of pictures are not really works of art at all. No doubt in most a careful analysis would reveal some trace of esthetic preoccupations, but for the most part the appeal they make is to quite other feelings.

For the moment I must be dogmatic and declare that the esthetic emotion is an emotion about form. In certain people, purely formal relations of certain kinds arouse peculiarly profound emotions, or rather I ought to say the recognition by them of particular kinds of formal relations arouse these emotions. Now these emotions about forms may be accompanied by other emotions which have to do more or less with what I call the instinctive life.

The simplest examples of this can be taken from music. If, as frequently happens, an unmusical child strikes six notes in succession on the piano, the chances are that no one would be able to perceive any necessary relation between these notes—they have been struck by accident, as we say. But if I strike the first six notes of "God Save the King," every one who is not quite music-deaf recognizes that they have, as one would say, a meaning, a purpose. They occur in such a sequence that after each note has been struck we feel that only certain notes can follow and, as the notes follow one another, they more or less adequately fulfil our expectation, *i.e.,* from the beginning the idea of a formal design or scheme is impressed on our minds, and anything which departed violently from that would be not merely meaningless, but an outrage to our sense of order and proportion. We have then an immediate recognition of formal design, of a trend in every part towards a single unity or complete thing which we call the tune.

Now let us suppose that you hear "God Save the King" for the first time; it is possible that you would get an emotion from the mere recognition of that formal system. I do not say it would be a very profound or important emotion, but it might be an emotion, and it would probably stir up no image whatever in your mind, would be associated with no particular person or thing or idea. But those particular notes have become associated with many other things in our minds, so that when they are played we no longer can fix our minds on the form, we are instantly invaded by the associated feelings of loyalty, devotion to country, boredom from the memory of tiresome functions, or relief that we can now at least leave the theatre. We shall say that that particular formal design of notes has become symbolical of numerous other things with which it has become associated.

Now this simple case presents in easy form some of the problems which confront us in works of art of all kinds. The form of a work of art has a meaning of its own and the contemplation of the form in and for itself gives rise in some people to a special emotion which does not depend upon the association of the form with anything else whatever. But that form may by various means either by casual opposition or by some resemblance to things or people or ideas in the outside world, become intimately associated in our minds with those other things, and if these things are objects of emotional feeling, we shall get from the contemplation of the form the echo of all the feelings belonging to the associated objects.

Now since very few people are so constituted by nature or training as to have developed the special feeling about formal design, and since everyone has in the course of his life accumulated a vast mass of feeling about all sorts of objects, persons, and ideas, for the greater part of mankind the associated emotions of a work of art are far stronger than the purely esthetic ones.

So far does this go that they hardly notice the form, but pass at once into the world of associated emotions

which that form calls up in them. Thus, to go back to
our example, the vast majority of people have no
notion whether the form of "God Save the King" is
finely constructed and capable of arousing esthetic
emotion or not. They have never, properly speaking,
heard the form because they have always passed at
once into that richly varied world of racial and social
emotion which has gathered round it.

And what is true of certain pieces of music is even
more true of the graphic arts. Here we have forms
which quite visibly resemble certain objects in nature,
and not unfrequently these objects, such for instance as
a beautiful woman, are charged for us with a great
deal of emotion. When to this we add that people are
far less sensitive to the meaning of visible formal design than they are to audible design, we need not be
surprised that pictures are almost always estimated for
qualities which have nothing, or almost nothing, to do
with their formal design or their esthetic quality in the
strict sense.

To satisfy this emotional pleasure in the associated
ideas of images which the mass of mankind feel so
strongly there has arisen a vast production of pictures,
writings, music, etc., in which formal design is entirely
subordinated to the excitation of the emotions associated with objects. And this is what we may call popular,
commercial, or impure art, and to this category belongs nowadays the vast majority of so called artistic
productions. On the other hand in each generation
there are likely to be a certain number of people who
have a sensitiveness to purely formal relations. To
such people these relations have meaning and arouse
keen emotions of pleasure. And these people create

such systems of formal relations and do not sacrifice willingly or consciously anything of those formal relations to the arousing of emotions connected with objects in the outside world. Their whole attention is directed towards establishing the completest relationship of all parts within the system of the work of art.

It so happens that these systems of formal relations the meaning of which is apprehended by a comparatively few people in each generation, have a curious vitality and longevity, whereas those works in which appeal is made chiefly to the associated ideas of images rarely survive the generation for whose pleasure they were made. This may be because the emotions about objects change more rapidly than the emotions about form. But whatever the reason, the result is that the accumulated and inherited artistic treasure of mankind is made up almost entirely of those works in which formal design is the predominant consideration.

This contrast between the nature of inherited art and the mass of contemporary art has become so marked that the word "classic" is often used (loosely and incorrectly, no doubt) to denote work which has this peculiar character. People speak of classical music, for instance, when they mean the works of any of the great composers. It is significant of the rarity of comprehension of such formal design that to many people classical music is almost synonymous with "dull" music.

Now what I want to put before you is that the purposes and methods of these two kinds of art and of the two kinds of artist that produce them are so different —in so many ways so diametrically opposed that when you set out to analyze the nature and function of art by psychological tests, you must know which kind you are dealing with and you must keep your results in separate pigeon-holes or else you will only make confusion worse confounded.

Before I go any further I will turn to what one or two of the psychological authorities have said on the subject. I quote the passage in his introduction to Psycho-Analysis in which Dr. Freud speaks of the artist. This is what he says:—

Before you leave to-day I should like to direct your attention for a moment to a side of phantasy-life of very general interest. There is, in fact a path from phantasy back again to reality, and that is—art. The artist has also an introverted disposition and has not far to go to become neurotic. He is one who is urged on by instinctive needs which are too clamorous; he longs to attain to honour, power, riches, fame, and the love of women; but he lacks the means of achieving these gratifications. So, like any other with an unsatisfied longing, he turns away from reality and transfers all his interest, and all his Libido, too, on to the creation of his wishes in life. There must be many factors in combination to prevent this becoming the whole outcome of his development; it is well known how often artists in particular suffer from partial inhibition of their capacities through neurosis. Probably their constitution is endowed with a powerful capacity for sublimation and with a certain flexibility in the repressions determining the conflict. But the way back to reality is found by the artist thus: He is not the only one who has a life of phantasy; the intermediate world of phantasy is sanctioned by general human consent, and every hungry soul looks to it for comfort and consolation. But to those who are not artists the gratification that can be drawn from the springs of phantasy is very limited; their inexorable repressions prevent the enjoyment of all but the meagre day-dreams which can become conscious. A true artist has more at his disposal. First of all he understands how to elaborate his day-dreams, so that they lose that personal note which grates upon strange ears and becomes enjoyable to others; he knows too how to modify them sufficiently so that their origin in prohibited sources is not easily detected. Further, he possesses the mysterious ability to mould his particular material until it expresses the idea of his phantasy faithfully;

and then he knows how to attach to this reflection of his phantasy-life so strong a stream of pleasure that, for a time at least, the repressions are out-balanced and dispelled by it. When he can do all this, he opens out to others the way back to the comfort and consolation of their own unconscious sources of pleasure, and so reaps their gratitude and admiration; then he has won—through his phantasy—what before he could only win in phantasy, honour, power, and the love of women.

I must ask you to believe that any criticism I make on this passage is not actuated by motives of personal pique. To be called introverted and on the brink of being neurotic does not seriously affect me. Indeed ever since I observed that the only people worth talking to, the only agreeable companions, belonged to the class that morbidly healthy, censorious people classed as neurotic and degenerate, these words have lost all terror for me. All the same I must declare that the portrait of the artist here given is drawn on the lines of a widespread popular fallacy about the "artistic temperament."

Most people lead dull, monotonous, and conventional lives with inadequate satisfaction of their libido and one of their favourite phantasies is that of the Bohemian—the gay, reckless, devil-may-care fellow who is always kicking over the traces and yet gets toleration and even consideration from the world by reason of a purely magic gift called genius. Now this creature is not altogether a myth—he or something like him does undoubtedly exist—he frequently practises art but he is generally a second-rate artist. He may even be a very brilliant and successful one, but he is none the less a very minor artist. On the other hand almost all the artists who have done anything approaching first-rate work have been thoroughly bourgeois people—leading quiet, unostentatious lives, indifferent to the world's praise or blame, and far too much interested in their job to spend their time in kicking over the traces.

Now all through this passage Dr. Freud is giving us the picture of such a brilliant, successful and essentially impure artist—I need not say that I use the words "pure" and "impure" in a strictly esthetic sense without any reference to sexual morality—*i.e.*, he is an artist who realizes the dream world wherein he and his admirers find an ideal satisfaction of their unsatisfied instincts. He creates images and situations which belong to this dream world wherein we are free to play the rôle which we all think we have somehow missed in actual life.

It is quite true that this explains nearly all contemporary artistic creation. You have only to think of the average novel, especially the feuilleton of papers like the *Daily Mail* and the *Daily Mirror,* and others, which supply every day their pittance of imagined romantic love to hungry girl clerks and housemaids. In fact I believe the most successful and widely read of these (mostly lady) novelists do really day-dream in print, as it were; nothing else would account for their astounding productivity. These people have the fortunate gift of dreaming the average person's day-dream so that the wish-fulfilment which comes natural to them coincides precisely with the wish-fulfilment of a vast number of the population. Other less fortunate writers have deliberately and consciously to concoct the sort of day-dream that they believe the public, want, and these can never be quite the best-sellers.

None of these conditions apply to any first-rate

novel—the novels that have endured do not represent wish-fulfilment to any considerable extent. They depend on the contrary for their effect upon a peculiar detachment from the instinctive life. Instead of manipulating reality so as to conform to the libido, they note the inexorable sequence in life of cause and effect, they mark the total indifference of fate to all human desires, and they endeavour to derive precisely from that inexorability of fate an altogether different kind of pleasure—the pleasure which consists in the recognition of *inevitable sequences;* a pleasure which you see correponds to the pleasure which we found in marking the inevitable sequence of the notes in a tune; in fact again a pleasure derived from the contemplation of the relations and correspondences of form. To give you instances—no one who hoped to get an ideal wish-fulfilment would go to *Mme. Bovary* or *Anna Karenina* or even *Vanity Fair*.

Another immense art industry of to-day is the Cinema, and here too wish-fulfilment reigns supreme. I remember an advertisement of a Cinema with the legend "Let us live a life in two hours." This was a clear appeal to the desire to realize ideally what reality had denied, and indeed there can be no doubt about the method and purpose of nearly all the films, at least such as are not definitely comic, since the comic introduces another problem which I cannot go into now.

By a process which is mere child's play in the dream life we instantly identify ourselves with the hero, and then what satisfaction we attain! With what incredible skill and what incredible good fortune we foil the villain's plot against the heroine, arrive in the nick of time to shoot him dead, and ride off with the heroine either insensible from fear or just able to cling to us for dear life as we cross terrible ravines on a fallen tree-trunk, scale precipices and crash through forests, and always with the certainty of ultimate and triumphant success! But I needn't labour the point; the theatre with its audience always clamorous for a happy ending is no less obvious a case.

What is more interesting is the question of the real artist's attitude to all this; for, in so far as he has to depend on his art for his living, he is under the hard compulsion of throwing a sop to the public, and therefore of giving some satisfaction to the dream-life in his creations. The whole question of the artistic conscience centres round this point. It so happens that some great artists have had rather easy artistic consciences. Dickens is a noteworthy case of this and you all know how he deliberately and consciously spoiled one of his novels by yielding to the clamour of the public and giving it a happy ending, though by doing so he broke the sequence which he knew to be esthetically inevitable.

But the mere fact that there is such a conflict between the artist and the general public is a proof that, qua-artist, the creator has other aims than that of wish-fulfilment and that the pleasure which he feels is not thus directly connected with the libido.

Freud, however daring some of his generalizations may be, is a man of scrupulous intellectual integrity, and he has generally avoided treating the question of esthetics and the artistic impulse, knowing, I suppose, that he has not the necessary sensibility and understanding. But other Psycho-analysts have gone further. Dr. Jung devotes a chapter of his psychological types to the artist. I wish I could criticize this, but I frankly confess I do not understand what it is about. Nothing that he says corresponds to any kind of experience which I or, I suspect, any of the artists I have ever known have ever had. In fact, I can find no connection at all with real experience so that I must simply leave it on one side, merely noting by the way that, according to Jung, Western Art implies an extrovert attitude and Eastern Art an introvert attitude (Freud you will remember makes all artists introvert). Anyone who knows Oriental and Western Art at all intimately must shudder at the temerity of any such generalization.

I quite recognize that a certain positive turn of mind makes me unfitted to follow Jung's speculations and that I am perhaps unfairly neglecting him. I turn to Dr. Pfister and here too, I will confess to a certain prejudice. I find, according to him, that psycho-analysis can only be safely practised by Christians,—all other religions are dissolved by the destructive activity of psycho-analysis—but the Christian religion has the mysterious power of remaining insoluble. This hardly reassures me that Dr. Pfister possesses that intellectual impartiality which Freud so rightly claims as the chief weapon of the man of science.

Well, Dr. Pfister has a chapter on Psycho-Analysis and Art. He had the opportunity to analyze a youth of eighteen, who had apparently come to him for treatment and who was frequently disposed to paint pictures. I will read you a description of a typical example "The Bridge of Death."

"A youth is about to leap away from a female corpse on to a bridge lost in a sea of fog, in the midst of which Death is standing. Behind him the sun rises

in blood-red splendour. On the right margin two pairs
of hands are trying to recall or hold back the hurry-
ing youth!"

Would you like one more, "Night's highest hope"?

"Night sits as a mother on a rock holding her child
on high. Around her lie 'spirits of the night' holding
out their hands to her like praying Mohammedans.
Rosy-tipped clouds announce the approaching dawn."

As a result of prolonged investigation of such works
Dr. Pfister arrives at the conclusion that:—

"Artistic or poetic inspiration is to be regarded as
the manifestation of repressed desires and, as such,
formed in accordance with the laws by which Freud
grouped the processes participating in the origin of
neurotic symptoms, dreams, hallucinations and related
phenomena, save that a whole is created, the deeper
psychological significance of which, however, is not
perfectly clear to the artist."

"Everything was present," he adds, "poetic creation,
substitution, dramatization. The most intensive use was
made of symbolism."

"Everything was present," I should add, except the
faintest glimmer of any artistic feeling. The one thing
I should know about this interesting young man's drawings would have been the extreme improbability that
he would ever be the least good as an artist.

Indeed from time to time my advice is asked about
the drawings of unhappy and dissatisfied young men
and women, drawings which are not altogether unlike
the improvisations of this Swiss boy, and I invariably
recommend them not to take up art, because I know
that real artists, even if they are destined to paint
highly imaginative works and to go mad in the end

like Van Gogh, generally begin by making an elaborate study of an old pair of boots or something of that kind.

I do not for a moment doubt the value of Dr. Pfister's analysis from the point of view of understanding the nervous troubles of his patient. I should think, indeed, that they would be in effect as useful as the study of his dreams, but, precisely in proportion as they were valuable as indications of the patient's dream life, they were worthless as indications of the nature of real art.

For I come back to this, that nothing is more contrary to the essential esthetic faculty than the dream. The poet Mallarmé foresaw this long before Freud had revealed the psychological value of dreams, for in his poem in memory of Théophile Gautier he says that "the spirit of Gautier, the pure poet, now watches over the garden of poetry from which he banishes the Dream, the enemy of his charge." You notice that in this connection he calls him deliberately the pure poet, knowing that in proportion as poetry becomes impure it accepts the Dream. You notice also that Dr. Pfister quite unknowingly betrays how little he knows what art is really about when he says of his patients' work that the most extensive use is made of symbolism. I have elsewhere expressed the belief that in a world of symbolists only two kinds of people are entirely opposed to symbolism, and they are the man of science and the artist, since they alone are seeking to make constructions which are completely self-consistent, self-supporting and self-contained—constructions which do not stand for something else, but appear to have ultimate value and in that sense to be real.

It is, of course, perfectly natural that people should

always be looking for symbolism in works of art. Since most people are unable to perceive the meaning of purely formal relations, are unable to derive from them the profound satisfaction that the creator and those that understand him feel, they always look for some meaning that can be attached to the values of actual life, they always hope to translate a work of art into terms of *ideas* with which they are familiar. None the less in proportion as an artist is pure he is opposed to all symbolism.

You will have noticed that in all these psycho-analytical enquiries into pictorial art the attention of the investigator is fixed on the nature of the images, on what choice the painter has made of the object he represents. Now I venture to say that no one who has a real understanding of the art of painting attaches any importance to what we call the subject of a picture —what is represented. To one who feels the language of pictorial form all depends on *how* it is presented, *nothing* on what. Rembrandt expressed his profoundest feelings just as well when he painted a carcass hanging up in a butcher's shop as when he painted the Crucifixion or his mistress. Cézanne whom most of us believe to be the greatest artist of modern times expressed some of his grandest conceptions in pictures of fruit and crockery on a common kitchen table.

I remember when this fact became clear to me, and the instance may help to show what I mean. In a loan exhibition I came upon a picture of Chardin. It was a signboard painted to hang outside a druggist's shop. It represented a number of glass retorts, a still, and various glass bottles, the furniture of a chemist's laboratory of that time. You will admit that there was not much material for wish-fulfilment (unless the still sug-gested remote possibilities of alcohol). Well, it gave me a very intense and vivid sensation. Just the shapes of those bottles and their mutual relations gave me the feeling of something immensely grand and impressive and the phrase that came into my mind was "This is just how I felt when I first saw Michelangelo's frescos in the Sistine Chapel." Those represented the whole history of creation with the tremendous images of Sybils and Prophets, but esthetically it meant some-thing very similar to Chardin's glass bottles.

And here let me allude to a curious phenomenon which I have frequently noticed, namely that even though at the first shock of a great political design the subject appears to have a great deal to do with one's emotional reaction, that part of one's feeling evaporates very quickly; one soon exhausts the feel-ings connected by associated ideas with the figures, and what remains, what never grows less nor evaporates, are the feelings dependent on the purely formal rela-tions. This indeed may be the explanation of that curi-ous fact that I alluded to, the persistence throughout the ages of works in which formal perfection is at-tained, and the rapid disappearance and neglect which is the fate of works that make their chief appeal through the associated ideas of the images.

At this point I must try to meet an objection which psycho-analysts are certain to raise. They will say that in my description of popular art I have used the word "wish" in the ordinary sense of a more or less conscious wish, whereas Freud uses wish of a desire which has been repressed from consciousness and remains active in the unconscious. The true Freudian wish is incapable of direct satisfaction. The typical kind of case is something like this. A middle-aged lady finds herself compelled at a certain hour of the day to go into a particular room and arrange all the objects in a particular way. She cannot explain the least why she does it and why she is compelled to perform this senseless act. By psycho-analysis it is discovered that in her extreme youth she was in love with her father and wanted to kill her mother, but that this desire was repressed from consciousness and came out later on in this peculiar and roundabout way. Perhaps both father and mother were dead at the period of her illness, and so any such fulfilment would be impossible but even if alive she has ceased to love her father or be jealous of her mother.

I admit that if you adhere strictly to the use of the word "wish" in this sense, it is quite possible that Cézanne's still-life pictures are a sublimation of some such repressed instincts. But you will notice that Freud himself when he talks of the artist neglects entirely his own definition of "wish." The wish in this case is the unsatisfied trying for "fame, power, money, and the love of women." Now these are not repressed wishes, they are, or may be, clearly allowed in consciousness, and they are capable of direct fulfilment. And he goes on to say that it is only because circumstances do not allow of their direct fulfilment that the artist takes refuge in the phantasy world. Similarly I can guess pretty clearly that Dr. Pfister's young man's inventions are inspired by unsatisfied sexual desire and this too is not repressed in the true Freudian sense. In fact I suspect that many difficulties arise from the habit of psycho-analysts of passing from the strict sense of wish to the ordinary sense without even themselves noticing how misleading the results may be. My criticisms, therefore, are based on the use that they themselves make of the word in speaking of art.

Now let me assume that you have granted me my main theory at least, in its general outlines—that you admit that while there is an art which corresponds to the dream life, an art in which the phantasy-making power of the libido is at work to produce a wish-fulfilment, there is also an art which has withdrawn itself from the dream, which is concerned with reality, and art therefore which is pre-eminently *objective* and *dis-interested,* and which therefore proceeds in the opposite direction from the other kind of art. If you will admit this, the most interesting problems suggest themselves for solution. What is the psychological meaning of this emotion about forms, (which I will call the passion for pure beauty,) and what is its relation to the desire for truth which is the only other disinterested passion we know of—what, if any, are their relations to the libido and the ego?

And here I will indicate a possibility which will have to be considered, a possibility which has often occurred to me, but with regard to which I have never come to any conclusion. I have admitted from the first the great probability, to me almost a certainty, that all psychic energy is divided ultimately from the instinctive life and has its source in the satisfaction, at however distant a remove, of some instinctive need or desire. I suppose, but I do not know, that you would trace the love of abstract truth to the reality principle, although, in its higher forms, it has long lost any biological value and has become an end in itself.

I should not be surprised if you were ultimately to trace the love of abstract beauty to the libido, but, even if you should, I should expect you to notice that its relation to that instinctive need is very different from the simple relation of the phantasy-making, dream-like quality of impure, image-making art. For whereas dream-art, if I may use the phrase, is nearly akin to the day-dream and may almost be reckoned as part of the actual instinctive life, the love of beauty implies an almost complete detachment from personality and from the wishes made by our unsatisfied libido.

Even if it derives from the libido, it does not seek to satisfy it directly in any way. None the less the question occurs: What is the source of the affective quality of certain systems of formal design for those who are sensitive to pure form? Why are we moved deeply by certain sequences of notes which arouse no suggestion of any experience in actual life? Why are we moved deeply by certain dispositions of space in architecture which refer so far as we can tell to no other experience?

One thing I think we may clearly say, namely, that there is a pleasure in the recognition of order, of inevitability in relations, and that the more complex the relations of which we are able to recognize the inevitable interdependence and correspondence, the greater is the pleasure; this of course will come very near to the pleasure derived from the contemplation of intellectual constructions united by logical inevitability. What the source of that satisfaction is would clearly be a problem for psychology.

But in art there is, I think, an affective quality which lies outside that. It is not a mere recognition of order and inter-relation; every part, as well as the whole, becomes suffused with an emotional tone. Now, from our definition of this pure beauty, the emotional tone is not due to any recognizable reminiscence or suggestion of the emotional experiences of life; but I sometimes wonder if it nevertheless does not get its force from arousing some very deep, very vague, and immensely generalized reminiscences. It looks as though art had got access to the substratum of all the emotional colours of life, to something which underlies all the particular and specialized emotions of actual life. It seems to derive an emotional energy from the very conditions of our existence by its relation of an emotional significance in time and space. Or it may be that art really calls up, as it were, the residual traces left on the spirit by the different emotions of life, without however recalling the actual experiences, so that we get an echo of the emotion without the limitation and particular direction which it had in experience.

But these are the wild speculations of an amateur. It is just here that we are waiting and longing for you to step in with your precise technique and your methodical control.

I do not pretend that either artists or art critics have made much of a job of esthetics. We have started innumerable theories and abandoned them again without getting at any very positive and assured results. But we have of late, I think, been able to make a little clearing in the approaches to these problems by analyzing a little more clearly than the older writers what goes on inside us when we are confronted by different kinds of works of art and by knowing, or trying to know, or thinking we know, what, as artists, we are after.

I expect and desire that you will test everything which we say about ourselves and our aims as ruthlessly as you test your patients' statements about their own motives, but at least I hope I have shown that it is important to know what class of objects we have in view when we talk of works of art; to know that, if you analyze the pictures of let us say the Royal Academy, your remarks may interest us on other grounds, but not for the light they throw on the esthetic process in itself.

THE HOGARTH ESSAYS

COMPOSITION AS EXPLANATION

BY

GERTRUDE STEIN

COMPOSITION AS EXPLANATION

THERE is singularly nothing that makes a difference a difference in beginning and in the middle and in ending except that each generation has something different at which they are all looking. By this I mean so simply that anybody knows it that composition is the difference which makes each and all of them then different from other generations and this is what makes everything different otherwise they are all alike and everybody knows it because everybody says it.

It is very likely that nearly every one has been very nearly certain that something that is interesting is interesting them. Can they and do they. It is very interesting that nothing inside in them, that is when you consider the very long history of how every one ever acted or has felt, it is very interesting that nothing inside in them in all of them makes it connectedly different. By this I mean this. The only thing that is different from one time to another is what is seen and what is seen depends upon how everybody is doing everything. This makes the thing we are looking at very different and this makes what those who describe it make of it, it makes a composition, it confuses, it shows, it is, it looks, it likes it as it is, and this makes what is seen as it is seen. Nothing changes from generation to generation except the thing seen and that makes a composition. Lord Grey remarked that when the generals before the war talked about the war they talked about it as a nineteenth century war although to be fought with twentieth century weapons. That is because war is a thing that decides how it is to be when it is to be done. It is prepared and to that degree it is like all academies it is not a thing made by being made it is a thing prepared. Writing and painting and all that, is like that, for those who occupy themselves with it and don't make it as it is made. Now the few who make it as it is made, and it is to be remarked that the most decided of them usually are prepared just as the world around them is preparing, do it in this way and so I if you do not mind I will tell you how it happens. Naturally one does not know how it happened until it is well over beginning happening.

To come back to the part that the only thing that is different is what is seen when it seems to be being seen, in other words, composition and time-sense.

No one is ahead of his time, it is only that the particular variety of creating his time is the one that his contemporaries who also are creating their own time refuse to accept. And they refuse to accept it for a very simple reason and that is that they do not have to accept it for any reason. They themselves that is everybody in their entering the modern composition and they do enter it, if they do not enter it they are not so to speak in it they are out of it and so they do enter it; but in as you may say the non-competitive efforts where if you are not in it nothing is lost except nothing at all except what is not had, there are naturally all the refusals, and the things refused are only important if unexpectedly somebody happens to need them. In the case of the arts it is very definite. Those who are creat-

ing the modern composition authentically are naturally
only of importance when they are dead because by that
time the modern composition having become past is
classified and the description of it is classical. That is
the reason why the creator of the new composition in
the arts is an outlaw until he is a classic, there is hardly
a moment in between and it is really too bad very much
too bad naturally for the creator but also very much
too bad for the enjoyer, they all really would enjoy the
created so much better just after it has been made than
when it is already a classic, but it is perfectly simple
that there is no reason why the contemporaries should
see, because it would not make any difference as they
lead their lives in the new composition anyway, and
as every one is naturally indolent why naturally they
don't see. For this reason as in quoting Lord Grey
it is quite certain that nations not actively threatened
are at least several generations behind themselves
militarily so æsthetically they are more than several
generations behind themselves and it is very much too
bad, it is so very much more exciting and satisfactory
for everybody if one can have contemporaries, if all
one's contemporaries could be one's contemporaries.

There is almost not an interval.

For a very long time everybody refuses and then
almost without a pause almost everybody accepts. In
the history of the refused in the arts and literature the
rapidity of the change is always startling. Now the
only difficulty with the *volte-face* concerning the arts is
this. When the acceptance comes, by that acceptance
the thing created becomes a classic. It is a natural
phenomena a rather extraordinary natural phenomena
that a thing accepted becomes a classic. And what is

the characteristic quality of a classic. The characteristic quality of a classic is that it is beautiful. Now of course it is perfectly true that a more or less first rate work of art is beautiful but the trouble is that when that first rate work of art becomes a classic because it is accepted the only thing that is important from then on to the majority of the acceptors the enormous majority, the most intelligent majority of the acceptors is that it is so wonderfully beautiful. Of course it is wonderfully beautiful, only when it is still a thing irritating annoying stimulating then all quality of beauty is denied to it.

Of course it is beautiful but first all beauty in it is denied and then all the beauty of it is accepted. If every one were not so indolent they would realize that beauty is beauty even when it is irritating and stimulating not only when it is accepted and classic. Of course it is extremely difficult nothing more so than to remember back to its not being beautiful once it has become beautiful. This makes it so much more difficult to realize its beauty when the work is being refused and prevents every one from realizing that they were convinced that beauty was denied, once the work is accepted. Automatically with the acceptance of the time-sense comes the recognition of the beauty and once the beauty is accepted the beauty never fails any one.

Beginning again and again is a natural thing even when there is a series.

Beginning again and again and again explaining composition and time is a natural thing.

It is understood by this time that everything is the same except composition and time, composition and the time of the composition and the time in the composition.

Everything is the same except composition and as the composition is different and always going to be different everything is not the same. Everything is not the same as the time when of the composition and the time in the composition is different. The composition is different, that is certain.

The composition is the thing seen by every one living in the living they are doing, they are the composing of the composition that at the time they are living is the composition of the time in which they are living. It is that that makes living a thing they are doing. Nothing else is different, of that almost any one can be certain. The time when and the time of and the time in that composition is the natural phenomena of that composition and of that perhaps every one can be certain.

No one thinks these things when they are making when they are creating what is the composition, naturally no one thinks, that is no one formulates until what is to be formulated has been made.

Composition is not there, it is going to be there and we are here. This is some time ago for us naturally.

The only think that is different from one time to another is what is seen and what is seen depends upon how everybody is doing everything. This makes the thing we are looking at very different and this makes what those who describe it make of it, it makes a composition, it confuses, it shows, it is, it looks, it likes it as it is, and this makes what is seen as it is seen. Nothing changes from generation to generation except the thing seen and that makes a composition.

Now the few who make writing as it is made and it is to be remarked that the most decided of them are those that are prepared by preparing, are prepared just as the world around them is prepared and is preparing to do it in this way and so if you do not mind I will again tell you how it happens. Naturally one does not know how it happened until it is well over beginning happening.

Each period of living differs from any other period of living not in the way life is but in the way life is conducted and that authentically speaking is composition. After life has been conducted in a certain way everybody knows it but nobody knows it, little by little, nobody knows it as long as nobody knows it. Any one creating the composition in the arts does not know it either, they are conducting life and that makes their composition what it is, it makes their work compose as it does.

Their influence and their influences are the same as that of all of their contemporaries only it must always be remembered that the analogy is not obvious until as I say the composition of a time has become so pronounced that it is past and the artistic composition of it is a classic.

And now to begin as if to begin. Composition is not there, it is going to be there and we are here. This is some time ago for us naturally. There is something to be added afterwards.

Just how much my work is known to you I do not know. I feel that perhaps it would be just as well to tell the whole of it.

In beginning writing I wrote a book called *Three Lives* this was written in 1905. I wrote a negro story called *Melanctha*. In that there was a constant recurring and beginning there was a marked direction in the direction of being in the present although naturally I had been accustomed to past present and future, and why, because the composition forming around me was a prolonged present. A composition of a prolonged present is a natural composition in the world as it has been these thirty years it was more and more a prolonged present. I created then a prolonged present naturally I knew nothing of a continuous present but it came naturally to me to make one, it was simple it was clear to me and nobody knew why it was done like that, I did not myself although naturally to me it was natural.

After that I did a book called *The Making of Americans* it is a long book about a thousand pages.

Here again it was all so natural to me and more and more complicatedly a continuous present. A continuous present is a continuous present. I made almost a thousand pages of a continuous present.

Continuous present is one thing and beginning again and again is another thing. These are both things. And then there is using everything.

This brings us again to composition this the using everything. The using everything brings us to composition and to this composition. A continuous present and using everything and beginning again. In these two books there was elaboration of the complexities of using everything and of a continuous present and of beginning again and again and again.

In the first book there was a groping for a continuous present and for using everything by beginning again and again.

There was a groping for using everything and there was a groping for a continuous present and there was an inevitable beginning of beginning again and again and again.

Having naturally done this I naturally was a little troubled with it when I read it. I became then like the others who read it. One does, you know, excepting that when I reread it myself I lost myself in it again. Then I said to myself this time it will be different and I began. I did not begin again I just began.

In this beginning naturally since I at once went on and on very soon there were pages and pages and pages more and more elaborated creating a more and more continuous present including more and more using of everything and continuing more and more beginning and beginning and beginning.

I went on and on to a thousand pages of it.

In the meantime to naturally begin I commenced making portraits of anybody and anything. In making these portraits I naturally made a continuous present an including everything and a beginning again and again within a very small thing. That started me into composing anything into one thing. So then naturally it was natural that one thing an enormously long thing was not everything an enormously short thing was also not everything nor was it all of it a continuous present thing nor was it always and always beginning again. Naturally I would then begin again. I would begin again I would naturally begin. I did naturally begin. This brings me to a great deal that has been begun.

And after that what changes what changes after that, after that what changes and what changes after

that and after that and what changes and after that
and what changes after that.

The problem from this time on became more definite.

It was all so nearly alike it must be different and it
is different, it is natural that if everything is used and
there is a continuous present and a beginning again
and again if it is all so alike it must be simply different
and everything simply different was the natural way
of creating it then.

In this natural way of creating it then that it was
simply different everything being alike it was simply
different, this kept on leading one to lists. Lists naturally for a while and by lists I mean a series. More
and more in going back over what was done at this
time I find that I naturally kept simply different as an
intention. Whether there was or whether there was
not a continuous present did not then any longer
trouble me there was or there was, and using everything no longer troubled me if everything is alike
using everything could no longer trouble me and beginning again and again could no longer trouble me
because if lists were inevitable if series were inevitable
and the whole of it was inevitable beginning again and
again could not trouble me so then with nothing to
trouble me I very completely began naturally since
everything is alike making it as simply different naturally as simply different as possible. I began doing
natural phenomena what I call natural phenomena and
natural phenomena naturally everything being alike
natural phenomena are making things be naturally
simply different. This found its culmination later, in
the beginning it began in a centre confused with lists

with series with geography with returning portraits and with particularly often four and three and often with five and four. It is easy to see that in the beginning such a conception as everything being naturally different would be very inarticulate and very slowly it began to emerge and take the form of anything, and then naturally if anything that is simply different is simply different what follows will follow.

So far then the progress of my conceptions was the natural progress entirely in accordance with my epoch as I am sure is to be quite easily realized if you think over the scene that was before us all from year to year.

As I said in the beginning, there is the long history of how every one ever acted or has felt and that nothing inside in them in all of them makes it connectedly different. By this I mean all this.

The only thing that is different from one time to another is what is seen and what is seen depends upon how everybody is doing everything.

It is understood by this time that everything is the same except composition and time, composition and the time of the composition and the time in the composition.

Everything is the same except composition and as the composition is different and always going to be different everything is not the same. So then I as a contemporary creating the composition in the beginning was groping toward a continuous present, a using everything a beginning again and again and then everything being alike then everything very simply everything was naturally simply different and so I as a contemporary was creating everything being alike was creating everything naturally being naturally simply different, everything being alike. This then was the period that brings me to the period of the beginning of 1914. Everything being alike everything naturally would be simply different and war came and everything being alike and everything being simply different brings everything being simply different brings it to romanticism.

Romanticism is then when everything being alike everything is naturally simply different, and romanticism.

Then for four years this was more and more different even though this was, was everything alike. Everything alike naturally everything was simply different and this is and was romanticism and this is and was war. Everything being alike everything naturally everything is different simply different naturally simply different.

And so there was the natural phenomena that was war, which had been, before war came, several generations behind the contemporary composition, because it became war and so completely needed to be contemporary became completely contemporary and so created the completed recognition of the contemporary composition. Every one but one may say every one became consciously became aware of the existence of the authenticity of the modern composition. This then the contemporary recognition, because of the academic thing known as war having been forced to become contemporary made every one not only contemporary in act not only contemporary in thought but contemporary in self-consciousness made every one contemporary with the modern composition. And so the art creation of the contemporary composition which would have been out-

lawed normally outlawed several generations more behind even than war, war having been brought so to
speak up to date art so to speak was allowed not completely to be up to date, but nearly up to date, in other
words we who created the expression of the modern
composition were to be recognized before we were
dead some of us even quite a long time before we were
dead. And so war may be said to have advanced a general recognition of the expression of the contemporary
composition by almost thirty years.

And now after that there is no more of that in other
words there is peace and something comes then and it
follows coming then.

And so now one finds oneself interesting oneself in
an equilibration, that of course means words as well as
things and distribution as well as between themselves
between the words and themselves and the things and
themselves, a distribution as distribution. This makes
what follows what follows and now there is every reason why there should be an arrangement made. Distribution is interesting and equilibration is interesting
when a continuous present and a beginning again and
again and using everything and everything alike and
everything naturally simply different has been done.

After all this, there is that, there has been that that
there is a composition and that nothing changes except
composition the composition and the time of and the
time in the composition.

The time of the composition is a natural thing and
the time in the composition is a natural thing it is a
natural thing and it is a contemporary thing.

The time of the composition is the time of the composition. It has been at times a present thing it has

been at times a past thing it has been at times a future thing it has been at times an endeavour at parts or all of these things. In my beginning it was a continuous present a beginning again and again and again and again, it was a series it was a list it was a similarity and everything different it was a distribution and an equilibration. This is all of the time some of the time of the composition.

Now there is still something else the time-sense in the composition. This is what is always a fear a doubt and a judgment and a conviction. The quality in the creation of expression the quality in a composition that makes it go dead just after it has been made is very troublesome.

The time in the composition is a thing that is very troublesome. If the time in the composition is very troublesome it is because there must even if there is no time at all in the composition there must be time in the composition which is in its quality of distribution and equilibration. In the beginning there was the time in the composition that naturally was in the composition but time in the composition comes now and this is what is now troubling every one the time in the composition is now a part of distribution and equilibration. In the beginning there was confusion there was a continuous present and later there was romanticism which was not a confusion but an extrication and now there is either succeeding or failing there must be distribution and equilibration there must be time that is distributed and equilibrated. This is the thing that is at present the most troubling and if there is the time that is at present the most troublesome the time-sense that is at present the most troubling is the thing that makes the present the most troubling. There is at present there is distribution, by this I mean expression and time, and in this way at present composition is time that is the reason that at present the time-sense is troubling that is the reason why at present the time-sense in the composition is the composition that is making what there is in composition.

And afterwards.

Now that is all.

PRECIOSILLA

Cousin to Clare washing.

In the win all the band beagles which have cousin lime sign and arrange a weeding match to presume a certain point to exstate to exstate a certain pass lint to exstate a lean sap prime lo and shut shut is life.

Bait, bait tore, tore her clothes, toward it, toward a bit, to ward a sit, sit down in, in vacant surely lots, a single mingle, bait and wet, wet a single establishment that has a lily lily grow. Come to the pen come in the stem, come in the grass grown water.

Lily wet lily wet while. This is so pink so pink in stammer, a long bean which shows bows is collected by a single curly shady, shady get, get set wet bet.

It is a snuff a snuff to be told and have can witer, can is it and sleep sleeps knot, it is a lily scarf the pink and blue yellow, not blue not odour sun, nobles are bleeding bleeding two seats two seats on end. Why is grief. Grief is strange black. Sugar is melting. We will not swim.

Preciosilla

Please be please be get, please get wet, wet nat-

urally, naturally in weather. Could it be fire more
firier. Could it be so in ate struck. Could it be gold up,
gold up stringing, in it while while which is hanging,
hanging in dingling, dingling in pinning, not so. Not so
dots large dressed dots, big sizes, less laced, less laced
diamonds, diamonds white, diamonds bright, diamonds
in the in the light, diamonds light diamonds door diamonds hanging to be four, two four, all before, this
bean, lessly, all most, a best, willow, vest, a green
guest, guest, go go go go go go, go. Go go. Not
guessed. Go go.

Toasted susie is my ice-cream.

A SAINT IN SEVEN

I thought perhaps that we would win by human
means, I knew we could win if we did win but I did not
think that we could win by human means, and now we
have won by human means.

A saint followed and not surrounded.

LIST OF PERSONAGES

1. A saint with a lily.
Second. A girl with a rooster in front of her and a
bush of strange flowers at her side and a small tree
behind her.
3. A guardian of a museum holding a cane.
4. A woman leaning forward.
5. A woman with a sheep in front of her and a
small tree behind her.
6. A woman with black hair and two bundles one
under each arm.

7. A night watchman of a hotel who does not fail to stand all the time.

8. A very stout girl with a basket and flowers summer flowers and the flowers are in front of a small tree.

SAINTS IN SEASON

See Saints in seven.

And how do royalists accuse themselves.

Saints.

Saint Joseph.

In pleading sadness length of sadness in pleading length of sadness and no sorrow. No sorrow and no sadness length of sadness.

A girl addresses a bountiful supply of seed to feed a chicken. Address a bountiful supply of trees to shade them. Address a bountiful supply to them.

A guardian.

In days and nights beside days are followed by daisies. We find them and they find them and water finds them and they grow best where we meant to suggest. We suggested that we would go there again. A woman leaning forward.

She was necessarily taken to be no taller.

A girl.

If she may say what she will say she will say that there were a quantity of voices and they were white and then darker.

A woman with two bundles.

If she did it to be useful if she did not even attract the same throne. What did I say. Did royalists say that they did not have this to say to-day.

Standing.

Measure an alarm by refusing to alarm them and they this not as a disaster but as a pretension. Do you pretend to be unfavourable to their thought.

Eighth.

If you hold heavily heavily instead. Instead of in there. Did you not intend to show this to them.

Saint.

A Saint.

Saint and very well I thank you.

Two in bed.

Two in bed.

Yes two in bed.

They had eaten.

Two in bed.

They had eaten.

Two in bed.

She says weaken.

If she said.

She said two in bed.

She said they had eaten.

She said yes two in bed.

She said weaken.

Do not acknowledge to me that seven are said that a Saint and seven that it is said that a saint in seven that there is said to be a saint in seven.

Now as to illuminations.

They are going to illuminate and every one is to put into their windows their most beautiful object and every one will say and the streets will be crowded every one will say look at it. They do say look at it.

To look at it. They will look at it. They will say look at it.

If it should rain they will all be there. If it should

be windy they will all be there. Who will be there. They will all be there.

Names of streets named after the saint. Names of places named after the saint. Names of saints named after the saint. Names of sevens named after the saint. The saints in sevens.

Noon-light for Roman arches.

He left fairly early.

Let them make this seen.

Louise giggled.

Michael was not angry nor was he stuttering nor was he able to silence them. He was angry he was stuttering and he was able to answer them.

They were nervous.

Josephine was able to be stouter. Amelia was really not repaid.

And the taller younger and weaker older and straighter one said come to eat again.

Michael was not able to come angrily to them. He angrily muttered for them.

Louise was separated to Heloise and not by us. So then you see saints for them.

Louise.

Heloise.

Amelia.

Josephine.

Michael and Elinor.

Seven, a saint in seven and in this way it was not Paul. Paul was deprived of nothing. Saint in seven a saint in seven.

Who.

A saint in seven.

Owls and bees.

If you please.

Paul makes honey and orange trees.

Michael makes coal and celery.

Louise makes rugs and reasonably long.

Heloise makes the sea and she settles well away from it.

Amelia does not necessarily please. She does not place herself near linen.

Josephine measures a little toy and she may be no neater.

Eleanor has been more satisfied and feeble. She does not look as able to stay nor does she seem as able to go anyway.

Saints in seven makes italics sombre.

I make fun of him of her.

I make fun of them.

They make fun of them of this. They make fun of him of her.

She makes fun of of them of him.

He makes fun of them of her.

They make fun of her.

He makes fun of them.

She makes fun of him.

I make fun of them.

We have made them march. She has made a procession.

A saint in seven and there were six. A saint in seven and there were eight. A saint in seven.

If you know who pleads who precedes who succeeds.

He leads.

He leads and they follow. One two three four and as yet there are no more.

A saint in seven.

And when do they sleep again. A ring around the moon is seen to follow the moon and the moon is in the centre of the ring and the ring follows the moon.

Sleeping, to-day sleeping to-day is nearly a necessity and to-day coals reward the fire. One two three four five. Corals reward the five. In this way they are not leaning with the intention of being a hindrance to satisfaction.

A saint in seven is told of bliss.

I will know why they open so.

Carefully seen to be safely arranged.

One two three four five six seven. A saint in seven.

To begin in this way.

Carefully attended carefully attended to this.

If we had seen if they had seen if we had seen what was in between, they went very slowly so that we might know but to be slow and we were not slow and to show and they showed it and we did not decide because we had already come to a decision.

Saints in seven are a very large number. Seven and seven is not as pretty as five and five. And five and five need not mean more. Now to remember how to mean to be gay. Gayly the boxer the boxer very gayly depresses no one. He seems he does seem he dreams he does dream he seems to dream.

Extra readiness to recall himself to these places. Thanks so much for startling. Do not by any means start to worship in order to be excellent. He is excellent again and again.

A saint can share expenses he can share and he can be interested in their place. Their place is plentifully sprinkled as they bend forward. And no one does mean to contend any more.

A saint in seven plentifully.

None of it is good.

It has been said that the woods are the poor man's overcoat but we have found the mountains which are near by and not high can be an overcoat to us. Can he be an overcoat to us.

A saint in seven wished to be convinced by us that the mountains near by and not high can give protection from the wind. One does not have to consider rain because it cannot rain here. A saint in seven wishes to be convinced by us that the mountains which are near by would act as a protection to those who find it cold and yet when one considers that nothing is suffering neither men women children lambs roses and broom, broom is yellow when one considers that neither broom, roses lambs men children and women none of them suffer neither here nor in the mountains near by the mountains are not high and if it were not true that every one had to be sure that that they were there every one would be persuaded that they had persuaded that they had been persuaded that this was true.

He told us that he knew that the name was the same. A saint in seven can declare this to be true.

He comes again. Yes he comes again and what does he say he says do you know this do you refuse no more than you give. That is the way to spell it do you refuse no more than you give.

He searches for more than one word. He manages to eat finally and as he does so and as he does so and as he does so he manages to cut the water in two. If water is flowing down a canal and it is understood that the canal is full if the canal has many outlets for irrigation purposes and the whole country is irrigated if even the mountains are irrigated by the canal and in this way neither oil nor seeds nor wood is needed and it is needed by them why then do the examples remain here examples of industry of cowardice of pleasure of reasonable sight seeing of objections and of lands and oceans. We do not know oceans. We do not know measures. Measure and measure and then decide that a servant beside, what is a servant beside. No one knows how easily he can authorize him to go, how easily she can authorize her to go how easily they can authorize them to come and to go. I authorize you to come and go. I authorize you to go. I authorize you to go and come.

SITWELL EDITH SITWELL

In a minute when they sit when they sit around her.

Mixed it with two who. One two two one two two. Mixed it with two who.

Weeks and weeks able and weeks.

No one sees the connection between Lily and Louise, but I do.

After each has had after each has had, after each has had had had had it.

Change in time.

A change in time is this, if a change in time. If a change in time is this. If a change in time.

Did she come to say who.

Not to remember weeks to say and asking, not to remember weeks to-day. Not to remember weeks to say. Not to remember weeks to say and asking.

And now a bow.

When to look when to look up and around when to

look down and around when to look down and around
when to look around and around and altered.

Just as long as any song.

And now altogether different.

It was in place of places and and it was here.

Supposing she had had a key supposing she had answered, supposing she had had to have a ball supposing
she had it fall and she had answered. Supposing she
had it and in please, please never see so.

As much even as that, even can be added to by in
addition, listen.

Table table to be table to see table to be to see to
me, table to me table to be table to table to table to it.
Exactly as they did it when she was not and not and
not so. After that perhaps.

She had a way of she had a way of not the name.

Little reaching it away.

As afternoon to borrow.

It made a difference.

This is most.

Introduces.

This is for her and not for Mabel Weeks.

She could not keep it out.

Introduces have and heard.

Miss Edith Sitwell have and heard.

Introduces have and had.

Miss Edith Sitwell have and had.

Introduces have and had introduces have and had
and heard.

Miss Edith Sitwell have and had and heard.

Left and right.

Part two of Part one.

If she had a ball at all, if she had a ball at all too.

Fill my eyes no no.

It was and held it.

The size of my eyes.

Why does one want to or to and to, when does one want to and to went to.

To know it as well as all there.

If a little other more not so little as before, now they knew and that and so.

What in execute.

Night is different from bright.

When he was a little sweeter was he.

Part two.

There was a part one.

He did seem a little so.

Half of to mention it at all.

And now to allow literally if and it will if and it does if and it has if and it is.

Never as much as a way.

How does she know it.

She could be as she sleeps and as she wakes all day. She could be as she sleeps and as she wakes all day is it not so.

It leads it off of that.

Please carried at.

Twice at once and carry.

She does and care to and cover and never believe in an and being narrow.

Happily say so.

What is as added.

And opposite.

Now it has to be something entirely different and it is.

Not turned around.
No one knows two two more.
Lose and share all and more.
Very easily arises.
It very easily arises.
Absently faces and by and by we agree. .
By and by faces apparently we agree.
Apparently faces by and by we agree.
By and by faces apparently we agree.
Apparently faces by and by we agree.

JEAN COCTEAU

Needs be needs be needs be near.
Needs be needs be needs be.
This is where they have their land astray.
          Two say.
This is where they have their land astray.
Two say.
Needs be needs be needs be
Needs be needs be needs be near.
          Second time.
It may be nearer than two say.
Near be near be near be
Needs be needs be needs be
Needs be needs be needs be near.
He was a little while away.
Needs be nearer than two say.
Needs be needs be needs be needs be.
Needs be needs be needs be near.
He was away a little while.
          And two say.

He was away a little while
He was away a little while
    And two say.

Part two.

Part two and part one
Part two and part two
Part two and part two
Part two and part one.
He was near to where they have their land astray.
He was near to where they have two say.
Part two and near one. Part one and near one.
Part two and two say.
Part one and part two and two say.
He was as when they had nearly their declamation
their declaration their verification their amplification
their rectification their elevation their safety their
share and there where. This is where they have the
land astray. Two say.

Put it there in there there where they have it. Put
it there in there there where they halve it.

Put it there in there there and they have it. Put it
in there in there there and they halve it.

He nearly as they see the land astray.

By that and in that and mine.

He nearly as they see he nearly as they see the land
he nearly as they see the land astray.

And by that by that time mine. He nearly as they see
the land astray by that by that time by that time by that
time mine by that time mine by that time. By that time
and mine and by that time and mine.

He nearly when they see the land astray.

By that time and mine.

Not nearly apart.

Part and not partly and not apart and not nearly not apart.

When he when he was is and does, when he partly when he partly when he is and was and partly when he and partly when he does and was and is and partly and apart and when he and apart and when he does and was and when he is.

When he is partly

When he is apart.

Particularly for him

He makes it be the rest of the day for them as well.

Partly partly begun

The rest and one

One part partly begun.

Partly begun one and one.

One and one and partly begun and one and one partly begun. Partly begun part partly begun part partly begun and one and part and one and partly begun and part partly begun.

Partly begun.

Did they need the land astray.

Partly begun and one.

Did they need the land astray and partly begun and one.

Did they need it to be the rest of the day did they need it to be the land astray partly begun and one part partly begun part part partly begun part partly begun and one.

They need it as they had it for themselves to be the rest and next to that and by this who were as it must for them.

He knew and this.

When half is May how much is May.

Whole and here there and clear shall and dear well and well at that. Well is a place from which water is drawn and what is drawn.

A well is a place from which out of which water is drawn and what is drawn.

A well is a place out of which water is drawn and water is drawn. A well is a place out of which water is drawn and what is drawn.

A well is a place out of which water is drawn.

A well is a place from which water is drawn.

They made it that they could be where they were.

Where they were when they were where they were.

He had it as is his in his hand.

Hand and head

Head and hand and land

two say

as

ours.

They make them they make them they make them they make them they make them they make them they make them at once.

And nearly when he knows.

As long as head as short as said as short as said as long as head.

And this as long and this as long and this and this and so who makes the wedding go and so and so.

It is usually not my habit to mention anything but now having the habit of addressing I am mentioning it as anything.

Having the habit of addressing having the habit of expressing having the habit of expressing having the habit of addressing.

A little away
And a little away.
Everything away.
Everything away.
Everything and away.
Everything and away.
Away everything away.
It is very extraordinary that it is just as interesting.
When it was it was it was there.
There there.
Eight eight and eight, eight eight and eight. Eight
eight and eight and and eight.
After all seeing it with that and with that never
having heard a third a third too, too.
When there a there and where is where and mine is
mine and in is in who needs a shred.
They needed three when this you see when this you
see and three and three and it was two more they must.
They must address with tenderness
Two him.

G. STEIN.

It was not always finished for this once.
Once or twice and for this then they had that and as
well as having it so that and this and all and now and
believe for it all when they and shall and when and
for and most and by and with and this and there and
as and by and will and when and can and this and this
and than and there and find and there and all and with
and will it and with it and with it and they and this and
there and so and I am in and all and all and if and if
and if and if and if and if now. Now need never alter
anyhow.

Anyhow means furls furls with a chance chance with a change change with as strong strong with as will will with as sign sign with as west west with as most most with as in in with as by by with as change change with as reason reason to be lest lest they did when when they did for for they did there and then. Then does not celebrate the there and then.

Who knows it.

I wish to be very well pleased and I thank you.

GERTRUDE STEIN.

THE END